WHEN
Variety
WAS KING

WHEN *Variety* WAS KING

MEMOIR OF A TV PIONEER

FEATURING JACKIE GLEASON, SONNY AND CHER, HEE HAW, AND MORE

Frank Peppiatt

ECW Press

Published by ECW Press
2120 Queen Street East, Suite 200, Toronto, Ontario, Canada M4E 1E2
416-694-3348 / info@ecwpress.com

LIBRARY AND ARCHIVES CANADA CATALOGUING IN PUBLICATION

Peppiatt, Frank G.

When variety was king : memoir of a TV pioneer : featuring Jackie
Gleason, Sonny and Cher, Hee Haw, and more / Frank Peppiatt.

Includes index.
ISBN 978-1-77041-157-9 (bound). ISBN 978-1-77041-029-9 (pbk.)
Also issed as: 978-1-77090-354-8 (PDF); 978-1-77090-355-5 (EPUB)

1. Peppiatt, Frank G. 2. Television producers and directors—Canada—
Biography. 3. Television producers and directors—United States—Biography.
4. Television broadcasting—United States—History—20th century. I. Title.

PN1992.4.P41A3 2013   791.4502'32092   C2012-907508-6

Editor for the press: Stuart Ross
Cover design: Ingrid Paulson
Text design: Tania Craan
Illustration: Tony Jenkins
All photos from the personal collection of Frank Peppiatt.
Typesetting and production: Carolyn McNeillie
Printing: Friesens   1   2   3   4   5

FSC
www.fsc.org
MIX
Paper from
responsible sources
FSC® C016245

ONTARIO ARTS COUNCIL
CONSEIL DES ARTS DE L'ONTARIO
50 YEARS OF ONTARIO GOVERNMENT SUPPORT OF THE ARTS
50 ANS DE SOUTIEN DU GOUVERNEMENT DE L'ONTARIO AUX ARTS

Canada Council   Conseil des Arts
for the Arts   du Canada

Canadä

Ontario
Ontario Media Development
Corporation

Made possible with the
support of the Ontario Media
Development Corporation

PRINTED AND BOUND IN CANADA

*I dedicate this book to my beautiful,
loving wife Caroline because she deserves it.*

TABLE OF CONTENTS

Chapter 1

✦

AND AWAY WE GO!

It was the strangest Saturday of my life.

The year was 1965. The setting was New York. My partner, John Aylesworth, and I were writing a pop-music show we had created called *Hullabaloo*. It featured all the big hit makers of the '60s — the Rolling Stones, the Supremes, the Mamas & the Papas. I was 36, John 34, which made us older than most of the acts on our show, so we could play grown-up to some of the drug-addled talent that came through the door each week.

John was about five foot ten, with straight blondish hair, intense blue eyes and a wonderful laugh. He did marvelous impressions of almost anybody in show business, but he had two left feet and no sense of rhythm. I was six three and gangly, with curly brown hair, hazel eyes and a gap-toothed grin. I had trouble doing an impression of myself, but I had rhythm and plenty of it. John hated sports; I loved them. I was a worrier; John assumed everything would turn out just fine. We were complete opposites, and it worked for us.

On this cold Monday in January our agent, Lester Gottlieb, showed up unexpectedly at the *Hullabaloo* office. Lester was a born-and-bred New Yorker, from his snap-brim fedora down to his wingtip toes. His sharp gray eyes were constantly shifting, sizing up everything. He always looked like he'd just had a haircut. People would ask him, "You just had a haircut, Lester?" I think his wife gave him a trim every morning, or maybe he was having an affair with a lady barber. I don't know how much Lester made as an agent, but I'll bet he spent at least half of it on clothes. Every week he sported something new. Not a button out of place, not a crease that wasn't razor-sharp. He carried an umbrella, rain or shine; summer or winter, he had a tan. He looked much younger than his 40-odd years and he considered himself a ladies' man. The ladies, however, hadn't been informed.

He lunged his umbrella at us as if it were an épée and said, "How'd you guys like to take a train ride to Florida this Friday?"

John and I looked at him, slightly stunned.

"Well?"

"Is this some kind of joke, Lester?" John asked.

"No, not at all," Lester said. "Jackie Gleason has requested that the two of you come up with some great ideas for a big special for him."

"Okay, but why does Gleason want us?" I said.

"Because Jackie Gleason is the agency's biggest variety star and variety is king of TV land and Peppiatt and Aylesworth are the crown princes."

I laughed. "Crown princes? That's over the top, even for you, Lester."

"Is Mr. Gleason willing to pay a princely sum for our week?" John asked.

Lester took off his winter fedora and threw a big smile at us. "You take the train Friday, meet with Jackie Saturday afternoon and come back Saturday night."

"And?" John asked.

"And all expenses and $5,000!"

"Each?" John and I said as one.

"For the team, guys, for the team. That is damn good money for a day's work."

"One day?" I said. "Will the great ideas be slipped to us under our door by the Fairy-Great-Idea-Godmother?"

"Come on, you guys can do it. You've got a whole week."

"The so-called one day's work just flew out the window," John said as Lester put his fedora back on.

"I take it that's a yes?" Lester smiled and held out his hand.

"Yes," we both said, and shook on it.

"See you Friday morning at Penn Station. Ten-thirty sharp."

"Why the train?" I asked.

"We can meet in the club car and go over what you guys have written."

"Sounds good to me," I said, knowing full well Lester the Debonair was terrified of flying. *What the hell,* I thought, *a train ride will be nice and relaxing.*

Lester smiled again and buttoned up his dark blue cashmere topcoat. "Don't be late." He touched the brim of his fedora with the tip of his umbrella and sauntered out of the office.

"Well," John said in a perfect Stan Laurel impression, "this is another fine mess you've gotten us into, Ollie!"

We spent the week writing *Hullabaloo* during the day and racking our brains for Jackie Gleason each night. By Friday morning, just in time to leave, we had written up what we considered a few good ideas.

On the way to Penn Station I asked, more than once, "We're as ready as we're ever going to be, right?"

"It's great stuff!" John assured me.

"From your lips to Jackie's ear, Johnny," I grumbled.

Lester was waiting for us at the gate. "And away we go!" he shouted. His Jackie Gleason impression was very bad, but indeed away we went.

Over lunch in the club car we pitched our ideas to Lester.

"Those are good," he said.

"What happened to *great*?" John asked.

"Don't worry, boys, it's in the bag," Lester said, taking a pack of cards from his pocket. "Anyone up for some draw poker?"

The two anyones, John and I, drew cards for who would deal. I proceeded to rake in $118 from John and Lester, which I then raked out for drinks and dinner for the three of us.

Later, in my roomette, I tossed and turned, finally drifting off to sleep with visions of Ralph Kramden, his rolled-up fist menacing my face: "To the moon, Frankie, to the moon!"

I WAS AWAKENED BY THE sound of a soft gong and a voice: "First call to breakfast." I was starving, so I didn't need a second call. I washed, shaved, got dressed, packed my small suitcase and went to the dining car. John and Lester were already seated, so I joined them and we all ordered breakfast.

"We'll be there in three hours," Lester said.

The idea of pitching comedy ideas so soon to the Great One himself set my stomach on fire. I canceled my order and spent the rest of the trip gnawing on my knuckles while Lester took a hundred bucks from John in gin rummy.

As we got off the train in Miami on Saturday, Sam Cohn came running across the platform. He looked scared to death and was tousled as usual. I think he sent his clothes to the cleaners to have them rumpled. There were the customary ink stains on his shirt, papers half falling out of his pockets, messed-up light brown hair, intelligent lively brown eyes and a beaming smile. He was Lester's boss but looked like his lackey. It was hard to believe that Sam was one of the most powerful men in show business. As the head of General Artists Corporation, a prestigious talent agency, he could make or break you. He ran the company with an iron — but slightly smudged — fist.

Sam rushed up to the three of us as we strolled down the platform. "What happened to you guys? You're late!"

"It couldn't be helped, Sam," Lester said.

"*We* weren't driving the goddamned train," John said with a grin.

"Anyway, what's the rush?" I said.

"Jackie's finished his golf game and he's waiting for us in the club-house. Just waiting. Don't you get it?"

"Get what?" John asked.

"He'll start drinking, and bye-bye meeting!"

"Jackie Gleason drinks?" I asked.

"Quit with the jokes, Frank," Sam said. "Come on, the car's right over there. Let's go!"

Now we were frantic. After a week of late-night work and the long train ride, Sam's "bye-bye meeting" put a scare in us. But we didn't have long to think about it. He made like an Indy 500 driver and soon pulled up to the clubhouse, tires squealing. Then he sent us ahead and went off to get himself a little less tousled.

Suddenly we came upon the biggest golf cart in the known golfing world.

"That's Jackie's," Lester said. "It's got a color TV, a full bar, and it's air-conditioned. Pretty snappy, eh?" His fingers lightly caressed the spotless white paint and blinding chrome trim.

"He could live in that," John said.

"Sometimes he does," Sam cracked as he caught up to us, tousled as ever. "The clubhouse is right in here." He motioned, opening the door for us, then started whispering. "Just follow me and smile. Jackie likes smiles."

We smiled as ordered and looked around. Everything was in rich red leather and expensive-looking dark polished wood, all of it floating on thick white wall-to-wall carpeting.

At the far end of the room, at a massive round table, sat Jackie, bigger than life. He was still wearing his golf clothes, a giant drink in one hand, a cigarette in the other. As we made our way over to him, Sam whispered that the man beside Jackie was the executive producer of Gleason Enterprises. He wore a very expensive Italian suit with a vest and glossy silk tie. I wondered if he played golf in that outfit. Sitting on Jackie's left were two other men who didn't rate Sam's whispered introduction.

"Would you care for a drink?" an African-American waiter dressed in red leather asked us before we sat down.

"Have a drink," Sam whispered. "Jackie likes it if you drink."

We ordered gin and tonics, and settled in across from Jackie and his gang. Here I was sitting opposite a man I'd admired and who'd made me laugh for years. He was Joe the Bartender, Reggie Van Gleason, the Poor Soul, and my favorite, Ralph Kramden, the New York bus driver. He wasn't making me laugh at that particular moment, though. His round, puffy face and crinkled blue eyes looked kind of mean and tired after his 18 grueling holes in an air-conditioned golf cart. But he *was* the Great One. Only a few years before, he was probably the biggest television star in America. "And away we go!" he'd shout, and light up America's Saturday nights for an hour. Right now he was sitting across from me in cashmere golfing clothes, his black hair neatly parted and slicked down. As he took a good solid pull on his drink, he glanced around the room. Then his eyes stopped glancing and looked directly at me. I guess he picked me because I was clutching a sheaf of papers full of possibly great ideas.

"Whatcha got, pal?" he growled.

Lester had explained to me that when Jackie called you "pal," it didn't mean he liked you or anything like that. He called everybody "pal" because he couldn't, or wouldn't, remember names. I wondered if he called his wife "pal." Anyway, I was Jackie's "pal" for the moment and he had asked for our best ideas. I shuffled a couple of papers and dived in.

"*The Honeymooners* as a two-hour musical!" I announced as confidently as I could. I looked up and everybody was nodding and smiling, even Jackie.

"We can take one of the best plots from a previous *Honeymooners* show, add singers and dancers, and give Jackie a song something like this . . ." I pointed to John, who stood up and, in a perfect Ralph Kramden voice, sang:

To the moon, Alice, to the moon.
And soon, Alice, to the moon.
That's the name of the tune, Alice.
To the moon, Alice, and soon!

Jackie gave the ditty a bit of a laugh, which was a cue for everyone to do the same, only louder.

"And right in the middle of the show," I continued quickly, "Jackie and Art Carney do a song-and-dance duet about the importance of their jobs." I pointed to John again.

"Who is more important, the bus driver or the sewer worker?" John said. "In the end, Alice is called on to decide and she picks the sewer worker, to which Ralph Kramden chimes, 'To the moon, Alice!'"

"That could be hilarious!" Sam exclaimed. There were more nods and grins.

"Will there be a lot of rehearsals?" Jackie asked.

"Jackie doesn't like rehearsing," Sam whispered in my ear, without moving his lips.

"That's up to the director, Jackie," I explained.

And Sam jumped in. "You could learn the songs on your own time and let Barney Martin do the same rehearsing like on your regular show."

Jackie seemed to like that idea. We found out later that Barney Martin was an actor who did all the rehearsals — even the dress rehearsal — while Gleason watched through a video hookup in his dressing room. Jackie not only hated rehearsing, he refused to participate. Barney came out okay a few decades later, playing Jerry Seinfeld's father on the hit comedy *Seinfeld*. But back to the meeting.

"That sounds like a damned good idea, Jackie," Sam said.

"We'll want the June Taylor Dancers, right, pal?" Jackie said to no one in particular.

"That goes without saying, Jackie," Sam said.

"And you know what?" Jackie said.

"No, what?" John asked.

Jackie raised his hand as if to answer and briefly seemed frozen. Then his eyes closed and his head nodded forward. He was sound asleep.

John was about to say something, but Sam shushed him and whispered, "Jackie doesn't like being awakened."

I couldn't believe what I was seeing. Seven grown-up men watching a fat man sleep. He even started to snore as we all waited, afraid to wake the Great One. The red leather waiter arrived with the drinks, but Sam frantically waved him away. Sam then got up, tiptoed noiselessly on the thick white rug and took the still-burning cigarette out of Jackie's fingers, stubbed it out in the ashtray and tiptoed back to his seat. Why he tiptoed I'll never know. An elephant stampede couldn't make a noise on that rug.

Four or five minutes went by. They seemed like four or five hours. Finally, Jackie moved in his seat and his eyes popped open.

"And you know what?" he said.

"No, what?" John asked, just as he had before the nap.

"I'll get Oscar Hammerstein to do the words and I'll write the music."

"Great!" Lester almost shouted, and everyone else nodded and smiled.

"What else you got, pal?"

I didn't answer right away. I was still wondering why in hell Oscar Hammerstein would dump Richard Rodgers for his big chance to write a *Honeymooners* television show with Jackie Gleason. *Stranger things have happened*, I told myself.

"Jackie's waiting, Frank," Sam whispered, nudging me.

"Oh, sorry." I started shuffling papers again and finally found my place. "We'll send out hundreds of invitations to a golf match between Arnold Palmer and Jackie Gleason. And," I continued before anyone could interrupt, "moving alongside the golf game, we'll have a flatbed truck, decked out like a pool hall, complete with a full pool table and Minnesota Fats. Between golf holes, Jackie plays a pool match with Fats."

"Wow!" Sam said.

Everybody nodded and smiled again, even Gleason, who took a good slug of his drink and lit another cigarette. "I'll tell you what, pal."

"What?" John asked as Gleason's eyes fluttered shut. "What?" John repeated, an edge creeping into his voice.

"Shush," Sam whispered, just as the red leather waiter returned with the drinks. Sam waved him away again.

"Okay," the waiter murmured. "I'm gonna need more ice, anyway."

I jumped up and grabbed the two gin and tonics from the waiter's tray. At least it gave John and me something to do while we waited for Sleeping Beauty.

That wait lasted almost 10 minutes. Nobody made a move. Suddenly, Jackie coughed himself awake.

"What?" John asked again.

"The caddies are gonna be showgirls, really sexy ones!" Jackie said.

"What a show!" Sam said.

"And a beautiful showgirl racks the pool balls for me and Fats!"

"Yes!" the well-dressed exec shouted, slapping his hand on the table.

"And we'll get Bob Hope or Bing Crosby to announce the golf and trade lines with Jackie," Sam said to more nods and pumps.

Then my partner spoke up. "The pool game should be announced by Jackie's co-star in *The Hustler*, Mr. Paul Newman."

"Perfect!" Lester said. Everyone slapped their hands on the table and grunted approvingly.

"Paul Newman will never do it," I whispered to John.

"I know it, but I want in on this Let's Pretend game."

I laughed and slapped my hand on the table, too.

"Okay, pal . . ." Jackie mumbled, then nodded off again.

The waiter, approaching again with a tray of drinks, did an immediate about-face and left. Sam did his tiptoe bit and removed another burning cigarette from Gleason's fingers.

Then the snappily dressed executive producer made a whispered announcement: "That's it, folks. Jackie doesn't like long meetings, so thank you all for a very successful meeting."

"But we have two more shows to present," John protested.

"Leave them here and I'll make sure Jackie sees them," Sam said. He patted me on the shoulder. "You guys did a great job and I'll be seeing you back in New York."

A sure kiss-off, if ever I heard one, I thought.

Lester motioned for us to get up and follow him. We floated out of the clubhouse on the thick white magic carpet, then took a taxi back to the station. The ride was much less scary than our trip with Sam.

"That was a sweet idea of yours, Johnny," Lester said.

"You mean Paul Newman?" I asked, incredulous.

"Yes, sir. Sweet."

"Are you kidding, Lester?" John said. "Do you really think Paul Newman, the big huge movie star, is going to stand outdoors on a moving platform and announce a pool game between Gleason and Fats?"

"Then why bring it up?"

"I thought the surprise might keep him awake."

"And it did, for about 12 seconds," I said.

Monday morning, John and I picked up on *Hullabaloo* where we had left off the week before, only now with greater appreciation of the acts we were writing for. No matter what they were smoking, snorting or shooting up, the rock stars of the '60s were down-to-earth, sober professionals compared to the Great One . . . and a whole lot more fun.

Chapter 2

✦

DEPRESSION WITHOUT A SHRINK

I WAS BORN IN 1927, a good year to be born. The '20s were still roaring and the stock market was soaring, but when I turned two, people stopped smiling at me and saying I was cute. I knew damned well I was still cute, but something really bad had happened to the grown-ups that year and they didn't see fit to discuss it with me. I found out much later that the stock market had crashed. I didn't hear the crash, but I sure as hell felt the shockwaves. Although my dad didn't have any stock, people he worked for had lots and lots, and the lots and lots became nots and nots. One night I was sleeping in my own bed in my very own bedroom in a very nice house in North Toronto; the next night I was sharing a bed with my parents in a tiny room in an east-end row house owned by my grandfather.

Duncan Grant was in his early 70s, but didn't look it. You knew he was a Scot as soon as he opened his mouth. I loved his accent and I deeply loved this tough old Scotsman. His pale blue eyes were friendly but wary. His wavy white hair was slicked back and parted, mostly to the side. His white moustache was always neatly trimmed. I think he still had his own teeth, but I couldn't be sure and was afraid to ask. He was very quiet, unless somebody stepped on his vegetable garden in the backyard and then you could hear him for blocks.

On New Year's Eve, Grandpa Grant would have my mother wake me up just before midnight and put me outside the front door and leave me there. This was the start of first fittin, a Scottish tradition my grandfather abided by because it meant good luck for the whole house for the coming year. The first person to knock on the door and enter the house after the strike of 12 had to be dark-haired and the youngest male. I'd stand on the front stoop, shivering in my jammies, waiting for the light over the door to come on. That was my signal to knock. The door would be opened by my grandfather, dressed in Grant-clan plaid kilt, a sporran, a Highland tam and scarf. He would hoist me up on his shoulders and lead a parade of relatives and neighbors through the tiny house, singing "Road to the Isles." He sipped at fine old Scotch whisky — first fittin was the only time of the year I saw him take a drink. After the procession, my mother would put me back to bed and the celebration downstairs went on well after I drifted off to sleep.

My father, Frank Peppiatt, was a big, strong, handsome man with curly black hair, a ruddy complexion, blue eyes and a big bright salesman's smile. He could tell a joke in almost any dialect and make you laugh, even if it wasn't funny. As he moved up in the world of business, he gave lectures on public speaking and salesmanship.

I, however, was not a chip off the old block. Early on I fell out of step with my dad. I don't know when or where it happened, but it did. He gave lectures to thousands of people but never bothered to sit me down and talk to me about what I was studying in school, or anything else. I loved sports — football, basketball and hockey. I played on one team or another year-round and I was good at it. But team sports were of no interest to my father. Occasionally, he came to watch me in sporting events, always hidden in the back — sometimes he told my mother and she told me he had been there and seen me, or so she said — but he never admitted to me he'd been there. That way he wouldn't have to praise me.

He was very good with his hands, always making things out of wood, repairing machinery. He tried and tried to teach me, to no avail. "The boy is all thumbs," I heard him tell my mother. It got so I would begin to feel queasy whenever I was anywhere near my dad's workbench. My father was also a passionate fisherman. As soon as the ice was out of the lakes, he would take my mother and me fishing. He would be pulling in bass or muskie by the bucketful, while I sat there, bored, holding my pole, with never a nibble on my line. It was frustrating for me and probably for him, too.

As I grew up, he wanted me to be successful, but only on his terms. I had to be a lawyer and that was that. A friend of my father told me it had broken his heart when I refused to go to law school. After that, even though I became very successful in show business, he didn't seem to care. He thought what I was doing was trivial. Maybe it was, but I loved it.

In spite of everything, I knew my father loved me, but he never said it. I loved him, but I probably never said it, either.

My mother, Sarah, was the complete opposite. She was shy and retiring, preferring to stay in the background and let my dad hold the stage. She was very pretty without the help of any makeup — sparkling green eyes, thick curly brown hair and a loving smile that said, "Everything's going to be all right." In her own quiet way, she was funny and smart. Her six sisters always came to her for advice on any problems they had. She also advised my father on many decisions that moved his career along. She was my mother and also my best friend. She refereed between my father and me whenever we had a disagreement, which occurred more and more often the older I got.

Back in 1929, we moved into 352 Glebeholme Boulevard, a semi-detached house with three tiny bedrooms and one bathroom. The house was heated by a coal furnace that had to be banked every night. Thank God I wasn't old enough to shovel coal! Our food was cooled with a 50-pound block of ice in an icebox — we had no Frigidaire, no phone, limited heat, no radio, but lots of coal in the bin and lots of coal dust in the air. The three bedrooms were occupied by my parents and me in one, my grandfather and my uncle Duncan in another. Dunc was my mother's younger brother and Grandpa's only living son. He was a spoiled brat — the apple of my grandfather's eye and he knew it. Dunc was blond and very handsome. He always wore a smirk as if he knew something and wasn't going to tell anybody what it was. Actually, he *did* know something — he had just graduated from the University of Toronto as a civil engineer. I didn't know what that was back then, but I did know they were mostly out of work.

The third tiny bedroom was occupied by my aunt Millie, one of my mother's six younger sisters. She was dating a fireman who was soon to be my uncle Bob. Millie was a real flapper, from her curly bobbed hair to her rolled-down stockings. She wore eye shadow, rouge and lipstick and didn't care who approved. She drank a bit too much, but what the hell, it *was* the Depression and she had a job. Aunt Millie worked at the T. Eaton Company department store, way downtown. I don't know what she did there, but that's where she did it.

Every Christmas my mother's whole family gathered for a turkey dinner, and Aunt Millie always drank to excess. After dinner Aunt Millie took a kitchen chair, planted it in a snowbank in front of the house, sat down with her legs stretched out in front of her and sang at the top of her voice "All I Want for Christmas Is My Two Front Teeth" and "Jingle Bells." Nobody said anything because, after all, Millie's merry melodies on the snowbank were an annual holiday event for the whole neighborhood. Eventually, she'd sing herself to sleep out in the frosty December air and a couple of uncles would bring her inside to thaw. All of my cousins and I thought it was great fun. But her husband, the fireman, did not agree.

Other relatives were constantly moving in and out of 352 Glebeholme Boulevard, as jobs came and went and the Depression moved slowly on. The one bathroom with a tub and no shower was like something out of a Marx Brothers movie every morning. Aunt Millie was always first in the bathroom and she locked the door. Uncle Dunc would rush into the hall: "Come on, Mill, I've got to go to work!"

"You don't have a damn job!" she'd yell through the door.

"But I've got to go!"

"Go in the sink in the cellar!"

"But I've got to go number two!"

My father would poke his head out of the middle bedroom. "Keep it down, you two. The boy's still asleep."

"I have to go!" Dunc would continue to the door.

"Go down to the gas station at the corner," Millie would shout back.

"Come on, Mill, Dunc has to go," my dad would say, "and I have to shave."

"Ha!" Millie would snort. "So you'll look good lounging around the house all day?"

Finally, my grandfather, with his Scottish burr, would come on the scene. "Let me into the damned bathroom, Millicent! I *have* a job and if I don't get the heck to work we won't *have* a bathroom to argue about!"

Meekly, Millie would open the door and Grandpa Grant would march in and slam the door behind him. I'd start to cry.

"Now see what you've done!" my mother would shout from our bedroom.

Uncle Dunc would scurry out the front door, heading for the gas station at the corner. Millie would go back to bed and my dad would shave in the cellar beside the coal furnace.

My grandfather had emigrated from Scotland before the turn of the century. He and my grandmother had 10 children — seven girls and three boys. Two of the boys died quite young of diphtheria, but the other eight children, including my mother, were constant players in my early years.

One cold winter morning, I looked out the living room window and watched my dad leaving to look for a job, as usual. As he walked by a neighbor's garbage can, something caught his eye. He stopped and pulled out a discarded tweed cap. He brushed some dust and dirt off the cap, put it on his head at a jaunty angle and went off down the street. When he came home that night he had a job — sweeping the showroom floor at the General Motors dealership on Bay Street. *Wow!* A job! Fifty dollars a month — we were rich! I guessed the jaunty tweed cap had done the trick.

A FEW YEARS LATER, I was doing well at school and everybody in the house was working. There weren't many ads in the Help Wanted section for civil engineers, so Dunc had joined the Toronto Police Force. Meanwhile, my dad was slowly starting to move up the General Motors ladder. Some money was coming in. The food tasted a lot better. It wasn't rabbit anymore or internal organs like lamb kidneys, beef heart, liver and lungs, baked, broiled or fried. Instead, our plates were heaped with roast beef, baked ham or roasted chicken.

On Saturday mornings, the kids on our block would go door-to-door, collecting fruit and vegetable baskets that we'd turn in at the stores on Danforth Avenue for two cents each. Once you collected 10 cents — five for the movies and five for penny candy — your Saturday afternoon was heaven. For five cents you got two cartoons, a feature film, a shoot-'em-up Western and a Flash Gordon serial.

About one Saturday every month, after we'd had our dinner, my grandfather would take my hand and say, "Laddie, we're going to the moving pictures." I didn't argue, so away we would go to see the same film I'd seen in the afternoon, without the Western and the Flash Gordon episode, but with a newsreel thrown in. I loved being with Grandpa. We would always stop for a chocolate soda at Small's Pharmacy on the way home. On one of these Saturday nights, when I had just turned 10, I had a confusing and serious question to ask him.

"Grandpa, the priest who runs the choir said he wanted to teach me how to masturbate. Is that okay?"

"And, laddie, what did you say to the priest?"

"I said I would ask my dad."

"And what did the priest say?"

"He said it would be a sin to talk of such things with a parent."

"Well, well," Grandpa said, smiling. "When the time comes, I think you'll be able to handle that thing by yourself without anybody teaching you."

The next day my mother sat me down and said, "Your father says you're not going to be in the choir anymore."

What a relief! My parents had found out about the priest, but I hadn't sinned because I had told only my grandfather, not either of my parents — who Grandpa told was his business. If fact, we never returned to that church. Every Sunday morning my parents and I would walk right past the church with that priest standing by the front door. My dad would wave to the priest and continue down the block to the Anglican church. I'm sure the priest knew where we were going, and why. And that's how I became a Protestant.

One Saturday I saw little Shirley Temple tap dancing with Buddy Ebsen in *Captain January* and I knew right then I wanted to be a tap dancer, too. Hollywood, here I come! I pushed brass thumbtacks into the heels and toes of my bedroom slippers and I tapped my way across the kitchen linoleum. What a great sound. Even though the tacks hurt like hell, it was worth it. My feet didn't agree, but you can't please everybody.

MY FATHER CAME HOME FROM work one day and announced that the car company had given him a promotion and they were moving him to Montreal. I thought the move meant just him, but apparently it meant my mother and me, too. Montreal — jeez! Another planet. I had my own little perfect world — one block on Glebeholme

Boulevard between Coxwell Avenue and Woodington Avenue. There were 11 guys my age on the one block, half of them my cousins, and we had a great time all year long. Street hockey with real apples, Saturday movies, snowball fights, fireworks on Victoria Day. We all went to the same school and did a zillion wonderful things together. And now I was never going to see all my grand old pals again. I cried. Apparently, I didn't cry loud enough or long enough, because before I could blow my nose, I was on a train with my mother and father, going like 60 to Montreal.

"When'll we get there?" I asked.

"When we get there," my dad said.

"When will that be?"

"The conductor will yell, 'Montreal next stop!'"

"When will he yell that?"

"I'm going to the club car to have a drink," my dad snapped at me, and strode up the aisle.

"Don't ask so many questions," my mother said.

"How can I find out stuff if I don't ask?"

"Look, your father is nervous enough about starting a new job in Montreal and —"

"When will we get there?" I interrupted.

"Stop it!" my mother cried, and smacked her knee in frustration. "Just look out the window and enjoy the countryside."

"There's nothing but snow," I said, slumping down in my seat.

I must have drifted off to sleep or gone snowblind, because next thing I knew a sharp, high-pitched voice announced, "Montreal Windsor Station in five minutes! Montreal next stop!" The conductor kept yelling his message as he hustled down the aisle and into the next car.

"Montreal in five minutes!" I called out.

"I heard! I heard!"

My parents were about to start a wonderful new life and I was being a huge pain in the neck, all because I had to move. I look back on it now and can't help but feel a little guilty. I was only 10, but I should have been more understanding. They were giving up twice as much as I was, and they had to be far more anxious. I did cut them a little slack as we settled in Montreal, but not enough.

After our train ride, we took a taxi to 5056 Victoria Avenue in an area called Notre-Dame-de-Grâce or NDG. I didn't like the looks of the street — too wide, houses too far apart, no verandas, no kids playing, a lot of snow and cold as hell. Inside, though, 5056 Victoria was fabulous, but I didn't let on to my mom and dad. I raced through the whole place — a big bright kitchen, a long hallway into a huge living room and dining room, three big bedrooms, a breakfast nook and one bathroom for just the three of us. After 352 Glebeholme Boulevard, it was a palace. We didn't own the place — we rented it for $70 a month, furnished. I knew I could get to like 5056 Victoria Avenue in one big hurry.

"Will I be sleeping with you?" I asked my parents.

My father looked at me and smiled. "Of course," he said, "we'll be leasing out the other two bedrooms to pay the rent."

I did a double take and turned to my mother.

"He's kidding. You'll have your very own bedroom."

I laughed, pretending I'd got the joke, and for just a second there, I really didn't. But that's the way it often was with my father's jokes.

The first morning my dad went to work he looked like he'd just stepped out of a men's fashion magazine — a beautiful gray fedora, a snappy-looking double-breasted gray flannel suit, white shirt, dark blue tie and shiny black oxfords. My father was ready for his first day of work at GM in downtown Montreal. No more dusty tweed caps fished out of a garbage can. Jaunty angle or not, that was all behind him. He slipped into his dark blue tweed overcoat, kissed my mother, patted me on the head and went out the front door, into a very cold and snowy brand-new life.

"Didn't your father look swell?"

"I'll say," I agreed, and wondered what my mom and I would do the rest of the day.

"You're going to your new school on Monday," she said.

"Yeah, I know, but can we go to the show on Saturday afternoon? There's a new Tom Mix movie and —"

My mother's frown stopped me in mid-sentence. She knelt down beside me and put her arm around my shoulders. "Frankie, I'm sorry, but nobody can go to the movies in Montreal until they're 16."

"Sixteen!" I shouted. "Is this a joke?"

"No. A few years ago on a Saturday afternoon a movie theater caught on fire and dozens of little children were killed. They passed a law — no one under 16 in any movie house in Montreal."

"This is horrible!" I paused with a catch in my throat. "I have to wait six years before I can see Tom Mix, Shirley Temple or Flash Gordon again?"

"That's the law."

"It's not fair. Six years. Rats!" I ran into my new bedroom and flopped onto my new bed. "Rats and double rats."

The next Monday, a bitterly cold day in January, I walked to Iona Avenue Public School. It wasn't far, but the cold crept right into my bones. If winter was cold in Toronto, Montreal was still colder — and no movies. The guys I met at school were okay, but after school they were all spread out, not all your pals on the same block like on Glebeholme. To make matters worse, I couldn't believe it when they told me at school I had to take French class. A 10-year-old learning French? What kind of a place was this? French class and no movies. None of the kids had ever heard of Shirley Temple or Tom Mix. What did they do on Saturday afternoons? Speak French?

I was depressed and so was my mother. Her best friends in Toronto were her six sisters whom she'd known and loved all her life. Montreal had no sisters to turn to for gossip, afternoon teas, bridal and baby showers, family Christmases and birthdays, plus all the other things girlfriends and families do together, week after week. In fact, it was much tougher on my mother than on me. I had school to attend five days a week. My mother had nothing. Sure, she made breakfast for my dad and me, packed my lunch to take to school and cooked hot dinners for us every night, but she was lonely.

ONE FRIDAY NIGHT IN MARCH, my father brought home two radios — a large DeForest Crosley for the living room and a small Bakelite for me in my bedroom. The radios changed my life forever and saved my mother's life. She played the DeForest Crosley all day while she cleaned, baked and vacuumed. *The Happy Gang* from Toronto every lunch hour, soap operas by the dozens, *Ma Perkins*, *The Guiding Light*, *Backstage Wife*, *Young Doctor Malone*. At night, we all listened to the big radio in the living room — *The Kate Smith Hour*, *Amos 'n' Andy*, *The Fred Allen Show*, *Fibber McGee and Molly* and, of course, Sunday nights at seven, *The Jack Benny Program*.

Every afternoon I'd race home from school to listen to my favorites on my radio in my very own bedroom: *Jack Armstrong, the All-American Boy*; *Speed Gibson of the International Police*; *Little Orphan Annie*; *The Lone Ranger*. Then after dinner I'd finish up my homework and go to bed early with *The Green Hornet*, *Suspense*, *Lux Radio Theater*, *Red Skelton*, *The Bob Hope Show*, *Mr. District Attorney*. Now it didn't matter that I couldn't go to the movies. Most of the programs would begin, "Live from New York . . ." and I thought New York must be a wonderful place to send out all these programs. They were even better than the movies because radio gave me my own movies in my head. For every show, I closed my eyes, heard the actors and imagined the scenes.

Sometimes in the newspapers or magazines I'd see photographs of people standing around microphones with sheafs of paper in their hands and the caption would say that it was such-and-such a radio show. Well, I knew they were lying because I'd seen that radio show in my head. The Green Hornet was Brit Reed and I knew exactly what his mansion looked like and his office at the newspaper with all the reporters spread out working at typewriters. They couldn't fool me with those pictures of actors just standing around. I would imagine the Lone Ranger, roaring across the prairie on his horse — "Hi-ho, Silver! Away!" — with his loyal Indian companion Tonto riding at his side. I told my father what I saw and he said with a bit of a sneer, "Do you honestly think the Lone Ranger and Tonto are riding the range, each holding a microphone with a hundred or so miles of cable trailing behind them?"

"Why not?" I answered, and slipped into my bedroom and tuned in to my world.

"Sarah!" I heard my father say. "I don't know if the radio was a good idea for the boy."

"Don't worry, Frank, he'll be fine. Hurry up. Bing Crosby's just started."

They had Bing Crosby while I had "The Flight of the Bumble Bee" and *The Green Hornet*. They couldn't see Bing, but I could see the Hornet racing through the city in his special car with his butler Kato beside him, ready to help him bust crime and save the world.

But it wasn't all entertainment. At that time, more and more radio newscasts were featuring a guy named Hitler over in Germany. I often heard my mother and father talking about him, but I figured this Hitler guy and Germany were a long way from Montreal. So what was the problem?

The problem turned out to be one *big* problem. I heard Hitler was taking over Europe and there could be a big war. The news seemed to get worse every day. I was 12 and I was getting scared. Boys waited to be called up. Maybe I'd have to join the army and fight this Hitler person. Did they take 12-year-olds in the military? I had no idea, but it was possible.

"Listen," my father explained, "you have to be 18 to join the army. Where'd you get that dopey idea they'd take a kid of 12?"

"Well, I'm big for my age."

"Forget it!" my father snapped. "We haven't even got a damn war yet!"

Before you could say, "We haven't even got a damn war yet!" we had one. Britain was at war with Germany and, of course, Britain's Commonwealth countries — Canada, Australia, New Zealand and the rest — joined Britain in declaring war on Germany.

The news, however, wasn't all bad in 1939. Because of my dad's good work over the past two years, General Motors had awarded him his very own Chevrolet/Oldsmobile dealership in his hometown of Newmarket, just a few miles north of Toronto. My mother was on top of the world — she was almost back in Toronto with her sisters. My dad was starting a business of his own and I discovered that Newmarket had one movie house that changed the bill twice a week, plus a Saturday-afternoon matinee with Westerns, cartoons and serials. And you didn't have to be 16 to watch them. We were moving back to Hollywood Heaven!

But heaven quickly turned into hell for my father. He had rented a gas station with three pumps, a big garage, an office and a large parking lot to display the sparkling new Chevvies and Olds he was going to sell. He put up a big sign over the garage that announced in bright blue letters: Peppiatt Motor Sales.

That same week General Motors stopped making cars and turned their plants over to the war effort. They built tanks, weapon carriers, ambulances, trucks and jeeps. Peppiatt Motor Sales had no motors to sell.

✦

Chapter 3

NEITHER A SALESMAN NOR A LAWYER BE

MY MOTHER WAS IN TEARS. "What are we going to do, Frank?"

"I'll tell you what!" my father said, smacking his hand on the kitchen table, "we're going to go to Toronto and get a job."

My mother started smiling through her tears. She was returning to Toronto and her sisters.

"Will we move back to 352 Glebeholme Boulevard?" I said.

"Your aunt Jessie and uncle Herb live there now with your cousins Grant and Donnie."

"Rats!" I muttered as my dad grabbed my arm.

"No rats about it," he said. "We're living alone, unless you want to start sleeping with us again?"

I shut up and shook my head.

My dad went to Toronto and got a good job almost immediately. Most of the young men had been called up for military service but my dad, at 40, was too old. He worked for Canadian Breweries and was in charge of selling O'Keefe beer in the province of Ontario. There was no chance that a beer company would stop brewing for the war effort. In fact, they increased production.

We settled in at 70 Melrose Avenue in North Toronto, near where I was born. Mom had her sisters back, and I had my radio and lots of Saturday-afternoon movies. I started high school nearby at a new building called Lawrence Park Collegiate.

The war news was not good. Hitler was dropping bombs all over England and hundreds of Canadian boys, including some of my cousins, were flying fighter planes. The Canadian army and navy were conscripting men as fast as they could. The Battle of Britain was underway. While my mother and father listened to Lorne Greene's war news broadcast, I was by my own radio listening to my usual *Green Hornet* stuff plus a wonderful show that was on the Canadian Broadcasting Corporation every Sunday night. The show was simply called *The Stage Series*. Directed by a very talented man named Andrew Allen, it featured fine Canadian actors and was written by Canadian writers — and damn well written, too. *The Stage Series* was nominated as one of the best North American dramatic shows every year. Some years it won the award, and when it didn't win, it usually came second to Orson Welles' *Mercury Theatre on the Air*.

My Sunday night played out perfectly for me. Six-thirty: *The Adventures of Ozzie and Harriet*; seven o'clock: *The Jack Benny Program*; eight o'clock: *The Charlie McCarthy Show*; and at nine I'd slip into bed and listen to the CBC *Stage Series* while my mom and dad listened to *The Kate Smith Hour*. One Sunday evening, we were having dinner and listening to *Ozzie and Harriet*, when right in the middle of the show an ominous voice broke in: "We interrupt this program for a special announcement. The Japanese air force has bombed the United States naval base and military headquarters at Pearl Harbor on the island Oahu."

"Not another war," my mother cried.

"Now the Yanks are really in it!" my dad exclaimed.

"Aren't they going to play the rest of *Ozzie and Harriet*?" I said.

"I sure as hell doubt it," my dad said. "Now America's in it and we'll get some help in Europe."

"Maybe it'll last until I'm 18 — then I can go."

My mother started to cry. "God, let's hope not."

My dad was right. America climbed right into the conflict, declaring war on Germany and Italy, while Britain and her allies, including Canada, declared war on Japan. The war in Europe had morphed into World War II. Would it last until I was 18? My mother hoped not, but I wasn't too sure anymore. (As it turned out, I was 17 when the war ended in Germany, but the Japanese were still hanging in there.)

Meanwhile, I was happy at Lawrence Park Collegiate, lettering in football and basketball and doing pretty well in my schoolwork. The French I had learned in Montreal gave me a leg up in Toronto. The only French I didn't know I learned from a beautiful girl, Sheila, and it involved kissing and other stuff. We were in love.

The war news was broadcast every day, but it seemed so far away and didn't invade our teenage lives. Not too much, anyway — we took a course in school called Aircraft Recognition in order to tell the differences between our planes and German planes. As if we'd ever see a German plane flying over Toronto. But we had to pass the exam nonetheless.

Several guys in my class and I helped the war effort by working on a farm in the summers. It was damn hard work — eight hours a day, six days a week on our knees, weeding row after row of lettuce, carrots and onions for 30 cents an hour. I don't think my knees were ever the same again.

And then one August day in 1945 I was kneeling, working a row of carrots at Holland Marsh, when the farmer I was weeding for came running out of his farmhouse, yelling, "They dropped the bomb! They dropped the bomb! Take the rest of the day off!"

I didn't know who dropped what bomb, but I would gladly take the rest of the day off. The farmer drove all the student workers back to the dorm where 25 or 30 of us lived, ate, slept and were loaned out to weed. As the news sank in, we realized the war would soon be over and we wouldn't be in it. Many of the guys were disappointed. I was secretly relieved.

We won the war in Germany and Japan, but I lost Sheila, my steady love of the past three years. A snappy-looking 25-year-old ace in the Royal Canadian Air Force turned her head, dazzling her with tales of dangerous missions flown all over Europe. How could I compete? I thought I was heartbroken, and that feels as bad as actually *being* heartbroken, believe me. But soon my heart was *really* broken when I found out Sheila was marrying the RCAF ace. She invited all of our friends — and me — to the wedding.

"If you go, you'll look like an idiot!" my good friend Tom Ryley said as we sipped cherry Cokes in Harold's Drugstore, a haunt for teenagers on Yonge Street.

"Are *you* going?" I asked.

"Sure, free food and she's having six single bridesmaids. Oh yeah, I'm going."

"Well, I'm going, too."

"Don't be dopey. You'll look like some kind of sad-eyed lapdog."

"I don't give a damn. She'll see what she's missing, marrying that squirt."

Tom laughed. "He's no squirt, Frank. He's a war hero. He won an award."

"Well, I made the all-star football team."

"Oh, that really helped win the war." Tom laughed again.

"Screw you, Ryley. I'm going!"

"Suit yourself," Tom said.

On the day of the wedding, I dressed up as snazzily as I could and went to the damn ceremony. Sheila got married without once looking in my direction. In the receiving line at the reception she kissed me — not a French kiss, a regular sisterly kiss — and I moved on down the line. As I wove my way through the guests, I ran into Tom Ryley.

"How you doing?" he asked.

"I guess it's really over," I said.

"Really over? You actually thought by coming here you had a chance?"

"You never know."

"Of course you know — everyone knows. It's been over for quite a while, Frank. Now stop hoping and start living!" he nearly shouted.

"I get it," I said. "I get it."

"I hope to hell you do."

Well, there I was. The war was over, high school was over and my love life was over. I had promised my mother I would go to the University of Toronto and get a degree. I had not promised *anyone* I would continue on to law school. I really enjoyed college. I got involved in theater with Don Harron and Norman Jewison, who I would run into again a little later along the way. I played on two championship football teams — Victoria College in 1945 and the Varsity Blues in 1949, the year I graduated.

"So you got yourself a b.a.," my father said. "What kind of a job does that set you up for?"

"I want to do something in entertainment."

"That's just stupid, wishful thinking. Go to law school. Lawyers always get a good job."

"Not lousy lawyers," I said, "and that's what I'll be, if I go to law school . . . a lousy lawyer!"

"How can you say that?"

"I believe I just did."

There was no way my dad and I would agree about my future. He was very explicit about law school — I was to become a lawyer with my name on some door. I, on the other hand, was in limbo. I knew I wanted to get into radio, but I didn't have any experience. At least I was in Toronto, the center of the Canadian radio broadcasting industry. But how to get in the door?

My father agreed to help me, or teach me a lesson, I wasn't sure which. He pointed out that advertising was a very important part of radio. Through a friend he got me a job with an advertising company that sold space on the exterior of Toronto streetcars. My salary was strictly commission. I reported to the head office (I found out later it was the *only* office) on a Monday morning. "You've got to look like you mean business!" my father had warned me. I strutted into the office with a big smile, a snappy shirt, tie and tweed sports jacket, ready to do business.

A well-dressed secretary led me into the boss's office. "I'm Jim Tanker," he said. "You must be Peppiatt." He looked like a boss. In a movie or a mob, he would probably be chosen as the boss. Piercing, almost black eyes, thinning hair combed over to not quite cover a bald spot, thin lips and a tanned, outdoor-looking face. He was about six inches shorter than me and didn't seem to like me looming over him. "Have a seat," he insisted. Then he gave me a list of prospective customers I was supposed to call on that very day, as well as the advertising rates for various numbers of streetcars running on various routes in the city. If the routes went through poor areas, the rates were lower.

He also gave me a list of surveys that proved hundreds of thousands of people would see the ads while they waited for streetcars and roamed the streets. I asked if the numbers were true. "That's not the point!" he barked. "You must make the customer *believe* they are true. Understand?"

I said I understood but I really didn't. Were the survey numbers made up? Who could check on that? Nobody. I started to understand. Anyway, out I marched with a list of potential customers and pages of magic numbers that proved something or other.

The first name on the list was Ted Davy's Used Cars on Danforth Avenue, near where I lived when I was a kid. I waited for a streetcar and as it stopped I noticed the ad posted on its side. *Wow*, I thought, *some guy made good money for selling that space.* Actually seeing the product I was going to sell bucked me up with a surge of confidence.

But the surge didn't last long. When I knocked on the door of Ted Davy's office, a man smoking a cigar answered. He was wearing a brown pinstripe suit, brown and white shoes and white socks — a 1949 fashion statement. His hair was slicked back and shiny like a freshly frozen skating rink. He was fat and his shirt collar looked like it was keeping his head prisoner. He gave me a big salesman's smile and held out his hand. "Interested in a car?" he said.

"No, I represent the outside-of-the-streetcar advertising company and I can give you —"

He pulled his hand away, dropped the big smile. "Not interested," he snapped, slamming the door in my face. I was left with nothing but a wisp of cigar smoke. He didn't even give me the chance to tell him about the thousands of people who would see his ad and hurry on downtown to Ted Davy's Used Cars.

My next call was at Stoney's Car Mart, about two blocks away from Ted's. The same thing happened. In only an hour and 20 minutes, I finished the entire list to a medley of slamming doors. I couldn't go back to the office, so I hopped a streetcar downtown and went to a movie.

Is there something basically wrong with my approach? I wondered. *My dad sells beer by the truckload and I'll bet he doesn't get doors slammed in his face.* I don't even remember what the movie was about, I was so depressed. I sat through the damn film twice to take up a decent amount of time before I went back to the streetcar office. When I walked in, the boss and two other guys in suits and fedoras were having a drink, celebrating because one of the guys had just sold a huge account to Loblaws, the big supermarket chain. The boss offered me a drink, but I turned it down. It felt kind of good, *me* turning something down for a change. I sat by quietly as the three men went on drinking and congratulating. The boss never asked me how I did on my first day. I found out much later that he had given me a list of names that nobody was ever able to sell. Who could outsell a used-car salesman? If I'd known that, I would have gone directly to the movie and seen it *three* times.

That evening, when I told my father how my first day had gone, he said, "You've got to push your way through the door and make your pitch. These car guys are used to that. That's the way *they* do business. You've got to know who you're selling to and sell their way. Understand?"

"Sure I understand, Dad, but I can't do it."

"I'll bet law school is a little more appealing after today. Right?"

"No."

"Now look, son, I think you —"

"I think you two should cool down," my mother said.

"He has to do *something*," said my father.

"For God's sake, Frank, he just graduated from the university. Give him a little room."

"Are you two speaking about me? I'm right here, folks."

"You see, Sarah, it's that kind of smart-ass talk that gets people upset."

"Gets *you* upset," my mom said, laughing. "*I* think it's funny."

In a way, they were both right. My dad wanted me to get into something solid with a secure future and my mom wanted me to have a little space to work things out in my own way. Naturally, I agreed with my mother because she was so much like me, but my dad wanted me to take the survey facts and figures the boss had given me and make them *sell*! The figures were probably perfectly legitimate, but I didn't believe them and I couldn't sell what I didn't believe. It was yet another source of frustration between my father-the-salesman and me.

Years later, I could dazzle a television network executive when I was selling him a show. I believed totally in what I was selling because John and I had created it and we knew our product inside and out. We didn't always make a sale, but we didn't stop believing, and to me that makes a hell of a big difference. My dad, though, could sell anything, whether he believed in it or not.

After my depressing start at the outside-of-a-streetcar advertising company, I drove a cab for a while on the midnight shift. My fares were mostly drunks and various ladies of the evening. I got along with the ladies well because, as my father said, I was a smart-ass and, as my mother said, I was funny. I made the ladies laugh as we cruised through the dark and empty Toronto streets. They never came on to me once and I kept my distance, too. We both knew they were way out of my price range, not that I was in the market for professional flesh — I've always been happy with amateurs. Don't mix business and pleasure, my mother always said. My cab driving made me some money and it was quite interesting.

One night, about 3 a.m., I picked up two ladies in front of the Royal York Hotel.

"How ya doing, Frankie?" one of them said.

"Fine as wine!" I said. "Where can I take you two beautiful babes?"

"Home, James — St. Clair and Avenue Road."

A damned good fare, I thought, and heard the girls laughing in back.

"What's so funny?"

"You tell him, Cindy."

"You won't believe this, kid," Cindy said.

"Try me."

"Well," Cindy began, "we got a call to go to a certain suite. It was a very posh place and this one guy was there in bed. Very politely, he told us to take off our clothes, which we did. Then he puts on very loud marching music and asks us to march around his bed while he masturbates with a cooked chicken! He provides the stuffing, if you get what I mean."

I nearly lost control of the damn cab. "And then?" I said.

"No 'and then,'" Cindy said. "There we were, stark naked,

marching around until he finished. Then we got dressed. He paid us with a nice tip and we left."

"Was the marching music still playing?"

"It sure was, and he was on the phone."

"Probably ordering another chicken," I said, and the ladies laughed all the way home.

One other very late night while I was driving south on Yonge Street, I was flagged down by a well-dressed man standing beside a limo.

"Our car's conked out. Can you take us?"

"That's what I do. Where to?"

"Just give me a minute," he said as he opened the limo door, and out stepped an unusually gorgeous and curvaceous lady — long blond hair, blue eyes and a very sexy mouth. She wore a tight-fitting something or other. I jumped out of the cab and opened the door for her.

"My name is Lady Annabelle," she said in a sexy whisper. "What's yours?"

I told her and she got into the cab followed by the well-dressed man, who was not only well dressed but movie-star handsome. He gave an address and, as I began to drive, I realized I was driving *the* Lady Annabelle. She was very well-known in late-night entertainment — and I don't mean the talk-show kind.

We arrived at a very expensive-looking apartment house. I hopped out and opened the door. "Thank you, Frankie," Lady Annabelle purred, and she swished into the building.

"Aren't you going in with her?" I asked the man.

"No, I'll just wait here with you. I'm her manager."

"But I've got fares to get."

"Don't worry, it'll be worth it," he said, lighting up a cigarette and sprawling back on the seat.

Manager? I thought. *Doesn't he mean pimp?* Oh well, it was none of my business.

The manager and I sat there for well over two hours, until finally Lady Annabelle appeared, looking as lovely as ever. The movie-star-looking manager told me to take them back to where the limo had conked out. When we arrived, the driver was waiting and the limo was up and running.

"So long, Frankie," Lady Annabelle said, getting into her limo. The well-dressed pimp paid me my fare along with a hundred-dollar tip. I just stood there with a stupid grin on my face as the taillights of the limo moved away into the night.

Wow! A hundred-dollar tip. Whatever she did in that expensive-looking apartment house must have been very, very special and I'll bet it didn't involve any marching band — but maybe a cooked chicken.

I DROVE THE CAB EVERY night for about two months and every week-day I tried to get interviews at radio stations for a job, any job. One day I was at CFRB, a big station on Bloor Street, waiting to see the personnel manager, when I bumped into a girl I had known at college.

"Frank Peppiatt," she said. "What are you doing here?"

"How about you?"

"Oh, I'm in charge of the record library and I dole out the discs to the DJs." Her name was Clarissa and she was quite pretty, in a preppy way.

"I'm here to see Mr. Dash about a job."

"He'll just tell you we're not hiring."

"Well, I'll just wait to see him."

"No point," she said. "You should try an advertising agency."

"I just went through that horror, Clarissa. No way!"

"Well, I happen to know that MacLaren Advertising is looking for someone."

"To sell space door-to-door, I suppose?"

"No, in the radio department."

"An advertising agency with a radio department?"

"Of course, silly, they all have one. Look, my aunt Jane works for MacLaren Advertising Bermuda."

"The island?"

"No, the shorts! Of course, the island. She's not in the radio department but she knows the people who are. I'll talk to her and see if I can get you an appointment."

"Clarissa, I love you!"

"No, you don't."

It was wonderful to have college classmates who believed in helping other college classmates. Clarissa's fabulous aunt was successful in getting me an appointment. It was wonderful to have aunts of college classmates who . . . well, you know. My interview was scheduled for Monday, September 6, at 10 a.m. at MacLaren Advertising on the third floor of the Sterling Tower on the southwest corner of Richmond and Bay. On Sunday, the day before, I took a streetcar downtown to look at the building and make sure I knew exactly where I was going. I didn't want to go into the wrong building and look like a sap.

The next morning I was up with the sun. I shaved, put on my white shirt and tie, my gray flannel pants, blue tweed sports jacket and shiny oxfords. Was I nervous? Scared to death! My mother made me my favorite breakfast.

"Where are you going?" my dad asked.

"Look for a job."

"Law school starts in two weeks."

"Good luck to it."

"See what I mean, Sarah?"

Being a Canadian, I was 15 minutes early and since the man I was meeting with was also Canadian, he expected me to be early. At 10 minutes to 10, his secretary showed me into his office. His name was Hugh Horler and he looked too young to be head of the radio department in a big advertising agency. *Must be really smart,* I thought. He was about five foot ten, very slim, black curly hair, heavy horn-rimmed glasses in front of intelligent brown eyes. His face seemed quite tanned but it could have been his natural coloring.

He smiled and put out his hand. "Hi, I'm Hugh Horler and you must be Frank Peppiatt."

"Yes I am, Mr. Horler."

"Call me Hugh, okay?"

"Okay, Hugh!" I shook his hand and he motioned for me to sit down opposite him at his desk. It was a big black shiny desk, no clutter, everything neat and tidy. I figured it wasn't that way to impress me — it was the way he wanted things. I made a mental note.

"I understand you just graduated from the U of T?"

"That's right."

"And you played on the Varsity Blues?"

"Yes, I did."

"And you want to work here."

"Yes, I do."

"I'd have thought you'd be going off to law school or something like that."

"You sound like my father."

He laughed and said, "Your father sounds like my father."

"He wanted you to be a lawyer?"

"No, a doctor."

"Same difference," I said. "And you wanted to do this?"

"Yes, and I did."

"Well, I'd like a chance to do it, too."

He laughed again. "Then you're really interested in advertising?"

"Not so much advertising as radio."

"That's good," he said. "Then you won't be interested in becoming an account executive."

"What's an account executive?"

"I've often wondered that myself. Come on, I'll show you around."

"Show me around? You mean, I've got the job?"

"Maybe," he said.

"Is that a nine maybe or a five maybe?"

"Closer to a seven," he said with a smile, and we walked out of his office.

He introduced me to Kay Dale, the head of traffic. She was a shortish, attractive middle-aged woman who looked efficient and acted efficiently. I met Doddie Robb, the chief copywriter, who, like Hugh, seemed young for such an important job, but Hugh assured me she knew her stuff. Next, I met Jeann Beattie, a copywriter, and recently the author of a novel called *Blaze of Noon*. She was in her late 20s, a very pretty brunette, tan and dressed in high fashion. *No shortage of pretty, interesting girls*, I said to myself.

Hugh then led me through a door and into my heart's desire — an actual radio studio. I completely forgot all the pretty girls I had just met.

"This is fantastic!" I said, staring into the studio, my eyes popping.

"Behind that large glass window," Hugh said, pointing, "is a complete control booth with facilities to record on tape or on acetate discs."

I looked through the big window and saw all the wonderful mechanics — a control board, a talkback microphone and large twin turntables.

"We can record all our demo commercials right here," Hugh said. "Do you think you could learn to handle this equipment?"

"I would sure as heck try my damn best!" I said, and Hugh Horler held out his hand.

"Then welcome to MacLaren."

"I got the job?"

"That's up to your negotiations with Mr. Ferris."

"Mister who?"

"Ferris. He's the vice president and secretary treasurer of the agency. I'll call him and tell him you're coming up to see him."

"See him where?"

"On the 10th floor, where the account executives live and breed."

"When?"

"How about right now?" He led me out to the elevators. "Just press 10." He left me standing there, waiting for the next car up.

On the 10th floor, the receptionist led me to Mr. Ferris's office. "Just through that green door," she said. "Good luck." I proceeded through the green door, wondering what luck had to do with it.

Mr. Ferris was a very tall man, taller than me, in his late 40s or early 50s. He had red hair, green eyes, a spatter of freckles across his nose and cheeks and wore a classy-looking houndstooth jacket. His office was enormous and plush.

"Hugh tells me you want to work in our radio department."

"Yes, sir, very much so."

"Well, sit down and we'll talk about it."

I wasn't quite sure what we were going to talk about, but I sat down opposite him and waited.

"Where have you worked before?"

"I just graduated from university and I've been driving a cab at night for the last couple of months."

"I see. And how old are you?"

"I'm 22."

"A 22-year-old university graduate and you want to start here at, sort of, the bottom?"

"I really want to work in radio."

"Is your father rich?"

"Far from it, sir, far from it."

"Well, it's your life, I guess. Hmmm, I'd be willing to start you out — let's see now — how does $1,100 a year sound?"

He probably thought I was going to negotiate with him, but I would have taken the job for nothing and driven a cab at night.

"Sounds fine, sir."

"When can you start?"

"Is now too soon?"

"You *are* eager. Go to it, young man, and good luck!"

I floated out of Mr. Ferris's office on a cloud. I had the job of my dreams. "Yippee!" I yelled in the empty elevator as it sped me to my brand-new life.

Chapter 4

✦

ENSLAVED TO THE AD MAN

"ARE YOU INSANE?" MY FATHER said. "You're a university graduate, not an office boy!"

"A junior-copywriter-slash-office-boy."

"That's just gilding a lowdown lily. An office boy at a measly $25 a week!"

"Eleven hundred a year," I said.

"Same difference."

"That's what they offered, Dad."

"Did you at least negotiate, for chrissake?"

"Couldn't get them any higher than $1,100," I lied.

"Frank," my mother said, "he's doing what he's always wanted to do."

"If I lost my job, we'd damn well starve!"

"Then I'd drive a cab at night," I said.

"And do the radio stuff during the day?"

"Yes."

"When would you sleep?"

"After dinner until midnight."

"Oh, really?"

"Yes, Dad, really."

"Will you two stop it!" my mother said. "You haven't lost your job, he doesn't have to drive a taxicab all night and he starts his new job in the morning. So let's drop it. Okay?"

"Well . . ." my dad mumbled.

"Okay?" my mother shouted. It was the first time I had ever heard her raise her voice like that.

"Okay, okay but . . ."

"But nothing. Just drop it!"

My father shut up, lit a cigarette and went out to the back porch.

"Thanks, Mom."

"If your father loses his job, *I'll* drive the damn cab!"

A few minutes later my dad came back inside and held out his hand. "Good luck tomorrow, son."

I shook his hand. My mother smiled and kissed him on the cheek.

I HAD TROUBLE SLEEPING THAT night. I kept seeing a whirling radio studio with tumbling microphones, spinning turntables banging into tape recorders and a jumble of all the other electronic gear I was going to operate. At last, I finally fell asleep, and even my dreams were full of what I was so eagerly looking forward to.

When I woke up, I bounded out of bed, washed, shaved, put on my clothes and headed for the kitchen to have breakfast.

"Is that you, Frankie?" my mother called out from my parents' bedroom.

"It's me, Mom. All ready for work."

"It's only five o'clock in the morning, for heaven's sake!"

"What bloody time does this MacLaren place open?" my dad said.

"I forgot to ask."

"Go back to bed for an hour or two," my mother said.

"I can't. I'm all dressed and shaved."

"If you hurry," my dad said, "I'll bet you can get to the office by six-thirty."

"I'm sure that's too early."

"No kidding. Go into the living room and read a book or something. I want some more shut-eye. Good night."

My mother came out of the bedroom, putting on her bathrobe. "Come on, we can have a nice long, leisurely breakfast. God knows we've got plenty of time."

I arrived on the third floor of the Sterling Towers at eight-thirty and the door to the office was locked. *Hmmm,* I thought, *I guess they don't open at eight-thirty.* I sat down on the floor with my back against the door.

I was half nodding off when the elevator doors opened and Kay Dale, the traffic manager, stepped out.

"We're going to have to get you a key," she said as she unlocked the door and let me in.

"Thanks. I wasn't too sure about the starting time."

"Usually 9 a.m. Can you type?"

"I did some typing in college, but I'm no typist."

"You don't have to be. I'll be giving you names of radio stations across Canada. You simply type them on labels, paste the labels on boxes, put recorded commercials in the boxes and they get picked up here and sent wherever. Got it?"

"Where does all this happen?"

"The recordings, the labels, the boxes and the typewriter are all in the control room of the studio. Got it?"

"Okay, I've got it."

"Then why don't you go back in the studio and wait for Al."

"Al?"

"Al Scott. He'll be teaching you all about the control room and the studio. Got it?"

By the end of the first week Al Scott had explained everything to me — how to operate the tape recorder, how to edit tape with a razor blade and adhesive tape, how to handle recordings on the acetate discs, set sound levels on the audio board and file tapes and transcriptions. He also showed me where the typewriter was, as well as Kay Dale's labels, boxes and commercial recordings.

"You catch on quick," Al said on Friday afternoon. "You're gonna be fine."

"Thanks for all your help."

"No problem," he said. "I won't be seeing much of you after today. On Monday I start up top, learning to be an account executive."

"Good luck, Al."

"And good luck to you," he said. "Have a nice weekend. It'll probably be your last." He waved and walked out to the elevators. I puzzled over his parting remark, figuring it was advertising lingo.

"AL SCOTT SAYS YOU'RE A really fast learner," Hugh Horler said Monday morning.

"That was very nice of him."

"He wasn't being nice. Al says what he thinks," Hugh said. "Has Kay Dale explained the recordings you'll be sending out for Imperial Oil?"

"Yes, and I *got* it."

"On Wednesday nights, starting this Wednesday, we have two shows on CBC — *Buckingham Theatre* for Buckingham Cigarettes and, right after that, *Comrades in Arms* for the Canadian army."

"I've heard them both."

"Good. I want you to be here and tape both shows. They're called air checks. Then you file the tapes and you're done. Okay? Do you have a key?"

"Yes, Kay Dale got me one."

"Good. Now, on Saturday afternoon you and I will meet here with Elmer Ferguson, Wes McKnight and Syl Apps."

"You mean the actual hockey stars who do the Hot Stove League commentary on the *Hockey Night in Canada* broadcast?" I said.

"The same. We have to plan the Hot Stove spots. Then we'll eat and go to Maple Leaf Gardens for the broadcast."

Now I knew what Al Scott meant about the "enjoy your weekend" stuff. "Wow!" I said to Hugh. "Syl Apps, the great centre, with Bob Davidson and Gordie Howe." I was in hockey heaven!

"You know hockey?"

"I sure do. I listen to Foster Hewitt and the Hot Stove League every Saturday night. Like everybody in Canada."

"Now you're going to *be* there!" Hugh said, smiling.

MacLaren had a lot of big-time clients: Imperial Oil for *Hockey Night in Canada*, Buckingham Cigarettes, General Motors, General Electric, Heinz soups, Mr. Christie's Biscuits, Peoples Credit Jewellers, the home of friendly credit, and a whole lot more. I loved Wednesday night alone in the office, taping the two shows. I loved it because the studio had a television set. I had never seen television before, except in a store window. The only station we could get in Toronto, at that time, was WBEN Buffalo, but that was just fine with me. They showed *Kraft Television Theatre*, a one-hour live drama from New York, and sometimes a boxing match. It was great.

Saturdays were exciting, too, sitting in as the Hot Stove League regulars planned the show, then on to Maple Leaf Gardens and Foster "He shoots, he scores" Hewitt. He was the best hockey broadcaster ever. Foster did the game from high over the rink in a hanging gondola. The Hot Stove League, which was broadcast between periods, was in a little radio studio under the stands. Every once in a while, Wes McKnight or Syl Apps would say, "Frank, find out where that new kid playing left wing for Detroit comes from," and I would rush out and go to the Detroit bench and find out that the kid was from Saskatoon and hurry back to the studio with my news. I loved it!

During the week, we recorded demo commercials almost every day and I was the audio engineer. Eventually Hugh let me produce the Heinz Soup commercials at the RCA Victor studio on the top floor of the Royal York Hotel. I use the word *produce* advisedly because all I did was take the commercial copy to the studio and listen to veteran announcer Herb May, who had been doing the Heinz commercials for years, smoothly record the copy with the RCA engineer at the control. I would carry the recorded commercials, along with a recording of *The Adventures of Ozzie and Harriet* that RCA had transcribed the night before, back to the agency. Three account executives would be waiting for me in the studio. I would play the commercials for them and then I'd play the episode of *Ozzie and Harriet* that Heinz sponsored in Canada. The three sober-faced executives would listen to the program and then announce to each other, "Good show! Yes indeed, good show."

I wondered what they would do if they *didn't* like the show. Phone Ozzie Nelson in Hollywood and complain? I mean, the show was already recorded and would air that night. What could they do? It was way too late to change anything. I wondered why they even ventured down from the 10th floor to listen to it. Hugh said it had something to do with "power." It wasn't until I got to Hollywood that I really understood what Hugh was talking about.

ONE DAY HUGH SAID WE had to meet with Jack MacGill, the head man at Buckingham Cigarettes.

"We have to smoke in the meeting," Hugh said.

"Hugh, I don't smoke."

"Just puff on it while we have the meeting."

"I don't smoke."

"Look," Hugh said, "this MacGill guy fired his milkman because he didn't smoke Buckingham Cigarettes. MacGill told me, 'If he doesn't smoke my brand, I won't drink his goddamned milk.'"

Halfway through the meeting I lit up a Buckingham. And after a few more meetings with Mr. MacGill, I was hooked for the next 30 years.

Another time, Hugh came into the studio one afternoon and seemed really excited. "I just sold Mr. Christie's a half-hour comedy show starring Wayne and Shuster!"

"That's fabulous. I love Johnny Wayne and Frank Shuster!" They were the biggest comedy stars in Canada.

"Well, that's good, because every Thursday night you're going to be the sponsor's rep on the show."

"You're kidding?"

"I don't kid," he said.

"Thank you!"

"Thank yourself."

It was a great experience, working on *The Wayne and Shuster Show*. Johnny Wayne was so full of humor — short with dark coloring, black wavy hair and big brown eyes that said, "I'm funny!" Frank Shuster was more of a straight man — tall, slick black hair, very businesslike brown eyes and smarter than Johnny, but not as funny.

I sat in on all the rehearsals and rewrites and learned a lot about writing comedy. The director of the show was Jackie Rae, a blond little bundle of energy who kept everybody's spirits up. Terry Dale was the singer, a very pretty redhead with a great voice. Herb May, my old pal from the Heinz Soup commercials, was the announcer. As the agency rep, I sat in the booth with Jackie Rae, soaking up the wonderful atmosphere of a weekly comedy radio show.

Soon Hugh Horler gave me a chance to try writing some of the show's Mr. Christie's Biscuits commercials. I came up with a character called the Count of Monte Christie: "I am the Count of Monte Christie, the father of Christie's Biscuits. I create them and send them into the world with a high degree of taste. My Christie's Biscuits know how to please and have been prepared with tender loving care. Biscuits for all ages, the way biscuits were meant to be. That's why Christie's Biscuits are smart cookies."

The sponsor liked my idea, so I started writing some of the commercials for the show. Every once in a while my commercials got laughs, and that was a thrill for me. One day during rehearsals Frank Shuster took me aside. "Frank," he said, "you write some funny stuff. You should consider writing it for people, not biscuits. Think about it." He tapped me on the shoulder and went back to rehearsal. Believe me, I thought about it, a lot.

That first year at MacLaren went by like a movie montage. *Hockey Night in Canada*, the Hot Stove League, *Wayne and Shuster*, *Buckingham Theatre*, *Comrades in Arms*, Heinz Soup commercials, plus all my studio work during the day, recording demo commercials and jingles and auditioning new announcers. I had been at MacLaren for a year or so when Hugh asked me to stay late one night and record a singing group that was owned and managed by a friend of one of the bosses upstairs. Hugh told me what they needed, so I hooked up one mike for the piano and another for the singers. Four teenagers walked in with their manager.

"Can you put the take on tape and on a disc?" the manager said.

"Sure. You guys go ahead and warm up and I'll set my levels. Okay?"

"They're called the Crew-Cuts, so just mark the recording 'Crew-Cuts Debut.'"

I found a good balance between the piano and the boys. "Okay," I said over the talkback. "Let's try a take?"

The group's sound had a nice blend, but I wasn't quite sure what they were singing.

"Hey nonny ding dong, alang alang alang. Boom ba-doh, ba-doh ba-doodle-ay . . ."

I thought it was pure nonsense and I'd never hear from these guys again.

I WAS JUST STARTING MY second year at the agency. I was in the studio, writing a Mr. Christie's commercial, when a young man walked in and introduced himself. "Hi, I'm John Aylesworth," he said, "and I'm working here now." I didn't know it then but that moment started a partnership that would last over 40 years — through seven marriages, five divorces, nine children, six grandchildren and over 1,500 television shows. We had a good batting average on television shows, but not so good on marriage. I was 23 and John was 21 — perfect ages to get things rolling. Hugh Horler had great confidence in us. He let John handle an afternoon show for housewives called *Listen Ladies*, starring Mona Gould.

When my own radio responsibilities took a summer hiatus, Hugh put me in charge of a Sunday-afternoon show called *The Peoples Credit Jewellers Community Sing Song*. The show was recorded in an open-air bandshell at Sunnyside Amusement Park on Toronto's lakeshore. The stars of the show were Joe Murphy, a local comedian, Art Hallman and His Orchestra, and a band singer named Marilyn Kent. One of my main tasks was to keep a close watch on the weather reports and determine if it was going to rain. If I decided rain was in the forecast for Sunday afternoon, we would transfer the show, minus the sing-song, to a radio studio uptown. Frank Gerstein, the owner of Peoples Credit Jewellers, was very proud of his show. Since admission was free, hundreds of people gathered at the bandshell every summer Sunday. "Popa," as Mr. Gerstein was called, would often show up at the outdoor show to see how his future "credit" customers enjoyed *his* show.

The first three Sundays were sunny and bright and the singsongs went extremely well — corny jokes from the Joe Murphy band members and from Art Hallman, songs from Marilyn Kent and much gusto from the sing-along audience with good old songs like "Roll Out the Barrel" and "Cruising Down the River." Early on the fourth Sunday, a clap of thunder woke me up. "God, please no," I said as I peeked out my bedroom window. It wasn't raining cats, and there were certainly no dogs yet, but I could hear them yelping in the distance. I phoned the radio station and the weather guy said it could clear up around noon — but then again, it might not. I borrowed my father's car and as I drove down Yonge Street to the radio studio, the full dogs and cats had begun to fall. I nearly hit a parked car trying to look up at the sky through the windshield.

"Any rain changes?" I asked the weather guy when I walked into the station.

"Looks like an all-dayer," he said.

When I walked into the studio, the engineer was there, waiting.

"I'm not sure if we're going outside or inside," I said.

"I figured that," he said. "I'm ready for whatever you decide."

"Thanks. Look, we'll rehearse here as usual and see what happens."

The musicians started to straggle in — Art Hallman, Joe Murphy and Marilyn Kent — and we started the rehearsal.

"Frank," the engineer said, motioning me to come closer. "It's still raining and you're going to have to decide in the next hour or I'll never have time to set up at the bandshell."

"I know. I know!" I looked over at the cast.

"So what's it's gonna be, Frankie boy, rain or shine?" Joe Murphy said.

I checked the window for the zillionth time and rain was still coming down, not as hard as before but pretty damn hard.

The station receptionist came into the studio and waved me over. She looked scared. "There's a crazy man on the phone. Says he's Popa Gerstein and he demands to speak to somebody with the show. I mean, he is *screaming*!"

I followed her to the front desk and she handed me the phone.

"Where the hell is mine show?" the voice on the line shouted.

"We're here at the studio, Mr. Gerstein. You see, it is raining and —"

"It's not raining here at the bandshell, damn it! It's nice and sunny and there's hundreds of customers here for a singsong. Where is mine singsong?"

"There's no time to get down there and set up."

"Set up, schmet up. I want mine singsong!"

"We have to broadcast from here at the studio. No time, Mr. Gerstein."

"You're fired!" he yelled. "*Everybody's* fired!"

"You can listen to your show on your car radio."

"I want mine money back! I want my singsong! These people waiting here to sing along will blame *me*!"

"No, they won't, sir."

"How do you know this?"

"I have no time to argue, sir. We go on the air in two minutes." I hung up in the middle of his scream.

I thought the show went pretty well, but I was scared to death. Popa Gerstein had fired me.

The next morning I was typing up some labels for Kay Dale when Hugh Horler walked in.

"I just had a bit of a stormy meeting with Popa Gerstein *and* his sons."

"Is he still mad?"

"Furious."

"It was raining at the studio, Hugh."

"And it was sunny at the lake."

"I had no idea."

"Of course you didn't, but Popa Gerstein wants me to fire the person who made the decision."

"He already fired me."

"Did you tell him your name?"

"No, he was yelling on the phone and —"

"I told him I fired the guy."

My heart sank. "Hugh, believe me, I —"

"And I told him I hired a new program supervisor named Frank Peppiatt. Try not to let this happen again." He tapped me on the shoulder and walked back to his office.

"Hey, Frank," Kay Dale called through the door. "I need those labels. These commercials have to go out this morning. Got it?"

"Coming up, Kay."

I was back at work. It didn't rain one single Sunday the rest of the summer and Popa Gerstein was smiling.

Chapter 5

✦

FROM AD MAN TO SUPERMAN

ON SEPTEMBER 8, 1952, TELEVISION came to Toronto, not just from Buffalo, but from the CBC station on Jarvis Street. Everybody at MacLaren was very excited. It was going to be a whole new visual world of advertising — we would *show* a man smiling as he puffed on his Buckingham cigarettes, *show* kids' faces as they happily slurped up Heinz soup, *show* the sparkle of a Peoples Credit Jewellers diamond ring on a woman's slender finger.

But all that showing meant the writer would no longer be king. We had to adapt, or get left behind on radio. Lorne Greene, the CBC news announcer, had seen TV coming and had started the Lorne Greene School of Broadcasting (later the Academy of Radio Arts) in a building right across from the CBC headquarters. Hugh Horler hired one of the academy's first graduates to head up MacLaren's new television department. His name was Peter MacFarlane, a sweet bright man, about my age, who seemed to know a lot about the new medium — or he knew about as much as Lorne Greene knew at the time. Peter was tall, lean and fair-haired, with inquisitive blue eyes and a firm handshake.

John and I became good friends with Peter, who laughed hard at our antics as I played straight man to John's fantastic imitations of

Stan Laurel, Jack Benny, Fred Allen, Arthur Godfrey and many other radio and movie personalities. In fact, Peter's loud laughter seemed a little over the top to John and me, since nobody else had laughed that much at our shenanigans, but we didn't complain. Peter had only been with MacLaren for about six months when the CBC asked him to produce and direct at the fledgling television network. Naturally, Peter jumped at the chance and, with Hugh Horler's blessing, he joined the CBC, along with other Lorne Greene academy graduates, including Norman Jewison, my friend from U of T.

Despite a few stumbles, such as showing the corporate logo upside down, CBC TV got things going in news, public affairs and some drama. Hugh and I were still doing the hockey radio broadcast and since Imperial Oil was also going to sponsor the hockey telecast, we were involved in that, too. But hockey would present a problem on TV. Hugh told me to sit in on the first test hockey TV broadcast. The director the network had chosen was Sydney Newman — a dark-haired, brooding man in his early 30s. He watched the first period between the Leafs and the Chicago Black Hawks without a comment until it was over.

"It's very fast, isn't it?" he said at last.

"You mean tonight's game?" I asked.

"No, hockey in general. Very swift."

"Yeahhh," I said, wondering if he'd ever seen a hockey game before.

"Next Saturday we'll set up the cameras here and I'll be directing from the remote truck."

"Sounds good," I said, and left to perform my Hot Stove League duties.

The following Saturday night, Sydney Newman had four cameras set up in various locations around Maple Leaf Gardens; he was in the remote truck with his technical director and camera switcher, who acts as second mate to the director. Typically, if there are four cameras, the control booth has five screens, one for each camera and a master screen that shows the actual broadcast. The director and the switcher see the different pictures that cameras one through four are taking and the director chooses the one he wants on the master screen. He might say, "Take one," and the switcher puts the picture from camera one on the master screen. So, the switcher is constantly following orders and, with his switching board, provides the pictures the director asks for. Hugh Horler and I were in the remote truck as observers when Sydney began directing the first TV hockey game.

"Camera one, give me a tight shot of center ice for the face-off. Good. Now, camera two, when the puck is dropped, you follow it with a panning shot. Okay! Here we go!"

The referee dropped the puck.

"Take two. Where the hell is the puck, two?"

"I've got it," camera three responded.

"Take three. Where is it?"

"I've lost it!"

"Camera one, go wide."

"On what?"

"The game! The game! For God's sake! Camera four, zoom in on the puck."

"I can't find it."

"Why is the crowd cheering?" Sydney yelled.

"The Leafs just scored a goal, Sydney," the technical director said.

"Did we get it?"

"He'll never get it," Hugh Horler whispered to me.

Sydney Newman never directed another hockey game, but he found his niche as head of drama production at the BBC in London. Drama was more Sydney's speed.

After analyzing our setup, Hugh Horler figured out what the problem was. You could not vocally direct a hockey game. It was just too damn fast. "We have to find a camera switcher who knows hockey and let him switch the cameras as the play progresses," he said. The CBC found that man. His name was George Retzlaff, and with him on board, television hockey in Canada was saved. George, by the way, became head of all sports for the CBC and introduced technical refinements that made the telecast even better.

Now that hockey was thriving, the CBC lacked only one genre on its television schedule — comedy. The station tried a few comedy shows, but they all came out flat. There were efforts to lure Wayne and Shuster into television, but Johnny and Frank weren't stupid. They had a very popular radio show at the time, so why jump into television before television knew which way to jump? Smart guys. What CBC needed was a couple of chumps.

One afternoon Peter MacFarlane dropped into our studio at MacLaren and invited John and me to lunch at a diner down the street. It was great to see Peter again, though I was a little puzzled as to the reason for his visit. But he was buying, so what the hell.

We ordered drinks and some lunch, and Peter took a deep breath. "I've been given the job of developing a comedy show and I need your help. I've been auditioning writers and I haven't found anybody as funny as you guys."

"That was just kidding around the office," I said.

"But very funny kidding around."

"Well, maybe but —"

"No 'maybe but,'" Peter said seriously. "I want you to write some comedy for me, and you *will* be paid."

"What kind of comedy?" John asked.

"At this point, I don't care, as long as it's funny. Will you try?"

"We get paid?" I said.

"Damn right!"

"Then I'd like to try it."

"Me, too," John said.

"You've got two weeks. See what you can come up with. Let's shake on it."

We shook hands all around, finished our lunch and went our separate ways.

"We can work at night here in the MacLaren studio," John said as we reached our office.

"Good idea, let's start tonight."

That night we both sat holding pencils and yellow legal pads, looking vacant.

"You want to write something about a bar?" John suggested.

"Like what?"

"I dunno, maybe two drunks trying to figure out how to get home."

"In a funny way?"

"Of course!"

"And what would that funny way be?"

"What are you gonna be, a critic or a partner?"

"Sorry."

"This is not easy."

"Whoever said it was is a liar," I said.

"Maybe it'll get better tomorrow night. At least we got a start."

"You call this a start?"

We went three nights like that — not writing a word and getting increasingly antsy. On the fourth night I remembered something John and I had joked about a couple of weeks earlier. We wondered what it would be like seeing comic book characters relaxing on their day off — Mandrake the Magician getting drunk and making things disappear and waking up with a hangover in jail; Orphan Annie and Daddy Warbucks playing poker with the Asp and Punjab, and when Annie wins all of Daddy Warbucks' bucks, she dumps him. We felt it might be funny, interesting and different.

"I would love to see Superman at home in a crappy apartment," John said.

"With a boozy mother," I added. "And a creepy father who couldn't care less about his prowess."

"We can write that," John said.

"So let's do it."

It took us four more nights of scrambling, arguing and staring, but we finally came up with something that might get a laugh or two.

"I'll make some copies," John said, straightening out the pile of papers.

"Not just yet. Read the thing back to me, okay?"

John cleared his throat, picked up our manuscript and started reading our very first effort in comedy.

"Superman at Home," John began.

Come up on SUPERMAN in his full Superman outfit, cape and all, walking along a residential street. As he walks he whistles and carries the evening paper.

Dissolve to the interior of a crummy living room. SUPERMAN's dad is smoking a cigar, reading the racing form in his undershirt and wearing a derby hat. Sitting near him is SUPERMAN's mother. She is very floozy-looking — hair in curlers, wearing a shapeless housedress and pouring herself a beer.

SUPERMAN enters.

SUPERMAN
Hi, Mom, hi, Dad. I'm home.

DAD
Big deal.

SUPERMAN
I saved a whole busload of citizens from toppling over a bridge into the river.

MOM
I'll drink to that!

DAD
So, what else is new?

MOM
We're getting tired of all this "Look up in the sky"!

DAD
"Is it a bird?"

MOM
"Is it a plane?" crap.

SUPERMAN
I can run faster than a speeding bullet. Leap tall buildings at a single bound.

DAD
So, where's the money?

SUPERMAN
I'm out to help people.

MOM
So, help your mom and dad!

DAD
You haven't made a dime out of that Superman junk.

SUPERMAN
I'm here to save the world.

MOM
How about saving a few dollars?

DAD
Join a circus, race the stupid bullet for bucks!

MOM
Yeah, Barnum & Bailey presents Superman!

SUPERMAN
Not so loud, Mom, people think I'm Clark Kent.

DAD
That's baloney, everybody knows Clark Kent is Superman.

SUPERMAN
They don't.

DAD
Do!

SUPERMAN
Don't!

MOM
Do.

SUPERMAN
Don't.

MOM and DAD
DO!

SUPERMAN
Can't we stop this wrangling and be a normal family?

DAD
That slut Lois Lane knows you're Clark Kent.

SUPERMAN
NO!

MOM
She told me she saw you changing in a phone booth.

SUPERMAN
No, no, never!

MOM
She's just stringing you along.

DAD
So she can get scoops for that rag, the Daily Planet.

MOM
Fish wrap.

SUPERMAN

I won't listen to this. I'm going to bed.

He turns to his right and a light comes up, revealing a phone booth lying on its side. Superman gets in and lies down.

SUPERMAN
Goodnight.

SUPERMAN closes door on phone booth.

DAD
What's good about it?

MOM
I never should have made that stupid suit and cape for him. I thought it was just for Halloween, but he's never taken the damn thing off.

DAD
You live, you learn.

MOM belches.

MUSIC PLAYOFF

"THAT'S GONNA BE FUNNY," I said.

"Sure sounds funny. I hope it plays funny."

"That's the director's and the actors' problem," I said.

It took yet another four days of rambling and staring until John came up with a great idea: "We make a stupid criminal, safe cracker or a thief, the star of his own show."

"Sounds good. Let's work on that," I said.

We fooled around with the idea for a couple more nights until we finally came up with *The Adventures of Rocky the Racketeer!* Sponsored by Gibson Getaway Cars, with Rocky doing his own commercials. "Go, Frankie," John said.

I put on a George Raft tough-guy voice. *"We'll be right back wid my adventures in a minute. Look, folks, if youse wanna be a successful racketeer or bank robber, youse gotta get you a Gibson Getaway Car. All de windows are bulletproof, the tires are bulletproof and the back seat and the trunk have been turned into a gas tank dat holds 300 gallons. Wit one tankful you can go 6,000 miles. Just tink of it, coppers chasin' you and all of 'em runnin' out of gas and you keep right on gettin' away. Youse can't lose, so drop into your Gibson Getaway dealer and try a test getaway in a Gibson. Remember, dey come in six shades of black. Now, back to De Adventures of Me — Rocky the Racketeer."*

"That sure sounds funny," John said.

"I think so," I said.

"Naturally we think it's funny, because we wrote it."

"I'd think it was funny even if we didn't write it," I said.

"But we *did* write it."

"If we didn't write it, would you laugh?" I asked.

"I'm not sure."

"There you go, John. No confidence in the material."

"The hell I don't!"

"You weren't sure," I said.

"I wasn't sure if we didn't write it, but we *did* write it."

"Did or didn't, I think it's funny."

"Didn't or did, so do I."

When we finally got that settled, John, who was a good typist, typed out three more copies. I went to the CBC building on Jarvis Street to deliver our skits. It was the high society of broadcasting. They had their own cafeteria, well-furnished offices and fully equipped studios that were radio broadcasting from coast to coast, day and night. Television was only an irritating itch on their backside.

"Be sure Peter MacFarlane gets this," I said to the receptionist.

"Who?" she said.

"Peter MacFarlane. He's a television producer."

"Oh, another one of these Lorne Greene TV academy grads."

"Yeah."

"I can't tell one from the other, they're all so wet behind the ears."

"Gimme back the envelope. I'll give it to him personally. Where's his office?"

"Whose office?"

"Peter MacFarlane's."

"Never heard of him."

I took the envelope back to MacLaren, slapped an address on it, making sure it read "*CBC Television*," and mailed the damn thing. I was sure they'd heard of Peter MacFarlane in the CBC TV mailroom.

Two days later Peter called us and wanted to meet in his office. I made sure to get the correct directions because I didn't want to tangle with Miss Information at the front desk again. We found our way to the Comedy Variety television offices, where they were just getting things started — there were folding wooden chairs, a couple of battered desks, some card tables and no carpets. Men and women were moving about, trying to look busy and purposeful.

When Peter saw us, he hurried over and slapped us on the back. "I knew you guys could write funny stuff."

"You really think it's funny?" I asked.

"A tad offbeat, but I *know* it's funny," Peter said, and introduced us to two other Lorne Greene TV academy graduates — Norman Jewison, whom I already knew from my U of T days, and Ross McLean. They both mentioned they had liked our comedy writing. Apparently, Peter had got some second opinions — you couldn't blame him.

"Maybe they want us to write more stuff," John whispered.

Peter led us to a large corner office where we met Don Hudson, the head of Comedy Variety. He was a very dapper dresser, with slicked-back wavy brown hair, brown eyes and a big welcoming smile.

"Good to meet you two," he said. "Peter's been talking you guys up to the sky."

"We're hiring him to be our agent," John joked. Peter and Don laughed as we all settled in on folding chairs.

"I'd like to get right down to business," Don Hudson said, and he motioned for Peter to begin getting down to whatever business Don was talking about.

"I've been auditioning people to be on this comedy show I'm supposed to get going and, believe me, the pickings have been lean," explained Peter.

"That's too bad," I said.

"Peter seems to think we should give you guys a crack at it," Don Hudson said.

"A crack at what?" John said.

"Doing the show," Peter replied.

"You mean like being *in* the show? *Us*?" I asked.

"We would do a test show with *you* doing the comedy *you* wrote," Peter explained.

Don continued, "It wouldn't be broadcast — just a test to see how you do. Peter thinks you can do it."

"But do *we* think we can?" I said.

"Why don't you sleep on it and let us know tomorrow," Peter said.

"Who can sleep?" John replied.

"How about we meet here tomorrow after you finish work?"

We both nodded and walked, as if in a trance, out of Don's office and down two flights of stairs to the street.

"What do you think?" John said.

"Let's talk to Hugh about it."

The next morning, after we had explained everything to Hugh Horler, he said, "It's up to you guys. You really don't have anything to lose."

"You don't mind?" I asked.

"Of course I mind, you're part of my team. Look, why don't you give this test-show audition thing a shot and see what happens."

"Suppose they like it and we get a show?" John said.

"Then I'll try to get Peoples Credit Jewellers to sponsor it."

We all laughed nervously and went about our day's work at MacLaren.

That evening, we met at Don Hudson's office and told Don and Peter we would do the test show. They both seemed thrilled, and why not — *they* didn't have to do it. Peter said he would schedule a time in two weeks when a studio was free and he would order the necessary cameras, lights and sound. We all shook hands again, and John and I returned to the empty MacLaren office.

"We've got to get a girl for the two scenes," John said as we settled down in the studio and started to really think about two weeks from now.

"I remember a girl who used to go out with a friend of mine."

"Is that all the acting experience she's had?" John asked.

"Don't be dumb. Let's see, her name is Florence Hancock."

"That'll look good in lights."

"Stop kidding around. She works in a stockbroker's office and she belongs to a little theater group called the Black Lock Players. I saw her play the lead in *Born Yesterday* — you know, the Judy Holliday part. She was hilarious."

"Seriously?" John said.

"Seriously, and I also saw her play the nutty mother in *You Can't Take It with You*."

"That's great," John said. "And she's a new face."

"Who the hell isn't?"

I got in touch with Florence and she said she would love to do the audition, as long as it didn't interfere with her day job.

Florence was not a glamour girl, but she was quite pretty, with a kind of schoolgirl quality. She was about five foot five, with short ash-blond hair, hazel eyes, a nice figure and an expressive face. She was smart, got the drift of any joke quickly and was very talented.

When we looked into a place to work, we were told that the CBC had no rehearsal space available, so my mom let us practice in our basement.

"What would you be rehearsing?" she wanted to know.

"Just some stuff for a TV audition."

"Sounds like fun. Don't be too noisy."

We started rehearsing every night after work, and by the fourth evening we started to feel as though it was pretty good.

"We better start learning our lines," Florence said. I had trouble memorizing poetry in high school and John said he wasn't much better. "Listen," Florence said, "you wrote the material, so you're already familiar with it."

"I hope so," I said.

"We need someone with the script to cue us, in case we go blank," John added.

"Maybe my mother could —" I started to suggest, but Florence jumped in.

"My boyfriend is in the Black Lock Players with me. He's a steward for Trans-Canada Air Lines and he could come with me every evening that he's free and help us with our lines."

"That would be swell," John said, and I could hear in his voice the fact that he didn't like that Florence had a boyfriend.

But it turned out the boyfriend was a big help, *and* he worked for free.

His name was Bernard Newbound, a tall, dark, good-looking guy, about our age. By the way, Mr. Newbound later changed his name to Bernard Slade and wrote a 1975 hit Broadway play, *Same Time, Next Year*. It was made into a movie a few years later, and Bernard Newbound Slade became a big-time playwright.

Florence Hancock also wanted to change her name — to Jill Foster. I was never sure if she didn't like the name Florence Hancock, or didn't want her parents to know she was playing Superman's boozy mother and Rocky the Racketeer's gun moll on TV. Anyway, she became Jill Foster and it was fine with us.

After a week, with the help of Bernie Newbound, we had learned our lines. Peter MacFarlane showed up in my parents' basement to see how things were going and to plot out his camera moves. He said the CBC hadn't established a costume department yet, so whatever costumes we needed had to be rented, and he was damned sure we weren't going to be able to rent a Superman suit. My mother, God bless her, came to the rescue. She dyed a pair of my long underwear blue and dyed a white sweatshirt blue to match, and she cut up some curtain material for a cape.

"What the hell have you got your mother doing?" my dad demanded.

"She's making me a Superman suit."

"Why?"

"For a TV audition."

"*You're* going to be Superman?"

"Yes. It's a comedy spoof."

"I'll bet it is," my dad said. "I thought you were working at MacLaren?"

"I am, Dad, but this is a big chance."

"Big chance? Wearing a dumb, homemade Superman suit?"

"It's not dumb and I've got to go and rehearse."

"Is that what's been going on in my basement all week?"

"Mom said it was okay."

"Oh, for God's sake, go ahead," he said, and yelled out to my mom, "*Sarah!* What the Sam Hill is going on with this kid?"

I painted a pair of white running shoes blue and got a graphic designer at MacLaren to draw the Superman logo on the blue sweatshirt. My dad was right, it did look dumb, but it was the best my mom and I could do. We were all set — Superman suit and cape, Rocky the Racketeer's snap-brim fedora and pinstripe suit. John and Jill had perfect-looking costumes for Superman's mom and dad and Rocky's right-hand man and sexy gun moll. We had our last rehearsal in the basement and went to sleep that night with the jitters.

On Saturday morning, we met Peter at the CBC television studio and walked through our two scenes for cameras, sound, lighting and props.

"You two okay with your lines?" Jill said.

"I think so," I said.

"Why don't we run through them over in the corner?" Jill suggested.

We went over everything four times and it came off without a hitch.

"Well, we're as ready as we're ever going to be," John said. "Why don't we get some lunch, come back here, get into our costumes and go for it."

"I'm just going to rest," Jill said. "I'm not hungry."

"Me neither!" I said. "If I eat, I'll throw up."

"It all starts at two o'clock," John announced, and we retreated to our dressing rooms to wait. We weren't scared; we just weren't hungry.

"OKAY, LET'S DO IT!" PETER said over the talkback microphone. "In five, four, three, two, one — *go!*"

Some CBC employees had heard about the test comedy show and a bunch of them crowded into one end of the studio. As we performed our scenes, they actually laughed. I looked up at the control booth and could see some engineers laughing, too. When Superman went to bed in the phone booth there was a really big laugh. The "Superman at Home" sketch must have warmed them up because they really seemed to enjoy "The Adventures of Rocky the Racketeer."

When we were done, Peter came down on the floor with a big smile. He kissed Jill on the cheek and patted John and me on the back. "I knew you two guys were funny but, Jill, you were wonderful."

"Thank you, Peter," Jill said. She smiled at John and me. "When the writing is funny, it's not hard."

"What now?" John asked.

"Well," Peter said, "all the CBC brass were watching you on a monitor in the boardroom and I'm meeting them in the morning."

"Put in a good word for us," I said.

Peter called us at MacLaren the next afternoon and asked us to meet him for dinner at the Little Denmark Restaurant, a favorite hangout for actors and writers and a real step up from the diner he'd taken us to a couple of weeks before. Peter was already there when we walked into the restaurant. He was alone. He stood up and motioned for us to sit down.

"How did we go over?" John said.

"Most of the people liked you."

"We can have Rocky the Racketeer take care of those saps who didn't," I said.

"Can we be serious for a moment?"

"Wait'll I rearrange my head to serious," John said, swivelling his head around. "Ahhh, there we go. Ready."

"The CBC offers the two of you and Jill . . ." He paused.

"What?" John and I said as one.

"Ten one-hour shows, called *After Hours*, to play live every Friday at 11 p.m."

"An hour, that's a lot of writing," I said.

"You don't have to fill the whole hour. You'll be working with Lou Snader. He's a filmmaker and he believes he has got the jump on TV. He has filmed a bunch of singers, just one song on each film clip — performers like Nat King Cole, Rosemary Clooney, Mel Tormé, Patti Page and lots more. We want you to do your sketches between

Snader's film clips and introduce them."

"Sort of like television disc jockeys," John said.

"Right. What do you think?"

"It might work," I said, and turned to John. "We'll have to talk to Hugh."

"Oh, you couldn't keep your jobs," Peter said.

"How are we supposed to live?" I asked.

"We'd pay you $50 for performing and $50 for writing, per show."

"Each?" we both said.

"Each," Peter said firmly.

We shook hands all around. We even included the waiter and a couple of customers.

Chapter 6

◆

STRIPTEASE AT THE BORDER

"You're quitting MacLaren?" my father cried, shaking his head in disbelief.

"Yes, Dad, we have our own TV show at the CBC," I said.

"That silly Superman stuff, I suppose?"

"That's only part of it."

"What's the other part?"

"Look, Dad, Hugh Horler said he'd take us back if this didn't work out."

"Back at the big $25 per?"

"I was making $50 when I quit."

"How much will you make at CBC?"

"It's $50 per show, but —"

"Frank," my mother spoke up. "I think this cross-examination is *over*!"

"My son could have been a lawyer, but he'd rather be a fake Superman!" he announced to no one in particular, and left the room.

Our first show was in three weeks, so John and I had to get a move on. First, we phoned Jill, formerly Florence, to find out about her availability.

"My boss has been great," she said. "He's letting me take off Thursday afternoons and Fridays to do the show. I can't believe it, it's so exciting!"

"It sure is," I said.

"And we'll send you the material," John said, "as soon as we finish writing it. You can look it over during the week. Okay?"

"That's perfect," she said, and hung up.

"I'm having a couple of problems at home," John told me, "so I'm going to rent a cheap apartment."

"I'll chip in on it," I said, "and we can use it as an office and do all our writing there."

John rented a little one-bedroom, three-story walk-up on north Bathurst Street, got some used furniture from his family and moved right in. One hundred and twenty dollars a month, $60 each. A good deal. I bought a used Chevy with the taxicab money I'd saved. John's place wasn't that far from my parents' house, so I drove there every day, and on Thursdays and Fridays I picked him up and we drove to the studio.

The "couple of problems" with his family that John mentioned turned out to be a lot more than that. Apparently, John had confided in Peter MacFarlane and Peter decided I should know, too.

"Do you know much about John's home life?" Peter asked.

"He never really talks about it," I replied.

"For a very good reason," Peter said. "John, his mother and father and two older brothers lived in a big, expensive house in a ritzy neighborhood."

"Forest Hill. I knew that," I said. "His father was a very successful doctor. A chauffeur drove John to school — that's why he never learned to drive. They were very rich."

"*Were* is the key word!"

"Were?" I asked.

"Just listen," Peter said. "One night John's father said he couldn't sleep and he asked John to bring him his sleeping pills. John fetched the pills and went to bed. His father downed the whole bottle and never woke up."

"Suicide?"

"Of course."

"That's so sad!" I said.

"That's not the half of it."

"What's the other half?"

"It turned out," Peter went on, "his father had been going to his medical office every day for the past three years, but he didn't see one single patient. He just went there every day to drink!"

"Didn't the family notice when he came home?"

"No, because his mother and two brothers were drinkers, too. By the time the father came home they were already well into it. Now, here's the part where the past tense comes in: as in, they *were* rich. While the fancy doctor had neither patients nor a sober breath, he was borrowing constantly on the big house, and from his life insurance and selling all his investments in order to buy booze, pay his medical-office rent and bring some money home for the family to live on. When he died, the family learned they no longer owned the house, the car, the chauffeur or anything else."

"Wow," I said. "So that's where John got the used furniture for our office."

"Well, at least he got something," Peter said.

"Why didn't he tell *me* all this?"

"You work with the guy seven days a week and I guess he didn't want you feeling sorry for him."

"At least we could have talked about it."

"John didn't swear me to secrecy, so you can bring it up with him if you want to."

"Yeah. I better get the air cleared," I said.

I felt so sorry for John that I didn't think too much about how and why he had never even hinted to me anything at all about this monstrous tragedy in his life. Still, I was a bit sore for being shut out so completely.

The next morning I brought it up with John. "Do you blame yourself for your father's death?" I asked.

"Not at all. Somebody else would have brought him the pills. I was just available."

"What a shame," I said, marveling to myself over his seeming nonchalance.

"Not really," he shrugged. "It came with the territory."

"Yes, but it's so damned sad!" I said, hoping to get some glimpse into my partner's emotions.

"Look, Frank, I'll tell you a story and then I don't want to talk about it again. Okay?"

"Okay."

"When I had just turned 20, I met this beautiful girl and I fell in love."

"Really in love?" I said, trying to pry loose some smidgen of feeling.

"Who knows? Anyway, we went out together for about three months. I met her mother, her father and two sisters, and she wanted to meet my folks. I talked to my mother and my brothers and told them I wanted to bring this special girl to dinner the next Sunday. They all said fine. My mom was very excited and started planning the menu. 'Crab bisque,' she'd announced, 'a roast of beef, creamed spinach, roasted potatoes and red wine. Then white wine with dessert. Then homemade lemon meringue pie with ice cream!' On Sunday afternoon, the roast beef was in the oven with the potatoes. The lemon pie looked wonderful. My mother was dressed beautifully, had her hair done, and both my brothers wore suits and ties."

"Sounds good," I said.

"It was. But I had to take a 45-minute streetcar ride to pick my girl up and a 45-minute streetcar ride back to our house. When we walked in the house, some wild jazz record was going, full blast. We went into the dining room and saw that the red wine for the roast beef was gone and the white wine for the lemon pie was gone. In the kitchen we found my mother and two brothers, completely blotto. The roast beef had somehow skittered under the kitchen table and my mother was slipping and sliding in the gravy that was spilled all over the kitchen floor. One brother was eating the lemon pie with his hands and my other brother was out cold on the countertop."

"My God! What happened?"

"The love of my life called her father, who drove over and picked her up, and I never saw her again."

"What did you do?"

"Believe it or not, I started laughing. The scene was so ludicrous. I realized they didn't do this to hurt me. They were just drunks. So let's forget it and start writing something *really* funny. Okay?"

"Okay," I said, but I didn't really believe all that family insanity could be so easily buried. I realized then that John and I would never be close, although he did open up to me one more time about his family a few months later.

He had mentioned he was going to Ottawa for the weekend, and I tried to persuade him not to go because we had lots of work to do. I insisted he tell me why he had to go.

"Okay! Okay!" he sighed. "I have to see my sister. Okay?"

I laughed. "You gotta do better than that, John. You don't have a sister."

"Yes I do!"

"You never once mentioned a sister."

"She's a lot older than my brothers and me. Since she married an Ottawa speechwriter, she hasn't been back home much. She's got two kids I've hardly ever seen."

"And now you've suddenly got to see them?"

"Well . . . yeah."

"Why? Tell me why."

"Okay! Okay! She's come down with polio and is in an iron lung."

"You're kidding, right?"

"Even I wouldn't kid about a thing like that!"

He was as close to tears as I ever saw him, but he didn't succumb. John went off to Ottawa, and the next Monday morning he was ready to work, as though nothing unusual had happened to him over the weekend. I didn't ask and he didn't tell. The only thing keeping our partnership together was the tough business of humor.

WE SOON LEARNED EXACTLY HOW tough writing comedy could be. The CBC saw to that by airing a live show in our studio, directly ahead of us — some kind of outer-space adventure thing. We had no more than 10 minutes to go in and help the stagehands carry out the space set and sweep up all the stray bits of Martian UFO space junk, then put up our sets and props. We had no time for rehearsal with cameras, so Peter had to hustle to keep us in frame. Our week of evening rehearsals in my parents' basement was all the preparation we had. Surprisingly, the first show went off smoothly. We even got some big laughs from the stagehands. There was no studio audience.

When the show was over, Peter, the CBC brass and the stagehands all congratulated us. John, Jill and I weren't exactly sure what had just happened. Had anybody actually tuned in, or were we only deluding ourselves? By Monday, piles of mail, mostly from teenagers and young adults, had come in. They had watched and they loved the show's zaniness. Knowing we were just starting, many of the critics gave us reasonable reviews. But the Toronto *Evening Telegram* critic *hated* us. Ron Poulton was his name and the son of a gun never let up. He kept slamming us every week.

"At least he's a loyal viewer," Jill said.

"Let's find out where he lives and steal his TV set," John suggested, only half in jest.

We pretended his barrage of bad reviews didn't bother us, but there was no denying that it hurt. Then Poulton went one step further: he asked his readers to send in critiques of our show and he'd print them. So, every day the *Telegram* ran hate letters about Peppiatt and Aylesworth. But the *Telegram*'s ragging campaign grew so venomous that it backfired. All the other news outlets printed letters of praise for our show from the highest ranks of the Toronto theater and cultural community.

That kind of support helped a lot and we kept going our zany way. My favorite running joke was how Superman changed from Clark Kent. Our shows were live and we had no time to change costumes from one character to the other and back again. Jill came up with the solution: Superman could just put on glasses and a fedora to become Clark Kent. Then John (as Perry White) and Jill (as Lois Lane) would accept the change immediately, even though Clark was still wearing my mom's homemade Superman suit. Superman would go around a corner, put on the glasses and fedora, walk right back into the scene, and Lois Lane would say, casually, "Hi, Clark, you just missed Superman." It worked perfectly and the audience loved it, thanks to Jill.

Three or four weeks into the show, the CBC dropped the Snader film clips. As it turned out, they didn't get as many as they'd been promised. I also doubt Rosemary Clooney and Nat King Cole would have been thrilled to be introduced by Superman or Rocky's gun moll.

After the fifth show, the CBC invited in a studio audience every week. Young couples and teenagers packed the place on Friday nights. They cheered and laughed. What a great feeling — real laughter! Then the CBC let us get really classy: they gave us an orchestra. It was only a trio — Rudy Toth on piano, Johnny Niosi on drums and Jack Kane, the leader and arranger, on clarinet. It wasn't much, but it was music to our ears. We had the set designer paint a life-size picture of a 16-piece band to back up our trio. It looked weird and kind of wonderful, watching the three live musicians playing in front of a big band that seemed to be playing, too. You were never quite sure.

Jack Kane impressed me right away. His musical arrangements made that trio sound like a big band. Jack wasn't very tall and he was pudgy, balding and wore thick glasses, but he was energetic and came across on camera like the really great guy he was. We quickly became the best of friends.

The next thing we added was our very own announcer, Rick Campbell. He was already on the CBC staff, so the price was right, and from time to time he helped us out by acting in sketches.

John and I were writing five days a week and rehearsing our performance two days. With the Snader film clips gone, we had a whole hour to fill every week. We had no social life, no girlfriends, no sex. Did we miss it? I don't know about John, but I loved the work so much that it was almost like sex. Not exactly the same, of course, but there was a thrill I got from what we were doing that I got from nothing else. Just like sex.

Don't get me wrong — I wasn't about to give up sex, but I wasn't about to give up the business of funny, either. If all of that makes any sense to you, please explain it to me. I've had more than one wife who didn't get it.

The show wasn't garnering blockbuster ratings, but people were talking about us and the CBC seemed pleased with our work. So pleased, in fact, that they extended the show for another 10 weeks. Our friendly television critic, Ron Poulton, wrote that the CBC had nothing else to put on, so they put on nothing. What a sweet guy!

One sketch we did about Canadian Customs earned a lot of talk and tons of mail. I played a Canadian Customs officer checking Canadians who were coming back from a weekend in Buffalo. Rick Campbell, our announcer, was the first traveler to come through and he was carrying a television set.

"You buy that in Buffalo?" I say.

"No, sir," Rick says innocently. "I took it over with me so I could watch some Canadian shows!"

"Okay," I say, and wave him through.

Then Jill Foster comes through, wearing a mink coat.

"You buy that fur coat in Buffalo?"

"No, I wore it over," Jill says, sexily.

"But it's the middle of summer."

"No wonder I was so hot. Thanks for the tip."

"You're more than welcome, sweetie pie," I say with a big smile, and wave her through, too.

Then John enters.

"Hi, Mr. Customs Man," he says cheerfully.

"Don't try to get in good with me!" I bark at him.

"I was only —"

"Only trying to *smuggle* something. Where'd you get that shirt?"

"In Toronto."

"Oh yeah, let's have a look."

I grab his shirtsleeve and pull the whole shirt off him through the sleeve of his jacket.

"Hey, that's a neat trick!" John says.

"Shut up. Take off your shoes. *And move it!*"

John hands me his shoes and I rip them to pieces, then look at them closely and toss what's left back to him.

"Hmmm, you're lucky; they were made in Montreal."

"I guess this is my lucky day." He lights up a cigarette.

"Where'd you get that cigarette?" I grab it out of his mouth. "It's *an American cigarette*!" I grab the neck of his jacket and start dragging him off. "Let's see how you like a Canadian jail!"

John starts crying, "I'll pay the duty!"

We wrote the shirt trick into the script, but the costume people said they couldn't find a way to do it, so I went home and worked it out myself. I finally figured that we could put the shirt over John's shoulders, leave it unbuttoned and hide it behind a tie, then pull both sleeves through the sleeves of his jacket so a little bit of the shirt cuffs could be seen peeking out. Then we buttoned up the jacket and everything looked normal until the whole shirt came through the jacket sleeve, leaving the tie still around his neck. It worked perfectly. I was proud until I found out later that burlesque comics did the shirt gag all the time. I may have reinvented the wheel, but at least I was smarter than the CBC costume department.

Early that summer the CBC asked John and me to fly to New York to watch some American TV. It was our first plane ride, our first time in New York, our first time out of Canada, all to see Kate Smith live. We didn't learn much but it was fun. When we landed back in Toronto and lined up to go through Canadian Customs, I noticed a couple of Customs guys pointing at us.

"Hey, you two," one of them called. "Over here, save you time."

We thought we were getting special treatment, Canadian television stars being escorted through Customs. *Wow!*

"Passports!" the taller of the two officers snapped.

"We only went to New York for three days. We don't need passports," John said.

"Who says so?" the shorter guy said, and went nose to nose with John.

"Nationality?" the tall guy demanded.

"Canadian," I said with a smile.

"Wipe that smirk off your face, Mr. Funnyman!"

"It's not a smirk, it's a smile!"

"How do we know you're Canadian?"

"We are! Honest!" John said.

"Let's see your birth certificate."

"We don't have it with us and we —"

"You're trying to sneak into Canada."

I pulled out my wallet. "Here's my driver's licence."

"That proves you can drive, not that you're Canadian. You two better come into the back room with us and we'll see what this is all about."

"See what *what* is all about?" John said.

The two Customs men herded us into a room and the tall guy announced, "Only way to solve this is a strip search."

"Solve what?" I yelled.

Five minutes later, John and I were standing in the middle of the room, stark naked.

"Well," the tall Customs agent said. "We didn't find anything, but this is a warning!"

John and I looked stupidly at one another and said in concert, "A warning about what?"

"Never do stupid skits about Canadian Customs on your dumb television show." Both Custom guys broke up laughing and left the room.

John and I got dressed.

"Well, how about that?" I said.

"At least we know somebody is watching our show," John said.

Chapter 7

✦

POLIO CLOWN

"I've got big news for you two saps!" Peter MacFarlane said as we gathered in his office. "Don Hudson wants you to star in *The Big Revue* next year."

"Wow!" I said. *The Big Revue* was a prime-time show with a big budget. No more sweeping up space junk. We'd probably get a raise.

"Yes, and Norman Jewison will produce and direct," Peter added.

"No way!" John said.

"We won't do a show without you, Peter!" I said. He was our mentor and had believed in us from the start. He gave us space. He understood our humor and let us run with it, but guided us with an invisible hand. Inexperienced as I was, I knew Peter was a rare talent.

"Look," Peter said, "I don't like it any more than you do, but that's the way it is."

"What'll you do?" I asked.

"I'm transferring to documentaries."

"Sounds like a lot of laughs," John said.

There was not too much to laugh about. A couple of years later, Peter and a camera crew were doing underwater photography in Georgian Bay, a very deep and dangerous body of water north of Toronto. A vicious storm blew up. Peter and the crew were never seen again. The only thing saved was their boat. We should have fought harder for Peter, damn it!

During our first *Big Revue* meeting with Don Hudson, he said, "We think the humor on the show should be a little less zany than you guys are used to. I mean, let's try some family humor — ordinary couples at home, doing ordinary things."

"But *funny* ordinary things," I said jokingly.

"Exactly," Don said. He wasn't kidding.

Oh well, we'll see, won't we? I said to myself. *At least I'll be getting $150 a show.*

For the first time in a very long time John and I had a full summer to relax. I went with some pals from high school to stay at Woodington House on Lake Rousseau. As soon as I walked in the front door, my eyes locked onto a gorgeous blond with haunting, ice-blue eyes. Her name was Nina. She was a model — I recognized her from a magazine ad and she recognized me from TV. We were both impressed, and we hit it off right from the first pitch. She was there with a group of her high school pals, and that night we all went to Bala for a big-band concert and dance. By midnight, Nina and I were skinnydipping in the Moon River. For the rest of that week we skinny dipped in my bed, day and night. Although writing and performing had provided all the passion in my life that I thought I needed, with Nina I was reminded how much better the real thing could be. But until work began on *The Big Revue* in the fall, John and I were unemployed.

Back in Toronto, Jackie Rae came through with a job for us at the Canadian National Exhibition Grandstand Show. We were assistant clowns to Fifi the Clown, a very popular entertainer in Toronto at the time. He always wore a ruffled, polka-dotted clown suit, a white face with enormous eyes and lips painted on it, a red skullcap and giant shoes. As popular as Fifi the Clown was in Toronto, I could tell Nina wasn't impressed with him or his assistants.

We rehearsed with Fifi every day in our full clown costumes. I wore a tramp suit, three-foot-long shoes, a red wig and a huge red round nose. We did a lot of chasing and tumbling and I struggled to keep the huge red nose on. Fifi fixed it with some of his special clown adhesive, assuring me the nose would come off easily with only a splash of warm water. So we resumed our rehearsal, practicing a crazy chase routine, when I fell down and couldn't get up.

"What's the problem?" Fifi the Clown asked.

"I can't move my legs!" I cried.

"We better get him to a hospital," Fifi said. "With this polio epidemic, we can't be too careful."

"Polio epidemic?" I said. "When did that start?"

"Where have you guys been — Mars?" Fifi said.

"Close," John said. "The CBC studios on Jarvis Street."

John and Fifi carried me to Fifi's tiny yellow VW clown car. They had to fold me in thirds to get me in, especially with those three-foot-long shoes. We were quite a sight, Fifi and I, as we sped up to the hospital's emergency entrance. "Take off the nose before you go in," Fifi the Clown said. I tried to pull it off, but it wouldn't budge.

The orderly who met us probably thought I was a candidate for the psychiatric ward. "Is the circus in town?" he asked, as he wheeled me into the ER.

"Your legs numb?" the doctor asked.

"I don't know what they are, but I can't feel anything," I said. I was really scared. Suddenly, the nurse broke out in uncontrolled giggles and soon the doctor joined her. "What's so damned funny!" I demanded.

"We've never seen a clown in here before!" the doctor said, trying to get himself under control. "Why don't you take off that nose?"

"I can't. It's glued on with special clown adhesive. If I pull it off, my real nose will come with it!"

The nurse, still laughing, wheeled me into the hall, while the doctor, also still laughing, went off to run some tests. Some other nurses in the hall began laughing when they saw me. "Is that wheelchair part of your act?" one of them asked.

"Maybe if he gets up, another clown will jump out from under the chair, then another and another!" another nurse said.

"I can't feel my legs!" I cried.

"Don't look at me," one of the nurses said. "I'm not gonna feel 'em for ya!"

"Take it easy, gals," my nurse said. "This clown probably has polio."

The two nurses sobered up quickly. "Sorry, we thought the circus was in town and entertaining in the children's ward," one of them explained.

Just then Fifi the Clown came flip-flopping down the hall, still in full costume. "How's he doing?" he shouted. The two nurses burst into laughter again and scurried away, holding their hands over their mouths.

The doctor returned, all seriousness this time. "It's polio, I'm afraid." Then he noticed Fifi the Clown and his face turned blue as he held back the laughter.

"Will I ever be able to walk again?" I asked.

Hiding his uncontrollable grin behind his clipboard, the doctor said, "I'm afraid we don't know for sure. We have to wait a week or two to see how hard the polio virus has zapped you. Right now, you need rest."

"Do I have to stay in the hospital all that time?" I asked, tears falling from my eyes, ruining my clown makeup.

"No, you can go home," the doctor said, regaining his composure. "I'll phone ahead so they'll be prepared for you. Do you have a ride?"

"Don't worry, Doc," Fifi the Clown said. "I'll drive him."

The doctor, on the verge of another laughing fit, mumbled, "Very well," and scurried away.

Fifi wheeled me through the hospital corridors, past stunned doctors and nurses. "Who sent in the clowns?" some wag called out. Even I laughed.

At home my parents and the family doctor were waiting for us out front. I introduced them to Fifi the Clown and my mother thanked him warmly for helping me. My father looked at my clown outfit, shook his head in disbelief and announced to no one in particular, "He could have been a lawyer!"

"All lawyers are clowns," Fifi said, and drove off to who knows where.

"Fifi seems like such a nice clown," my mother said, always looking on the positive side.

"At least you can take off that damn nose," my father said, reaching in to yank it off.

"Owwwww!" I cried. "It's glued on with special clown adhesive!"

When they got me into bed, the doctor prodded my legs with a needle. "Feel anything?" he asked.

"No, I don't, and I'm scared," I said.

"Of course you are. But it's quite possible your feeling will come back to normal."

The doctor returned every other day and prodded my legs. A couple of very nerve-racking weeks went by, until one day I shouted, "I think I feel something!"

"Are you sure you aren't imagining it?" the doctor said.

"I don't think so. Try again." I closed my eyes and he gave me a jab. "I feel it! I feel it!" I was so loud they probably heard me over on the next block.

My parents rushed in. "There is feeling," the doctor told them, "which means the polio virus just numbed the spinal cord. He's going to get better quickly now."

"Thank God!" my father said.

My mother wept.

By the end of the summer I was completely recovered. The clown nose had finally fallen off and so had my romance with Nina. She ended up marrying a big movie star.

It was time to pour all my passions into *The Big Revue*. John and I hired Alfie Scopp to help with the writing and to join the cast. Alfie was long and lean, with friendly brown eyes. I had met him at a poker game of up-and-coming actors that also included Robert Goulet, and I had seen his work in a Spring Thaw revue at the Royal Ontario Museum theater. He was a very funny guy, both onstage and at the poker table. We became great friends and have remained so ever since. Alfie, John and I worked well together. We had a similar sense of humor and we all knew we had to get things done fast. Television waits for no man.

As our first order of business, we made an outline for a big scene that would include the whole cast. Before we filled it out, we had John read it back to us so that Alfie and I could make comments and John could make additions.

"Okay, Johnny, let's hear it and see if we got something," I said.

John cleared his throat and started: *"Uncle Jackie's Used Servants Lot."*

"I like it so far," Alfie laughed, and John continued.

"We come up on a set decorated like a used car lot with flags and signs. Fifteen or 20 cast members dressed like butlers, maids, cooks and chauffeurs lined up like used cars. John walks in front and does his Arthur Godfrey impression and starts selling." (In 1954 Arthur Godfrey was one of the biggest stars on American television and he was considered the top TV salesman. John's impression of Godfrey was so dead-on that it gave the sketch an added boost of satire.) *"John moves to Frank, who is dressed like a butler."*

"Hey, Johnny," I broke in, "mention that I act very snooty and react to everything you say about me."

He made some notes. *"John points at Frank in the butler suit and continues, 'Right here, my friendlies, we've got a 1949 butler who's still got a lot of miles left in him. His past owner was a little old lady who hardly ever used him. He's in mint condition and the price is right.'"*

"The maid should be next," Alfie interjects.

"Right," John says, and moves to a pretty dancer dressed as a French maid. *"And right over here is an imported* 1950 *French maid. Look at these lines, sleek and dependable. Ready to go* and *she's equipped with an automatic power smile.'* He walks to Alfie, who is dressed like a chauffeur, looking very knowing and worldly. Here's a prewar beauty, a 1938 chauffeur. He can go from zero to 60 in 10 seconds. Sure, he's a little old, but a classic, in great shape, a lean machine, no spare tire. All the used servants in Uncle Jackie's lot have had a complete checkup and are guaranteed for up to three years.'

"And I think that's it," John said.

"You forgot the cook," I said.

"Turn the page," Alfie added.

"Oh, yeah." John continued. *"Listen to this, my friendlies, if you're looking for a used cook who can make meals go further in these tough times, look no further.' John stops beside Jill, who is dressed like a cook and is very self-confident. 'This* 1950 *cook right here can stretch your use of milk and wine. She can get you three meals to the gallon. That is excellent mileage.' Now the orchestra starts and everybody sings: 'If you need a butler, a chauffeur, a maid or a cook, drop in on us and have a real good look. We've got bargains on butlers and chauffeurs galore. You can't go wrong at Uncle Jackie's big store. So hurry on down and see what we got at Uncle Jackie's Used Servants Lot. That . . . is . . . the . . . spot! Oh, yeahhh!'"*

"Music play off. As everybody waves goodbye," I said. "Tomorrow we'll smooth this out. I think we hit funny."

"It's not exactly a family situation," Alfie added.

"Once they see this material, they'll forget about the family situations," John said.

By the end of the first week we had put together lots of other material. We showed it to Norman Jewison.

"It's all very funny," Norman said, "but do you think the used servant bit will go over people's heads?"

"Some people, maybe," I said, "but I think most of the audience will get it."

"Don't get me wrong. I love it, but it's really pretty far out." Norman chuckled. "Three meals to the gallon. That *is* funny!"

"So, we'll give it a try, okay?" Alfie said, and we left Norman's office before he stopped chuckling.

Rehearsing the used servant sketch was the most fun because it included the whole cast, and on the first show it gave us a team feeling. Norman had everything decked out like a used car lot and John was doing his hilarious impression of Arthur Godfrey.

"Take five," Norman announced, and we all relaxed, had a smoke or a coffee and started gabbing.

"What happened? Did they fire you off the *Community Sing Song* show for the rain-decision thing?" a female voice said behind me. I turned and a smiling Marilyn Kent was standing there.

"Did Art Hallman and His Orchestra fire you?" I answered, and we both laughed.

"Who are you, Peppiatt or Aylesworth?"

"Take your pick."

"I'm thinking Peppiatt because I heard Norman call you Frank."

"And you're Marilyn Kent."

"Actually, I'm Marilyn Fredrickson."

"That's nice. Why did you change your name?"

"Too long to fit on the coming attractions sign."

"That sounds like an excellent reason. I'm sure your folks understand."

"Let's get back to work, people," Norman announced.

"This is a really funny sketch," Marilyn said.

"Thanks. Say, can you tell me if Samuel Hershenhorn has already written the music for the closing jingle in the scene?"

"He doesn't write music. He just conducts."

"Will he arrange it?"

"No, he's just a conductor."

"Then he should be working on a railroad," I said. I was surprised someone with so little training could have such an important role in *The Big Revue*. Unfortunately, it was painfully obvious in the show that there was no musical cohesiveness. I missed Jack Kane. He composed, arranged *and* conducted. He did it all. And he was my best friend.

Our first show went very well — though not without some bumps. The used servant sketch got big laughs, but the other sketch we wrote about a vain private eye just lay there like a bad alibi.

"I thought it was funny when we wrote it," Alfie said in the dressing room.

"So did I!" John added.

"I sure wish you guys had been in the audience," I said.

After the show most of the cast went across Jarvis Street to the Celebrity Club — a pub frequented mostly by the arty crowd, of which we were now bona fide members.

"Hey!" Marilyn Kent called out when we walked in.

"Why, Marilyn Fredrickson, imagine meeting you here."

"Oh, I come here often," she said.

"That's great, because so do I. Why don't you wait here while I get myself a drink and join you."

I looked back at her, waiting, while I ordered a drink. She looked really good — long blond hair, blue eyes and very shapely in a clingy blue silk-like dress. She was also wearing glasses. *Glasses?* I didn't remember her wearing glasses during the show. But then, why would she, when she was out there singing a romantic song? I knew she would wait for me. And the glasses suited her — gave her a kind of "I'm smart" look. Or was I talking myself into something? Actually, I thought she kind of liked me. *Hold it, Frankie,* I thought, *she hardly knows you. Well, I can start fixing that right now!*

And so it began.

Chapter 8

✦

HURRICANE WEDDING AND OTHER DISASTERS

SINCE WE WERE ON *The Big Revue* only every other week, I actually had time for a social life. Marilyn Kent quickly filled it up.

"I hear you've got a new girlfriend," my mother said one morning at breakfast.

"I guess you could say that."

"I think your mother just did," my father said.

"Right and, uh . . . yes," I said.

"A band singer, I'm told," my mother said.

"Whoever told you that was dead wrong. She used to be a band singer and now she's a featured soloist on *The Big Revue*."

"I hear band singers are pretty wild — all that traveling with all those men," my father said.

"I guess I better watch my step."

"She married?" my mother asked.

"No, and she's not a divorcée."

"How old is she?"

"My age, 26."

"She's that old and never been married, son?"

"I'm that old and I've never been married."

"Don't think all your aunts and uncles haven't noticed *that*!" my mother said. "All of your cousins are married."

"Well, I commend them and hope they'll all be very happy."

"That smart talk is not called for," my dad said. "Marilyn Kent's her name. Right?"

"Her real name is Marilyn Fredrickson. Her father was a professional hockey player with the Bruins."

"Frank Fredrickson?" my dad asked.

"The very same."

"Oh, he was something, an all-star and great goal scorer!"

"Does that lessen the band-singer stain?"

"Relax, son!" my mother said. "If you've found someone, we're happy for you."

"Mom, I'm not sure if I've found someone or if someone's found me. Just let us work it out. Okay?"

"Pass the peanut butter," my father said, putting a period on the conversation.

My relationship with Marilyn was going along much better than the show. The CBC brass, Don Hudson and Norman Jewison kept pushing us to do more material that appealed to a family audience. Everyone but John and I seemed to have some sort of pipeline to a certain family audience that told them exactly what they wanted. After a few shows and incessant prodding, we relented and hired a very good actress, Peggi Loder, to play John's wife, and Jill would play mine. The two couples would live next door to each other, high up in a large apartment building.

We tried each week to write one sketch about the comic doings of these two couples. John, Alfie and I had trouble writing this gentle *Father Knows Best* type of comedy, and God knows, John and I had no idea, no training or experience in life to guide us on how to act the two roles. It turned out to be mostly unfunny and boring. The CBC executives, it seemed to me, assumed we would magically turn into Jackie Gleason and Art Carney, or Lucy and Desi — stars of the biggest U.S. television comedies that year: *Cavalcade of Stars*, where *The Honeymooners* characters made their debut, and *I Love Lucy*. But it would have taken an act of God to make that happen and I knew damn well God wasn't stupid enough to try it.

We were still getting laughs out of our more zany stuff. One idea for a nutty sketch came to me while listening to "Life Could Be a Dream" by the Crew-Cuts on the radio. It was the same number I had recorded at MacLaren nearly three years earlier and it was now the latest overnight sensation, zooming its way up the pop charts. I called the sketch "Real Gone With the Wind." I was Rhett Butler, sitting at the piano and describing a Civil War battle. I said, ". . . and the cannons exploded! . . . SH-BOOM SH-BOOM . . . and the rifles fired . . . YA-DA-DA DA-DA-DA DA-DA-DA DA . . . and the cannonballs hit the steeple bell tower . . . HEY NONNY DING DONG ALANG ALANG A LANG . . ."

The sketch got huge laughs from everyone except Don Hudson and his bosses, who had never heard of this big hit or the Crew-Cuts. They had been too busy staying in touch with their "family audience," who had also somehow managed never to have heard the record that was being played constantly on every radio station and jukebox in the world.

Norman Jewison went along with the powers that be, but he also understood that our comedy strengths lay elsewhere. He tried his best to help our two couples come alive and be reasonably funny, to no avail. By the end of the season, John and I were completely demoralized. We thought our comedy careers had crashed and burned.

It was an advertising executive named Bill Byles who picked us up out of the ashes. He brought Lever Brothers to the CBC as a sponsor who wanted to do a half-hour comedy-variety show, starring Peppiatt and Aylesworth. We couldn't believe our luck. Neither could the CBC. Lever Brothers was the largest soap manufacturer in North America. Suddenly, we were golden again in the CBC executive suites. Our old boss from MacLaren, Hugh Horler, had quietly set up the deal. It was payback for the years I worked for him, round the clock in seven-day, $25-weeks, with no vacations.

John and I raced over to Alfie's house to tell him the good news. As it turned out, Alfie had something to tell us. He had auditioned for a Canadian version of the American kids' show *Howdy Doody* and had landed the job as Clarabell the clown — he'd be doing five one-hour shows a week for at least 26 weeks at a fivefold raise in pay. We wished Alfie good luck and said goodbye. It was a tough goodbye, because Alfie Scopp had become a good friend, and his wife, Doe, was the very best pal of my lady friend, the band singer.

Norman Jewison was selected to produce and direct our new half-hour show. That made me uneasy. As hard as Norman had tried to liven up our hopeless *Big Revue* family sketches, his loyalties had always seemed divided. But I did talk him into hiring my friend Jack Kane to arrange and conduct the big band on the new show. That made me feel much better. At least the music would be first-rate. Norman told us the show would be called *On Stage*. He didn't know who thought up the name and told us not to ask. It was probably the same guy who thought up *The Big Revue*!

At our next meeting with Norman he dropped the bomb. "I met with the advertising agency and the sponsor," he said, "and they told me they really enjoyed the sketches we did on *The Big Revue* about the two couples. They'd like that to be a regular spot on the show."

John and I were dumbfounded! Finally, I stuttered, "Are . . . are . . . you kidding us, Norman?"

"No, they seemed very excited about it."

"Excited about *what*?" John asked.

"Look," Norman said, "I know it's not your favorite thing, but we will be doing *two* sketches per show."

"We have real trouble writing that couples stuff and now we don't have Alfie."

"I know," he said, "and I have a suggestion. A Canadian comedy writer named Reuben Ship has moved back here and he could help us."

"What's he done?"

"He co-created *December Bride* starring Spring Byington and *The Life of Riley* with William Bendix."

"Wow," I exclaimed. I knew these popular American series — they were big.

"What's he doing back here?" John asked.

"He was called to testify in front of the House Un-American Activities Committee about some socialist club he had belonged to in the '40s. Anyway, he refused to divulge the names of the members."

"So what happened?" John asked.

"Well, because he was in the States on a green card and was still a Canadian citizen, they put him on a train and shipped him back here. Not only that, he's lost all his royalties and income from those big hit shows."

"Let's hire him!" I said.

"And he can do the couples stuff!" John added.

Reuben Ship was a very nice man — slim, dark complected, with black eyes that shone like his black hair. Norman hired him, but either the CBC, Lever Brothers or the agency wouldn't let him have a credit. We never found who decided this.

"Why the hell not?" I asked Don Hudson, who was still head of Comedy Variety.

"Well, you know," he said, "the McCarthy thing."

"What's that got to do with Canada?" John asked.

"Just leave it! Okay, guys? That's the way it's going to be."

And that's the way it was. Reuben didn't seem to mind, though. I guess he'd been through a lot worse. "At least I've got a job," he said. "At least my wife sold our house in L.A. and she's bringing some money up here when she arrives with our two little girls."

"You mean, they shipped you out and left your wife and kids to scramble?" John asked.

"That's right, and they dumped me off at the train station in Windsor in the middle of winter."

I guess the credit thing was trivial by comparison.

Back at CBC, Don and Norman thought we needed some female comedy input, so they hired an Englishwoman who had written comedy in London for the BBC. We interviewed her and she seemed very bright. Most importantly, she knew her way around a joke. Her name was Jo Kowin and she *was* allowed to have a credit.

We had the whole summer to wait for our first show and in that time my relationship with Marilyn ripened. John, meanwhile, had started going with a girl named Jean. Marilyn and Jean strongly disliked each other, so I didn't see much of John that summer. But one day he called me out of the blue and asked me to lunch.

"How come the lunch?" I asked, sitting down across from him at the Bathurst Diner.

"Are you in love?"

"I don't know, but I'm enjoying myself."

"Me, too . . ."

"Are *you* in love?" I asked him.

"I don't know how you're supposed to feel! I can't tell."

"Me, either."

We ate in silence for a few minutes.

"I think I want to get married!" John blurted out. "It's time."

"You serious?" I asked.

"I think I'd like to try it."

"Try it?" I said. "There is no try. When you say, 'I do,' you do."

"I suppose you do," he said.

"Of course you do. Are you going to ask her?"

"How about you?" he asked.

"Why would *I* ask her? She's *your* girlfriend."

"Don't get funny, this is serious. We're talking marriage."

"Not *we*, pal. *You're* talking marriage. Leave me out of it!"

"You mean you don't want to get married and have kids?"

"Eventually, of course."

"Eventually?" he said. "You just turned 27. It's getting a little late."

"You sound like my mother."

"You're lucky you have parents who care about you."

"I know," I said, and I shut up. I realized that his getting married meant he could have a real family again, or maybe for the first time ever. I hoped it would work out for him.

And true to his word, John and Jean got married soon after. At the reception, Marilyn and I were drinking champagne and feeling the romance and excitement of the whole event.

"I think it would be really nice if we got engaged," I said.

"Is that a proposal?" she asked.

"I, uh . . . believe it is."

"You're such a romantic, Mr. Peppiatt. I think it would be *really* nice, as you put it, too."

We drank to it and I guess we were engaged. I couldn't afford a ring at that time, so I gave her my Psi Upsilon fraternity pin. A real romantic, indeed. I met her parents over the phone from Vancouver and she had dinner with my parents in early September.

"She's just right for you," my mother said.

"When is the wedding?" my dad asked.

"We haven't discussed it," I said. "I've got a lot on my plate right now. The new show starts in two weeks."

"I'm looking forward to meeting Frank Fredrickson," my dad said. "He's in the Hockey Hall of Fame."

"We know that, Frank," my mother said. "Let the boy work out his own future. Do you think you might get married soon, dear?"

"You're our only chance for us to be grandparents," my father added.

"I'm taking all that into account. Marilyn and I will talk it over, okay?"

They both smiled and nodded.

I took Marilyn out to dinner that night. "My parents are really pushing the wedding thing," I said.

"So are mine."

"Why don't we make everybody happy and get married?"

"That would make me happy, too," Marilyn said.

"Include me in on that," I said, and I leaned across the dinner table and kissed her.

We decided on October 15 for the wedding. We had no particular reason for choosing that date; we just did and that was that. We both informed our parents. Marilyn and my mother started making a list of wedding guests.

Meanwhile, I was busy every day with John, Reuben Ship and Jo Kowin. One day, Jackie Rae of the *Wayne and Shuster* radio show and the Canadian National Exhibition appeared at our writing session to inform us that he had been appointed head of TV Comedy Variety.

"What about Don Hudson?" John asked.

"He's been given another job," Jackie said.

"Well, we all wish you good luck," I said as we all shook his hand.

"And good luck to you guys," Jackie said. "I'll leave you alone to create your magic."

"I wish it was only magic we had to produce and not humor," John joked, but nobody laughed.

The change gave me some hope. I knew that at least Jackie Rae had a sense of humor. Maybe he wouldn't hold us to the family sketches the way Don Hudson had.

MARILYN AND I CHOSE A church near my parents' house and we decided to have our reception at a little hotel on Yonge Street, just south of St. Clair.

"Why that dinky little hotel?" my dad asked.

"That's all I could afford, Dad."

"All *you* could afford? The bride's father is supposed to pay for the wedding *and* the reception!" he said, anger in his voice.

"Marilyn's dad is having a tough time. He can't afford the airfare from Vancouver as well as the reception."

"I don't like that! Not a bit!" my dad said. "You're going to end up supporting those people. They could move in with you!"

"I doubt that. Her dad is just having a rough patch — he'll be fine."

"Just mark my words, sonny boy!" When my dad called me "sonny boy," which he rarely did, it meant I should sit up and take notice. I usually did, but this time I didn't.

I rented a nice little two-bedroom apartment in Leaside, a Toronto suburb. My mother and father furnished it for us as a wedding present and we were all set.

OUR FIRST *ON STAGE* SHOW went well. We did a couples sketch with a lot of humorous confusion about who was supposed to go to whose house for dinner. The scene got good laughs, but afterward the sponsor's rep said we made the two couples look stupid. He told us to write more believable family situations.

"Fuck him!" Reuben Ship said. "Does he think the characters that Gleason and Carney play are rocket scientists? They're stupid and damn funny."

What did they want from us? It was hard to figure — I was hopelessly confused. Why had they hired us? How was I going to get through 25 more shows with "believable family situations"? Work was no longer the all-encompassing passion I had felt while doing *After Hours*.

At least I was getting married in a month, so there was passion in my personal life. There was also nervousness, extreme nervousness, which was only somewhat calmed by Marilyn's excitement as she prepared for the big day. She was not working, but it didn't seem to bother her. We didn't have time for a proper honeymoon, just one night in a very nice hotel on Lake Ontario, then back to rehearsal the next day. We were both trying to figure out why we had chosen October 15, but it was too late now. The bridal train had left the station.

On the morning of the wedding, I was awakened by the sound of heavy rain falling on the roof. I looked out the window and saw the trees on the street bent almost in half from the roaring wind.

"I hope the weather clears before the ceremony," I said as I sat down to breakfast.

"I don't think so," my dad said. "They're calling it a hurricane."

"You're kidding!"

"No, he's not," my mother said. "The radio news says it's going to get worse."

"Hurricane Hazel, they're calling it," my dad added.

"Nice name for a hurricane — alliteration and everything."

"It's not too late to call it off, *sonny boy*," my dad said, looking me dead in the eye.

For a brief moment my heart felt a warm sense of relief. Did I really, really want this marriage? What was my father saying? Did he have reservations about Marilyn, too? Was Hurricane Hazel giving me an out, or warning me? Then my head took over and directed me to practicalities. "Come on, Dad," I said. "Do you want to start calling a hundred guests and telling them to forget it? We can't let a little rain spoil everything."

"A little rain?" my father exclaimed. "It's a damn hurricane, for chrissake!"

The ceremony and reception went off without a glitch, and our honeymoon night at the fancy hotel dispelled my doubts about the marriage. As I drove to rehearsal the next morning, the hurricane accounts on the radio were horrendous — people drowned, houses swept away, the whole west end of the city under water. Meanwhile, I was awash in nuptial bliss.

"Let's start with the Bengal Lancers sketch!" Norman announced, as I walked into the studio.

The sketch was pretty funny, but it sure wasn't family-oriented. "How the hell can plain ordinary Canadian families relate to British soldiers mucking about in goddamned India?" the Lever Brothers rep said. Jackie Rae and his CBC bosses came at us from all directions, demanding: "Husband-and-wife comedy!" "Fun with neighbors!" "Family situations!" "Real people reacting to real people." "Real situations in the home!" Even some media critics chimed in, although others liked the Bengal Lancers sketch.

We tried, damn it, we tried. The four of us wrote some funny family things, but John and I weren't good enough actors to make them come to life. The season dragged on and became nothing but drudgery. I was falling into a deep funk when something wonderful happened: Marilyn was pregnant.

"Are you feeling okay?" I asked her.

"Of course, I feel great. I'm only about three weeks."

"Pregnant?"

"Yes, and you sound more nervous about this than I do and I'm the pregnant one."

"I know. It's all so new."

"It better be, unless you've been married before," she said with a smile and a soft punch on my arm. We both laughed. I left to meet the other writers to try and write some realistic family fun.

ON STAGE CAME TO AN end and I mean *end*. The sponsor canceled the show after 20 weeks and hired Denny Vaughan and His Orchestra with singer Joan Fairfax. Denny sang and played family-type piano and it was safe. No funny stuff, just good, family musical entertainment under the direction of Norman Jewison. He was the only one who didn't lose a job.

On our first day of unemployment John and I met at his place to figure out what to do now. It turned out that his wife was pregnant also.

"I think we should stop performing and stick to writing," I said.

"I don't know about that, we were getting pretty good," John said.

"Pretty good enough to get canceled. We're lousy actors, John!"

I finally convinced him to give up the acting and just write.

"What'll we write?"

"Whatever they pay us for."

There were a number of new musical variety shows about to start in the fall, so we let it be known we were available to write and not perform. There were no agents for television writers or performers in Canada then. The CBC was the only shop in the whole country where we could sell our wares. They told us these new shows had a budget for only one writer, or two writers willing to split one writer's money. We were both married and expecting babies. Both families living on one salary was out of the question. John was offered a job on *Cross Canada Hit Parade.* He also had an idea for a news-panel show that he wanted to develop. I encouraged him to go for it. Soon, Jackie Rae hired me on to write *The Jackie Rae Show.* Jackie hadn't performed since he was a child in vaudeville with his brother and sister as one of the "Three Raes of Sunshine." I convinced Jackie to hire Jack Kane on as music director.

"I thought Jackie Rae was head of the CBC Variety Department?" John said.

"He was."

"How did he get his own show?"

"I guess he gave it to himself."

"Can he do that?"

"It seems so, Johnny."

Reuben Ship went on to write a fabulous radio play for the CBC called *The Investigator,* based on the Army–McCarthy hearings. The show was a big hit. Someone recorded it and sold millions of copies all over the world. Reuben didn't make a dime out of it but he sure got back at the vicious old senator.

John's news-panel show became *Front Page Challenge*, a huge hit that ran over 30 years. CBC gave John no credit or royalties for the show — he threatened to sue. CBC said that if he did, they'd simply cancel the show and put all those people out of work. John walked away.

John wasn't the only one to feel the injustice of CBC arrogance. About that time, many writers, performers and directors began referring to the CBC as "the Kremlin."

On a side note, Jo Kowin, the comedy writer from England who had been brought in to write for *On Stage*, married Fred Davis, a trumpet player who became the host of *Front Page Challenge*.

I was the only writer on *The Jackie Rae Show*. Since it was basically a musical show, I didn't have a whole lot to write — some snappy dialogue between Jackie and a guest lady singer, Jackie's opening and closing remarks, medleys for Jackie and our regular singing group the Four Grads, and every once in a while I would appear as a character whom Jackie would interview for, hopefully, comedic effect. That was about it.

"We need some rock-and-roll guests," Norman Sedawie, our director, said at a production meeting.

"This is not a rock-and-roll show," Jackie Rae snapped. He set great store by his singing (out of key though it was) and would not share the spotlight with a hip-swiveling rocker.

"It's a rock-and-roll world right now, Jackie," Sedawie said.

"He's right, Jackie," I added.

"The Four Grads can do rock-and-roll," Jackie said.

"Not really," Jack Kane said. "You need somebody whose bag is rock or the kids will see right through it."

"Why don't we invent our own rock-and-roll star," I suggested. Everybody looked at me like I was some kind of nut. "I'm not kidding.

I'll bet we could get away with it."

"And how the hell could we do that?" Sedawie asked.

"Well, Jack can sure make a rock-and-roll arrangement," I said.

"No problem," Jack Kane said. "All I need are some amps."

"Let the Grads be backup singers."

"Yeah, and then what?" Jackie asked.

"I'll bet I could change my whole look with dyed hair, a glitzy rock outfit and special makeup, and have a dentist make a plate of teeth that fit over mine. Give me some sexy moves, a guitar with fake strings, and there we be."

"But you can't sing," Jackie pointed out.

"Has that stopped half of the rock stars?" I said. *Or you, Jackie*, I thought, then said aloud, "I'll sing quietly and let the Grads do a backup voice-over."

There was complete silence in the room until Jack Kane spoke up. "It just might work."

"We could start an advertising campaign that we've discovered a new star," Sedawie said.

"All the TV newspaper columns would pick it up," Jackie added. "I've got a great dentist on Eglinton Avenue who would get a real kick out of being included in this."

"Make an appointment as soon as you can," I urged.

"We'll have to let Anna the makeup girl in on this, but nobody — absolutely nobody — else should know. Okay?"

Jackie nodded and okays echoed around the room. It was a go!

The dentist made me a beautiful set of upper false teeth that fit firmly over my real ones. On our next show, Jackie announced that our new rock star, Bryce Patton, would make his first television appearance the following week. Jack Kane picked a rock song that wasn't too rangy, and the Grads, a rock guitarist and I rehearsed all week. The strings on my guitar were fake and silent, so I learned to play along with a real musician. It *looked* great. On the day of the show, I came in early and Anna was waiting for me in the dressing room. She put in the fake teeth.

"Wow, that makes a huge difference!" Anna said. She then whitened up my hair and added highlights to my face with makeup. "There, how do you like it?"

I didn't recognize myself in the mirror. I had become Bryce Patton. I put on tight, shiny silver pants and a satin black-and-white-striped shirt.

"Ready for rehearsal, Mr. Patton," the stage manager said as I stepped out of my dressing room.

"Okay, sir," I said. I'd known this particular stage manager for years and now he didn't recognize me.

"Follow me, Mr. Patton, the stage is this way."

"Thank you," I said with kind of a Texas twang.

We entered the studio, where Norman Sedawie and Jackie Rae were standing in a spotlight in front of a lattice-like set.

"Welcome, Bryce," Jackie said, holding out his hand.

"Pleasa meetcha," I mumbled.

"I wouldn't know it was you," Jackie whispered.

"It's not," I said, and smiled with my brand-new teeth.

"You ready for a rehearsal, Bryce?" Norman Sedawie asked.

"I sho am."

"Let's do it!" he yelled, and he and Jackie left me alone in the spotlight.

Jack Kane's rock-and-roll intro sounded great and I did a little wiggling, bumping and twirling my guitar. The Four Grads began to sing and I sang along without being out in front. I slithered my hips and smiled. The practice with the live guitar really paid off because I mimed the finger work almost dead on. When we came to the big finish, I grinned and took a bow.

"Okay, Bryce. Relax in your dressing room until showtime," the director said over the talkback.

After the show aired, I got 10 fan letters from teenagers. The CBC brass and the sponsors were thrilled that we had discovered our own Canadian rock star. I appeared on the next two shows and my fan mail began to fill sacks. Dot Records called to say they were interested in signing me. After my third appearance, a TV critic in Winnipeg recognized me and called me an impostor, demanding that the CBC apologize for this big fake. Bryce was out of the bag and it caused a national furor.

Alex Barris was one of the few critics to support our little gag. "This 'Hoax,'" he wrote, "which lasted a few weeks did no harm — other than to injure the vanity of a teenage public so devoid of taste that it will cheer anything now without even bothering to examine its merits."

But the CBC didn't see it that way. They insisted Jackie and I appear together on the next show and apologize to Canada. I pulled out my fake teeth, cut my guitar strings and said I was sorry. The audience in the studio had given me a standing ovation. We might have been found out, but we created a great deal of interest in the show. We were even mentioned in *Variety*, the American show-business newspaper of record.

But all of the publicity was to no avail. The CBC canceled us. Jackie Rae took a montage of film clips from his show, flew to England and got a job as the star of the British version of *Name That Tune*. This time he didn't hire himself — someone else did the deed.

MY FAVORITE JACKIE RAE SHOW was the one in which I brought on Robyn, my beautiful baby daughter. She was only a month old. I held her up to the camera. "Folks in Vancouver," I said to my in-laws, "I'd like you to meet your granddaughter." The orchestra played an impressive chord. "Our very special guest star, Miss Robyn Peppiatt!" I guess I said it a little too loudly because she started to cry; but she was, to me, the best guest star we ever had on the show.

During the last month of *The Jackie Rae Show*, Jack Kane and I worked out an idea to close every episode. We put the whole band on camera, dressed them like a '30s or '40s big band, used music stands emblazoned with the letters J.K., suspended a big mirrored ball spinning over their heads, had Jackie Rae as the singing emcee, Jack Kane as the leader and the Four Grads dressed like Glenn Miller's big band, the Modernaires. Our lady guest that week would be the girl singer, and each week we would pay tribute to a different big band. The segment really caught on, but it didn't save the show. However, it did great things for Jack Kane.

The CBC offered Jack a weekly big-band show, *Music Makers*. He told them he wanted me to write the show and they agreed. I got $200 a week — just enough to support my family, which was soon to grow to four — and I didn't even have to appear on camera. Equally important, I could put passion into my work again. Jack Kane was a natural for television because he was instantly likeable. He wasn't handsome, but his happy round face and sparkling brown eyes said, *Trust me, I'll entertain you*. And he always did. The members of his band believed in him and loved him. He arranged every single note they played and he conducted his big band with energy and authority. He seemed to enjoy every musical bar from jazz, to soft pop, to symphonic and big-band swing. He did it all.

Word soon got around North America, through jazz joints and music magazines, that Kane was able and you got treated with class on his show. That first year, names like Woody Herman, Buddy Rich, Lionel Hampton, Cab Calloway and the Four Freshmen appeared with the Music Makers, and they all had a ball. I was the only writer on the show and I worked closely with Jack on interesting production numbers for the band. The show had a happy feeling, one that came across to the audience and the sponsor, who renewed the show for a second year.

"We made it, Frankie boy!" Jack said.

"*You* made it, Jack, and you thankfully dragged me along with you."

"Come on," he said, "you made the show different, funny and exciting. Frank, I couldn't have done it without you. That Christmas show where you had the kids of all the guys in the band on their own tiny bandstand, using smaller versions of the instruments their fathers played! It was great!"

"Thanks, Jack. Next Christmas my daughter Robyn will be a year and a half and we'll put her behind a typewriter in the bandstand."

"And my daughter Fern will conduct!" We shook on it, and at Christmas that's what happened. It also happened that Marilyn was pregnant again. The New Year looked just fine.

ONE VERY COLD JANUARY DAY, Jack and I were at his house working out some routines when he tossed me a copy of the morning paper.

"'Eydie Gormé from *The Tonight Show* will be here all next week,'" I read aloud.

"She'd be great on the show and she used to be a band singer," Jack said. "She's terrific. You think we can get her?"

"We can try. Let's you and Marilyn, Claire and I go and see her opening night, and we'll talk."

"We'll take a shot."

Eydie Gormé's opening set, backed by a small Toronto jazz group, was wonderful. After enthusiastic applause from the packed house, Eydie and her manager came over to our table. Eydie was an attractive woman with curly black hair, dazzling brown eyes, a fabulous figure and a wonderful friendly laugh. Ken Greengrass, her manager, was very well dressed, dark complected, with straight black hair parted at the side and a little-dab'll-do-ya shine. He looked very wise and gave us the once-over before he accepted our invitation to sit with us.

"I hear you've got quite a show," Ken said.

Jack came right to the point. "We're on the air every week and we'd love Eydie to join us the night after you close here."

"Buddy Rich told us he had a ball working with you," Eydie said.

"I think we could work that out," Ken Greengrass said.

"But you have a big band, and I don't have any big-band arrangements," Eydie said.

"I think *we* can work *that*!" Jack said with a grin.

"You arrange?" Ken asked.

"He sure does! The best," Marilyn said.

"Eydie's been dying to get a big-band arrangement for 'Be Careful, It's My Heart.'"

"You want it to swing?" Jack said.

"Oh, yeah!" Eydie said. "Oh, yeah!"

"A nice key change after the first chorus?"

"You are talking my language, Mr. Kane."

On the morning of the show, Jack introduced Eydie and Ken to the band and the TV crew, then tapped his baton on his music stand. "Shall we go from the top?"

"Be my guest," Eydie said.

The intro started with a swinging vamp by three trombones and the rhythm section. Eydie looked over at Ken and nodded with a big smile. Jack cued Eydie and she dove right into the song. Eydie wanted to swing and the arrangement sure as hell swung. The whole studio was jumping as she and the band exploded into the second chorus, then a big exciting ending faded down to a trombone vamp, with Eydie wailing along.

The band applauded, the staff and crew applauded and Eydie threw her arms around Jack.

"Jack! That was fantastic!"

"So were you."

"Can we buy that arrangement?" Ken asked.

"It's not for sale."

"Why?" Eydie asked.

"Because I'm giving it to you. It's a gift."

Then *Ken* hugged Jack.

Eydie did the show two more times. Once she brought a friend up with her. His name was Steve Lawrence; Jack arranged a great duet for them. Then, Steve and Eydie brought Jack to New York to arrange some songs for their first album together, which turned out to be a smash. Steve and Eydie were regulars on Steve Allen's original *Tonight Show*, and they were semi-regulars on Steve Allen's variety show on Sunday nights at eight. During the 12-week summer hiatus of the variety show, NBC allowed Allen's production company to produce a replacement show. This was standard practice for all successful prime-time network variety programs. Steve and Eydie were given the summer replacement slot by Steve Allen. Ken Greengrass offered Jack the job of musical director. Without telling me, Jack insisted I be hired as a writer and they agreed.

Wow! I was going to New York!

Chapter 9

✦

I TAKE MANHATTAN AND MANHATTAN TAKES ME

On the two-and-a-half-hour flight to New York, Jack and I were so high with excitement that our energy alone could have kept the plane up in the air. Jack's wife, Claire, was with us and every bit as thrilled. I was really sorry that Marilyn hadn't come along. Although we had hired a live-in nanny to help with Robyn and Marney, the new baby, Marilyn didn't want to come to New York, even for a short visit. She had a strong hatred for the United States.

Before I had met her, she had been hired to sing with Red Ingles and His Natural Seven. With big fanfare in all the papers, Marilyn had left Canada to meet up with Ingles' band as it swung through the Kentucky leg of its national tour. About a month later she quietly returned to Toronto. She never told me, or anyone else I know of, why she left the band. Whatever happened had apparently been so horrible that her hatred of Red Ingles' band had grown into an extreme antipathy to the entire United States of America. So Marilyn had not been pleased about my going to work in New York, though she was pleased I wouldn't be unemployed the whole summer.

At the New York airport, Jack and Claire hailed a cab and were off to their hotel on Central Park. I took a separate taxi because my apartment was farther downtown. A friend of mine had a sister and brother-in-law with an apartment in New York that would be empty for the summer. They rented it to me at a reasonable rate, which meant I could send most of my paycheck home to Marilyn each week. I felt lucky indeed.

"Twenty-six Houston Street," I said to the cabby.

The cab didn't move. The driver slowly turned to face me. "Twenty-six Houston Street?"

"That is correct."

"Do you know where that is?"

"Of course, it's in Manhattan."

"On the Lower East Side, mister."

"So?"

"That is a very dangerous area, sir, and you don't look like someone who would go there."

"I've rented an apartment there for the summer."

"Someone paying you to stay there?"

"Don't be silly. Let's go."

"Okay, sir, but don't say I didn't warn you."

He put the cab in gear and gunned it into the traffic. I thought about what I knew of the Lower East Side. It was all from the movies: *The Dead End Kids*, *Angels with Dirty Faces*, Leo Gorcey, Huntz Hall, Jimmy Cagney, Humphrey Bogart. All tough-guy movies, but that was only in the theaters. This was 1958. Was the cab driver trying to scare me? We traveled over a big bridge, then onto a freeway beside a river. "Where are we now?" I asked.

"We're on the FDR Drive along the East River."

"It's not the Hudson River?"

"No, that's on the other side of the island."

I could see all the skyscrapers zipping by and wondered when we would turn right and go into the city. He finally turned off and we passed some old-looking apartment buildings and some dingy corner stores that had seen better days.

"Kind of a run-down area," I said, looking around warily. This was definitely *not* how I had imagined New York City when I was a kid, glued to my radio back in Montreal.

"I told you, mister," the cabby said.

As we drove along farther, the neighborhood got worse — men sleeping in doorways, drunk-looking people arguing on the street at the top of their voices, tenement houses with rusted iron fire escapes.

"Here we are," the cabby said. "Twenty-six Houston Street. Actually, it ain't a bad-looking building, considering."

"Considering what?"

"Where it is. I think it's owned by some union."

I paid the fare and hoisted my suitcase onto the sidewalk.

"If you need a cab, you sure ain't gonna find one around here, so you should walk over to Seventh Avenue where there's more traffic."

"Thanks."

"Good luck, sir," he called as he drove away.

I had been sent two keys by my friend's brother-in-law, one for the front door and one for the apartment door. They both worked, thank God, and I entered a quite nice-looking apartment — small rooms, but furnished with taste. I closed the door behind me and noticed four chain locks and a large bolt-action lock. I'd never seen anything like that before. The apartment was stuffy and I couldn't find any air-conditioning boxes, so I opened the bedroom windows and got a nice breeze off the East River. I unpacked, watched some TV on a tiny black-and-white set, made a grilled cheese sandwich and went to bed.

It had been a long, busy day and I was asleep very quickly. But I soon woke up with a start, just as fast. Something was biting my face and arms. I switched on the bedside lamp and discovered a covey of large bugs buzzing around the room and more of them flying in through the open window. I was their Friday-night BBQ. I jumped out of bed, slammed the window shut, grabbed a magazine from beside the bed, rolled it up and started swatting the huge bugs. I ran around swatting until my arm was limp. I think I killed a couple dozen of the invaders before I slumped down on the bed like a wounded warrior. One last bug was still flittering around on the floor. I stomped him good.

I found a broom in the kitchen, swept up the attackers into a dust-pan and flushed them down the toilet. I breathed a sigh of relief until I looked into the bathroom mirror. There were large red welts on my face and shoulders. The dastardly bugs had done a job on me, but good. Frantically, I rooted through the medicine cabinet and found a jar of Noxzema. I spread the cream all over my face and shoulders and went back to bed looking like a French mime. The Noxzema helped, but the itching was horrible. Luckily, I was so tired that in spite of the bug bites and the renewed stuffiness in the bedroom, I fell fast asleep again.

The next morning I looked like I'd just gone 15 rounds with Joe Louis and lost big time. Most of the itchiness was gone, but the hideous welts were bigger than ever. I wrapped ice cubes in towels and held them to my face, then wrapped my face in hot towels and smeared on more Noxzema. Nothing seemed to help. I shaved the best I could, showered and dressed up in a shirt, tie and blazer. At least from the neck down I looked halfway presentable. I was going uptown to a fancy restaurant to meet with Nick Vanoff, the producer of *The Steve Allen Show* and *The Steve Lawrence and Eydie Gormé Summer Show*. I needed to make a good impression.

I walked 14 blocks before I saw a taxi. Fourteen blocks full of drunks passed out in doorways. At least, I hoped they were only passed out. There were strange old ladies asking for money and mysterious odors coming out of open windows. I was really sweaty after that walkathon. Now I didn't look so good from the neck down, either. I flagged down the cab.

"Youse sure youse got money to pay?" the cabbie said before unlock-ing the door.

"Of course," I said, and showed him a 20.

He let me in and sped off. "Whatcha doin' down here?"

"It's a long story. Just take me to 53th Street and Seventh Avenue."

"Youse got it, buddy." He wove through the slummy streets until we turned right onto a big boulevard.

"Seventh Avenue?" I asked.

"The very same. Now we gotta go about 50 or 60 blocks."

It was Saturday, so there was no traffic. He gunned us uptown, making every light, and squealed to a stop at the restaurant.

"Thanks." I paid him. "Do you have the time?"

"Uh, let's see, twelve-fifteen."

The lunch was for twelve-thirty, so I was 15 minutes early, which was just perfect. Actually, for a Canadian, it was right on time. Inside, the air conditioning was a welcome smack in my hideous, swollen face. The place was all red leather, mahogany and white tablecloths. Very classy. Now, *this* was more like what I had imagined back in Montreal. I had arrived!

"May I help you, sir?" the head guy asked.

"I'm meeting a Mr. Nick Vanoff for lunch and —"

"Why, yes, he and his party are not here yet, but follow me."

His party? I thought. *Hmmm.*

The headwaiter led me through a very crowded room to a large corner table.

"Mr. Vanoff should be here shortly. May I get you a cocktail?"

"A gin and tonic."

"Coming right up, sir."

I didn't usually drink at noon, but what the hell, I'd been in a fight. I sat there sipping my drink.

"Frank Peppiatt, I presume?" a friendly voice said.

I looked up. "Mr. Vanoff?"

"Nick, for God's sake — Nick!" he said, and sat down. "So, you got settled okay?"

"Yes. Fine."

"What happened to your face?"

"I had a disagreement with some bugs."

"So, the look is not permanent?"

"I sure as hell hope not."

The headwaiter appeared, leading Jack Kane and two other guys.

"The rest of your party has arrived, Mr. Vanoff."

"Hi, Frankie," Jack said. "What the hell happened to your face?"

"Later," I said.

Nick introduced me to our director, Dwight Hemion, a tallish blond man with a crewcut and a round happy face. He resembled the ruby-cheeked kid from the Campbell's Soup ads. He had big blue eyes, freckles and a nice handshake.

"And this is Bill Dana, your writing partner for the summer, Frank." Bill was very short, well built with black wavy hair, impish brown eyes, a dark complexion and a knowing smile.

"Jack here tells me you know what you're doing," Bill Dana said, shaking my hand.

"You'll soon find out," I said.

You could tell Nick was a take-charge guy by the way he carried himself like an AKC champion terrier and led the conversation. He was taller than Bill but shorter than Dwight. He had a mass of lustrous black hair, dark piercing eyes and, when he wanted to use it, a great friendly smile.

"What happened to his face, Greek?" I heard Dwight whisper to Nick.

"Don't call me Greek! I'm Macedonian and why don't *you* ask him."

We all ordered lunch and sat back as Nick outlined the production.

"Johnny Bradford, our head writer, will be flying in from L.A. later today."

"Johnny Bradford?" Jack Kane asked.

"He's the head writer on *The Dinah Shore Show*," Nick said, "and supposed to be damn good. At least, that's what his agent tells me. Johnny would like to see Bill and Frank at his apartment Sunday evening. You guys free?"

Bill and I nodded.

"He'd like to meet you both and get things straightened around before we all start working at the Steve Allen office on Monday morning. Okeydokey?"

We nodded again.

"Here's the address." Nick handed each of us a slip of paper. "It's on Madison Avenue around 73rd Street. He'd like you there about eight-thirty."

That was the sum and substance of our first meeting. It also included the best damn grilled chopped sirloin I had ever tasted.

Bill Dana and I let the other guys grab their cabs. When they were gone, Bill asked, "I hope you don't mind me asking, but what the hell happened to your face?"

I related my night of the bug invasion to him.

"That's terrible!" he said. "Why did you get an apartment way down there?"

"I didn't know it was way down there."

"You should move."

"I've already paid for the whole summer in advance."

"Well, if we have to work late, you can bunk in with me those nights. You don't want to be going home after dark in that area."

"Thanks, Bill, that would be great."

"Okay," he said. "I'll meet you tomorrow night at eight, and keep your damn windows closed."

"Before I go, do you mind if I ask you something?"

"'Course not."

"How much would I be making on the show?"

"You mean, you don't know?"

"I don't have an agent and —"

"You came all the way down here, with the bugs, renting in wacko town, without knowing how much you'd be paid!"

"I'd do it for nothing, but I couldn't afford that, so I —"

"You're making four-fifty a show."

"Four *hundred* and fifty?"

"No, four dollars and 50 cents. Of course 400. Are you kidding me?"

"No. I just didn't know."

"And you don't have an agent, so you get the whole thing."

"Wow. Four-fifty — hundreds. Wait'll I tell my wife."

"Go home and tell her now. See you tomorrow."

"And thanks," I said.

"Don't thank me, I'm not paying you."

"My dad never made this much."

"Neither did mine," Bill said with a chuckle.

I hailed a cab and gave him the address.

"You know where that is?" the driver asked.

"Yes, I know, but I gotta go, okay?"

"Okay, mister, but I'm just dropping you off. I'm not getting out or nuttin'."

"I understand. Let's go!"

Bill became a big star a few years later. He created a very funny Latin American character called José Jiménez, who played in comedy clubs, big nightclubs, in Las Vegas, on *The Ed Sullivan Show* and, of course, regularly on *The Steve Allen Show*. He was a very talented man who became my friend and helped me find my way.

Back downtown I was just putting my key in the front door when the door opened and an elderly man made his way out.

"New tenant?" he asked.

"Yes, for the summer."

"Welcome!" he said. "Did you hear about da knife fight on the corner last night?"

"No, I believe I missed it."

"The police was here and everything."

"And everything?"

"Oh, yeah!" he said, and went out the front door. I took the elevator to my floor and couldn't believe I'd missed a good old knife fight and *everything*. I shuddered at the thought and entered my new summer home.

The next evening, when Bill Dana and I were going to Johnny Bradford's place, I asked him, "Do you know why we're seeing this Bradford guy so late?"

"No, but I find it kind of interesting," Bill said with his knowing smile.

"In what way?"

"I'm not sure. We'll see."

At Mr. Bradford's apartment a formally dressed woman opened the door.

"Johnny?" she called. "The boys are here."

"Hi, guys, I'm Johnny Bradford and this is my wife, Glenna." To his wife we were the boys and to Johnny we were the guys. I guess they didn't care what our real names were. Don't get too familiar with the help. "Come on in and meet some friends of ours."

While his wife was formally dressed, Johnny was very, *very* formally dressed in a tux. I guessed he was in his mid-30s, a little prematurely gray, a beautiful tan, hazel eyes that crinkled at the corners from the L.A. sun. He was clean-shaven with a perpetual half smile.

"These are the boys I'll be working with on the show," Bradford told his two friends, who were also formally dressed. We shook hands with the couple, but nobody ever said who they, or we, were. "There's writing material on the kitchen table," Bradford said to Bill and me. "We're all going to the Copa for dinner and the show. We'll see you two when we get back."

"What do you want us to do?" Bill asked. "No guests have been booked yet."

"Just fool around with some smart talk between Eydie and Steve," Bradford said with a dismissive wave of his hand, and the four night-clubbers left for the Copacabana.

"What was that all about?" I asked Bill.

"Showing us who's boss."

There were two yellow legal pads and a pile of sharpened pencils on the kitchen table. Bill and I sat across from each other and stared. Eventually, we wrote some dialogue between our two stars, but our hearts weren't really in it. After all, it was late, we hadn't eaten, we were sitting in a strange kitchen on Madison Avenue — and I didn't know about Bill but I was confused as hell.

Johnny Bradford and his wife arrived back home at 1 a.m. Bill and I were yawning at the kitchen table.

"How you guys doing?" Bradford asked. "You get to know Steve and Eydie a little better?"

"I know Steve and Eydie," Bill said flatly. "I've worked with them on *Steve Allen* for three years!"

"I know them, too," I added. "I've worked with them on a show in Canada, three or four times."

"They have shows in Canada?" Bradford chuckled. "Just kidding! You guys have had a good night of thinking things over, so why don't you get on home and I'll see you in the morning."

"Here?" Bill asked.

"At the office."

Bill and I both breathed a sigh of relief and left.

"You better bunk in with me tonight, kid. It's too late for you to go down there."

"Thanks, Bill," I said. "But let me ask you something."

"Shoot."

"Is this the way you work here in New York?"

"Not unless you want to get fined by the Writers Guild of America."

"Thank God."

NICK VANOFF WAS ALREADY IN the office, along with two secretaries, when Bill and I walked in the next morning. "How'd your meeting with Johnny Bradford go?"

"There was no meeting, Nick," Bill Dana said. "We met Johnny, his wife and two friends for about 11 seconds. Then they went to the Copa."

"That was it?"

"He left Frank and me with paper and pencils to write some smart talk and sort of get to know Eydie and Steve."

"That's interesting!" Nick said.

"What the hell is interesting about it?" I asked.

"It's probably his way of getting things started."

"Well, he started on the wrong foot with us," Bill said.

"Take it easy, you two. Give Johnny a break. He's never worked in New York before. He's wed to Hollywood. Just relax and take it easy. Okeydokey?"

"Okay," Bill said, and I nodded.

"You know," Nick went on, "Johnny's brother wrote 'The Christmas Song' with Mel Tormé."

"Too bad his brother wasn't available," Bill snapped.

Johnny Bradford came into the office a little later with another man. "This is my adopted son," he said. "He's going to act as my secretary." The son looked about my age. The adoption angle seemed like a really cheap way to get a secretary, but what did I know, it was probably a Hollywood thing.

Nick showed Johnny his new office and Bill showed me our office, which was Bill's old *Steve Allen Show* office. Nick called all three of us into his new office, which was Steve Allen's old office. "So far, I've booked Don Adams for the first show. He'll do a monologue and

I'd like something written for Don and Steve or Don and Edyie and Steve. I still need a musical guest. On the second show I've got Shari Lewis and her puppet, Lambchop. I think it would be cute and funny with a spot where Steve meets Lambchop. She's a pretty good singer and it might develop into a trio with Shari, Steve and Lambchop. I still need another guest for that show. On show three, we have singer, dancer, actress Janis Paige and we —"

"I'll handle that," Johnny Bradford broke in.

"Oh?" Nick said.

"I know Janis and I've written a great piece of special material that would be perfect for her. It goes, 'I can't act. I can't dance. I can't sing. But I can't quit, because I'm a star.'"

"Sounds good," Nick said. "Can we hear it?"

"I'll have my office send it in from L.A."

"Great," Nick said. "That's as far as I've gotten. I'll keep you all in touch. You can start on a couple of spots with Don Adams and Shari Lewis and Lambchop. Okeydokey?"

Johnny followed us into our office. "You guys know Don Adams, right?"

"Just know he's funny. I've never met him," I said. "But Bill has worked with him a lot."

"Then you two handle that scene with he and Eydie or, possibly, Steve."

"Fine," Bill said.

"Bring it in to me when you finish." He walked out.

"Yesiree, boss," Bill whispered, "and it's Eydie and *him*!"

We ordered in cheeseburgers for lunch from a place Bill liked called the Primeburger.

"These are really good."

"I told you," Bill said. "I wouldn't steer you wrong."

Just then Nick stuck his head in the door. "I'll be back in a couple of hours. I'm taking Johnny Bradford to lunch at 21. He's never been there before," he said, and moved quickly away.

"Neither have I," I said to no one in particular.

When Nick got back from 21, he poked his head in our doorway again. "I've booked Salvatore Baccaloni on the first show," he said. "They're sending over his bio."

"Salvatore Baccaloni. What luck!" I said sarcastically. "Who the hell is Salvatore Baccaloni?"

Bill smiled and proceeded to give me a few lessons in classical music. He knew what he was talking about. Bill's brother was the concert master of the Boston Symphony and Bill knew his opera. "Salvatore Baccaloni, Frankie, is the primo basso with the Metropolitan Opera. He is also well spoken, humorous and sings his ass off."

"That's swell, but what'll we do with him?"

"Eydie has an unbelievable range, and I think our special-material man, Artie Malvin, could come up with a great duet for Baccaloni and Eydie."

"*And*," I added, "Don Adams could drive Steve nuts by inferring that he has held Eydie back all this time. She could have been a world-renowned opera diva."

"That could be funny, Frankie boy, funny. Let's talk to the boss about this."

"Which one — Nick or Johnny?"

"Let's not step on toes too early," Bill said. "We'll talk to Johnny."

Johnny said he loved the idea. "This Salvatore whosit, is he really with the Met?"

"Why the hell would I lie?" Bill asked, a little annoyed.

"I'll talk to Artie Malvin and get things going," Bradford said. "I'm sure Artie'll want to talk to you guys, too."

"And we'll keep working on the Steve–Don Adams spot," Bill said.

"Drop it on my desk when you finish."

We received a memo the next morning concerning a production meeting for the following afternoon and everyone was included, except Bill and me. The two of us walked briskly into Nick's office.

"Is there any reason Frank and I aren't in on the production meeting?"

"Take it easy," Nick said. "Johnny prefers that the creative area flows through him. Too many voices at the meeting causes confusion. Okeydokey?"

"Okeydamndokey!" Bill muttered as we marched back to our own office.

The next afternoon all the production meeting invitees passed our office and said hello.

When the meeting was over, Nick approached us. "Hey, guys, how's it going?"

"It's going," Bill said.

"Johnny Bradford and Artie Malvin came up with a great idea for Eydie and Baccaloni. They're going to —"

"We know," I spoke up.

"Johnny told you?"

"No," Bill said, "*we* told *him*."

"Oh," Nick said. "Whatever . . . Uh, it sounds good." Nick had chosen Johnny Bradford as the head writer, brought him here from Hollywood, set him up in an apartment on Madison Avenue and he wasn't ready to admit there was anything wrong in that, just yet.

In spite of the tension behind the scenes, the first show went very well. Good reviews and fair ratings. The second show was in rehearsal at the NBC studio in Brooklyn. Bill and I were sitting in the audience bleachers, watching Shari Lewis and Lambchop rehearse her spot. Shari was a famous ventriloquist and comedian, but Dwight Hemion, our mild-mannered Campbell's Soup Boy director, was having a problem getting the shot he wanted.

Dwight's voice came over the PA. "Shari."

"Yes, sir," Shari said.

"Can you hold Lambchop up a little higher?"

"I don't think so, sir."

"Why not?"

"Then, sir, people will see that my hand is manipulating Lambchop."

"I think people know that, Shari."

"I prefer to believe not, sir."

"Okay, Shari, then can you lower your head so that we can see the two of you in close-up in one frame?"

"That changes the dynamics of Lambchop being my pet."

"Then I'll just stay on a big, wide shot."

"It's your decision, sir."

"Take five, everybody," Dwight announced. He came down to the floor, sat with us in the bleachers and lit up a cigarette. "You know what?" he said.

"What?" I said.

"I'm going to roll a fucking camera right over her!"

In spite of Dwight's troubles with the lady, the show was very good and Shari Lewis got big laughs.

The morning after the show, Nick waved us into his office. "Janis Paige is coming into town the day after tomorrow. What'll she do?"

"She's going to do Johnny's special-material number, 'I can't dance, I can't sing, I —'"

"She won't do it!" Nick broke in. "She told Johnny Bradford she didn't like it."

"She could do a number from *The Pajama Game*," Bill said. "She starred in the thing."

"That is a super idea," Nick said, grabbing his phone. "Get me Janis Paige in Hollywood."

Janis Paige came into town, and when Nick asked why she didn't want to do Johnny's number, she said she didn't know what he was talking about.

"He never even talked to her?" I asked.

"Apparently not," Nick said.

"Why the hell would he do that?" Bill said.

"One of them is crazy," Nick said. "But we'll get by . . . and by the way, you guys are in on all the production meetings from now on. Okeydokey?"

"Okey . . ." I said.

"And dokey," Bill added.

Nick didn't scream at anybody about the Janis Paige incident, but now he made damn sure he knew where the ideas were coming from.

Johnny Bradford went back to L.A. before we'd even taped the last show. He said he had meetings and things to attend to. I'm sure he did. I wished good luck to him *and* especially to the folks he was going to be working with. They'd need it.

After we finished the final show, Nick Vanoff called me into his office. "Frank," he said, "I'd like you to meet Leonard Stern, the head writer of *The Steve Allen Show*."

"Good to meet you," I said, and shook his hand.

He was a tall man and sharply dressed. He had thick black hair graying at the temples. He looked Turkish — heavy eyebrows, brown eyes and angular facial features. He was smoking a long, thin, black cigarillo and he smiled at me through the smoke. "Pleased to meet you, Frank," he said. "Peppiatt — is that French?"

"French Canadian," I replied.

"You speak French?"

"Patois. But I can be understood in France."

"Well, Bill Dana and Nick here tell me you're a damn good writer."

"That's very nice. Thank you Nick."

Nick nodded with a smile.

"We would like you to join us on *The Steve Allen Show* as part of our writing staff."

"I would like that, too!"

"Your immigration is okay? Green card?"

"Yes, it is."

"You start in two weeks in this very office. Welcome."

Wow! *Steve Allen*, one of the biggest shows on television. Every Sunday night on NBC with Louis Nye, Tom Poston, Don Knotts! *Wow!*

✦

Chapter 10

BROWN CHRISTMAS WITH BING CROSBY

WITH JUST A COUPLE OF weeks before I had to report to *The Steve Allen Show*, I flew back to Toronto full of good news.

"That's wonderful, darling," Marilyn said, "but why do you have to work *there*?"

"They're paying me $750 a week! It's enough for us all to move to a really nice place down there. It'll be great!"

"But you can work right here."

"There's only one network in Canada. In New York there are three and they pay three times as much money. Here the CBC controls who works, who doesn't and also controls the money, by the throat."

"The CBC has been very good to you, Frank."

"Yes, they gave me work and allowed me to learn a lot, but there's no future for a decent living wage! We owe it to our children and ourselves to live better than we ever can on CBC wages. Come on, darling, we'll have a ball in New York!"

"I just don't want to live down there! That's the end of it. No more. End of discussion!" Marilyn rubbed her belly — she would be going into labor any day now with our third baby. But at this moment, she was more than upset: she was a stone wall.

Ever since I'd been a little kid and thrilled down to my socks by all the shows I heard on the radio, I had dreamed of going to New York, where most of them were broadcast, and somehow getting involved. Now the center of the television world was also in New York. Steve Allen had given me a personal invitation and I was damn well going to the party, with or, if necessary, without Marilyn. I would not give up my dream. I would not give up the work I loved to do so damned much. I would not be held back. I proposed a deal to her: she would go into the hospital, give birth and bring our new baby home to a big house in Toronto that I would buy and furnish for her. But the money for all this could only come from my work on *The Steve Allen Show*. No CBC job could give her all that.

She accepted.

What followed was the most insane two weeks of my life. I put a down payment on a four-bedroom house in Downsview, a suburb in the north end of Toronto, then packed up our apartment, Robyn, Marney and our Scottish nanny, Tommy, and had it all moved in and unpacked when Marilyn came home with our new baby, Melissa. Marilyn was delighted and so were the children and Tommy.

I was delighted, too — I had a beautiful new baby, *and* I was going back to New York!

Jack Kane was very happy for me when I told him about my new job. "We'll really, really miss you on *Music Makers*. It'll be a dull show without you."

"Look," I said, "I'll be flying home every Sunday night and I'll meet you every Monday and we can do some work on your show. I don't want any payment. I'll be happy to help."

"You're a real friend, Frankie. Thanks."

Norman Jewison called and asked me to write with John Aylesworth on *Your Hit Parade*, but I turned him down due to my contract with NBC. He was impressed that I was signed up for 26 weeks on a big U.S. prime-time network show like *Steve Allen* — I was the first Canadian of my generation to land a steady gig on U.S. television. I could hear the wheels spinning in Norman's head as he wished me luck.

In New York I rented a cheap, tiny room with no TV in the Victoria, a not-quite-fleabag hotel at 51st and Seventh Avenue — no bugs, only three blocks from the office, no big cab fares every day: a step up from the previous summer. I was lonely, but Birdland, the premiere jazz club, was just down the street. I spent many evenings sipping a beer at the bar and listening to the best jazz in the world.

My first day at work was, to say the least, eventful. Leonard Stern, the head writer, took me in to briefly meet Steve Allen, who was friendly and charming and asked me to please write funny. Then Leonard introduced me to the other writers. There were three teams: first Arne Sultan and Marvin Worth, two very short, bouncy guys full of life and about my age; next, Bill Dana and Don Hinkley. Bill, of course, I knew, but I hadn't met his partner. He was a quiet man with wispy blond fringes of hair, blue eyes, freckles and a warm, open smile. The other team consisted of Stan Burns and Herb Sargent, who had started with Steve Allen on the NBC *Tonight Show*. Stan, a born wisecracker, was a big weightlifter with a broad, open face; Herb was a tall, handsome guy who didn't smile much, but it didn't take long to find out that he was the best comedy writer in this and probably any other office. Herb would have a long, storied career, ending in co-creating (uncredited) and head-writing *Saturday Night Live*.

I noticed at once that there was a strain between Herb and our boss, Leonard Stern. Herb was married to the gorgeous movie actress Geraldine Brooks, and Stern was married to her not so gorgeous, not so famous older sister, Gloria. Herb didn't like the fact that his boss was his brother-in-law — a brother-in-law who told Herb how to do what Herb did better than anyone else on the planet. I often wondered why Stern had been hired in the first place. I knew he had written two or three *Ma and Pa Kettle* movies, and while they were funny, they were not smart, Steve Allen funny.

Later on my first day, Steve had gathered the writing staff to talk about the coming season, when a very loud, raucous laugh drowned him out. William O. Harbach, our producer, stormed into the room, smacking his cane on every desk. "Hey, everybody's here!" he shouted. "Let's get the whole world laughing!" Everyone cheered. He was the handsome, tall, blond, blue-eyed son of Otto Harbach, who had written a bunch of Broadway musicals including *No, No, Nanette* and *Roberta*, plus a great many hit songs, including "Smoke Gets in Your Eyes," which he had given to his son and our producer, Bill, for a wedding present. That song had set William O. up as a very rich man. His infectious, upbeat style and enthusiasm served as an antidote to the dysfunctional strife always simmering between brothers-in-law Stern and Sargent.

"You're going to like Harbach," Bill Dana said. "He does some strange things, but he's okay."

"What kind of strange things?"

"I jumped into a cab with him once and he said to the driver, 'Circle 6-5100 and step on it.' The cabby just looked at him dumbfounded."

"What happened?"

"Circle 6-5100 is the phone number of the William Morris Talent Agency and I guess Bill thought the phone number was clear enough."

"Is that where he wanted to go?"

"That is correct. And one day Bill was on the phone with somebody he was meeting for lunch. His last words before he hung up were, 'Okay, Dave, I'll meet you in five minutes at the corner of Walk and Don't Walk.' As he ran out of the office, his secretary ran after him, trying to explain that there were over 10,000 street corners in New York with Walk and Don't Walk signs."

"What happened?"

"His secretary phoned the guy and explained that her boss meant the corner of 48th Street and Seventh Avenue."

"Did she explain it to Bill?"

"Why bother? The guy met Bill where he said he would, on the corner of Walk and Don't Walk."

On the second day of my new job, a strange-looking man came into the office and dropped a large envelope on every writer's desk. When he got to me he asked, "You the new writer?"

"Yes, I just started this week."

"Here's your plug list," he said, then handed me an envelope and left.

"What the hell is a plug list?" I asked Bill.

"A list of people or products who want their names or brands mentioned on the show."

"And then what?"

"He pays you in cash or booze."

"For just saying the name?"

"No, it's got to be part of a sketch or monologue, and it has to sound natural."

"Is that legal?"

"Probably not," Bill said with a smile. "But most of the shows do it."

"Have you done it?"

"A couple of times."

"And you got paid?"

"I was given a case of champagne for the whole office."

"What did you plug?"

"I did a commentary about Dinah Shore and her new fan club."

"Dinah's Club?"

"You got it."

"And here's Diner's Club still on the plug list."

"Right, along with Arpège perfume, French champagne — you've got to say French, not just champagne — plus three or four liquor brands, two Congressional committees —"

"Congressional committees? Why would they be on the list?"

"They can't buy commercial time and they want exposure, so . . . hello, plug list."

"I don't feel comfortable with that, Bill."

"Look, there are new names on the list every week, but don't worry about it. If something comes to mind while you're writing, drop one in, and if the shoe fits, it pays off."

"I'll keep it in mind," I mumbled. I didn't like the sound of the plug list, but what did I know? It was only my first week. Dinah's Club and a case of French champagne, hmmm. A few years later the "payola/plugola" scandal broke. There were Congressional hearings, resulting in legislation outlawing the practice. I'm glad I was never involved.

That same day, Bill Harbach, our producer, stormed into the office, again thwacking his cane on every desk. All the writers gathered around him. "Great news, boys! Great news! I just booked Chester Moses for the week after next! Make him funny! Make him *funny*!" With that, he thwacked a few more desks and was out the door.

There was a long silence. I had no idea who Chester Moses was and I kept quiet, waiting for somebody to clue me in. Slowly, everyone admitted they had not heard of Chester Moses. Herb Sargent took a poll of all the secretaries and production assistants. None of them had heard of Chester Moses, either. Leonard Stern went into Steve Allen's office. Steve was no help. All the major talent agencies were called, but none of them had Chester Moses on their roster. We all went home that evening, completely buffaloed. The next day Bill Harbach again bounded into the office, cane a-thwacking.

"What have you guys got for Chester Moses?" he said.

No one spoke up.

"Well? What have you got?"

Stern cleared his throat and mumbled, "We're not sure who Chester Moses is, Bill."

"What!" Harbach shouted. "Everybody knows who Chester Moses is! He parted the Red Sea, for chrissake!"

A sigh of relief filled the room. "Oh, you mean *Charlton Heston*!" Stern said.

"Charlton Heston, Chester Moses — same difference," Bill Harbach said with a shrug. It made perfect sense to him. Maybe he'd met Chester Moses on the corner of Walk and Don't Walk.

"Great!" Leonard Stern said. "We'll have something for Mr. Heston on your desk by the end of the day, Bill."

EACH TEAM OF WRITERS HAD its own office. I didn't have one because Leonard Stern wanted me to be a roving writer, one week helping one team and the next week another. I felt like a substitute teacher, but I was hardly in a position to complain. Although I helped with some of the comedy, I was just an intruder. My strength was in coming up with concepts. Now, everyone else came up with concepts and I dropped in to add a line or two.

Some weeks Leonard didn't even put me in with a writing team. He asked me to write intros for Steve, so I sat in the outer office with the secretarial staff and wrote introductions for guest singers, dancers and movie stars like Peter Ustinov, Lloyd Bridges, Martha Raye and George Sanders.

Occasionally, Steve did a piece on the show called "The Answer Man." He would be given an answer like "Miss America." Then he would think hard and come up with a question. "Let's see . . . " he would muse. "The answer is Miss America, and the question is . . . 'What do you hope happens when they drop an atomic bomb? Miss America!'" I came up with an answer a couple of weeks into the show. "Goldilocks and the Three Bears" was the answer. The question was, "Name a lousy Chicago backfield?" It got a big laugh. Years later, Johnny Carson did the same schtick, but wearing a turban.

One morning Herb Sargent patted me on the back. "Nice going, kid!" he said. "Or should I say what everybody's calling you — Snowback."

My mother, Sarah, my father, Frank, and me.

My wedding day, 1957.

Me and my three little darlings — Marney, Melissa, and Robyn, 1958.

*Robyn, Marney, and Melissa with friends on the **Hullabaloo** set in 1964.*

The Jackie Rae Show *in 1955: Jack Kane, Jackie Rae, and me.*

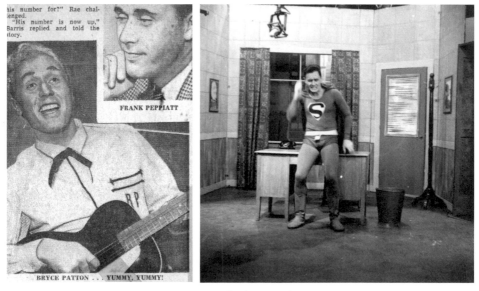

Me as Bryce Patton.

It's a bird, it's a plane, it's me on After Hours!

Cast photos for After Hours *(from left): Jill Foster, me, John Aylesworth, and Rick Campbell.*

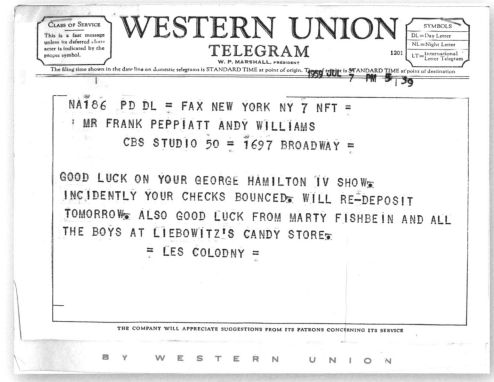

Our agents at William Morris wishing us well, sort of.

Our little summer show breaks into winter. Clockwise from left: Gordie Tapp, from Toronto; a Hee Haw Honey; Buck Owens and Roy Clark; another Honey; Lulu Roman; another Honey; Grandpa Jones; and (center) Stringbean.

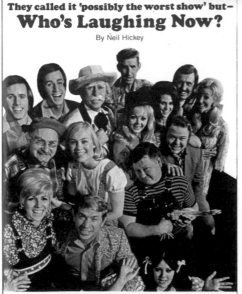

(Top row, left to right): Hagar twins, Gordie Tapp, Stringbean, and Archie Campbell with three Honeys.

John and me with Nancy
Sinatra at the Mother
Goose Special *in 1964.*

Jack Kane and I take our first bite out of the Big Apple.

John, Archie Campbell, and me arriving in Nashville in 1969 to shoot our first Hee Haw show. They promised us round-trip transportation.

Me and my second wife, Valerie, in 1975.

The Hee Haw *10th anniversary party in 1978 at the brand new Opryland Hotel in Nashville. From left: John Aylesworth, me, Sam Lovullo, Roy Clark, Gunilla Hutton, and Buck Owens.*

John, me, Nick Vanoff, and Sam Lovullo.

John, Nick, and me.

Caroline, grandchildren Liam and Laura, and me.

Four grandchildren (left to right): Stuart, Liam, Laura, and Freya.

Caroline and I pretend we're back in Canada during Christmas in Florida, 2011.

I asked Bill Dana what the "Snowback" thing was all about.

"You know what a wetback is?"

"Because I'm from Canada?"

"I guess," Bill said. "Don't let it bother you."

But it did bother me. A few weeks later, when *Variety* reported that two Canadians, Norman Jewison and John Aylesworth, had been hired to write and direct the new *Your Hit Parade* show in New York, I was delighted. The next morning there was a big sign on the office bulletin board: "Snowbacks invading TV from the north." When Norman and John arrived in New York, I took them to lunch near my office. Stan Burns saw me and I introduced him to them. I got back to the office after lunch and a new sign was already up. It read: "Snowbacks meeting secretly and planning to freeze us out."

I got the joke, but it irritated me, though not as much as the fact that I wasn't getting anywhere. I was still on the bench, waiting to get into the game and pitch ideas. I had been a first-string football player all through high school and university. I loved the rough and tumble of competition — I was not the kind of guy who warmed benches. If all that weren't bad enough, I was exhausted by the commute to Toronto every weekend. I loved seeing the girls, but tension was growing between Marilyn and me. Why couldn't she move to New York? Or even visit me once in a while? It seemed so selfish to me. But then, she felt that my ambition was selfish. It was becoming a running argument. What on earth had Red Ingles done to make her so frightened of the United States? The fact that I spent a large part of my weekends in Toronto working with Jack Kane on *Music Makers* did not help smooth things out between Marilyn and me, either. Finally, I told Leonard Stern I would like him to let me out of my contract after 13 weeks.

"What's the problem, you unhappy?"

"No, but I'm not happy, either."

"Can I help in any way?"

"Look, I know you have your way of working, but I feel like a relief pitcher. I'm living in one lousy room in a fleabag hotel. I miss my wife and kids."

"Why don't you move down here?" he asked. "You've got a real future in this town."

"That's a whole *other* problem," I almost shouted, "and I'm tired of that Snowback crap!"

"It's all in fun," he said, grinning.

"Maybe for you!"

"What'll you do?"

"I'll go back to the snow and do another show."

After show 13 I got my last check, packed my bags and grabbed the old "North Star" back to Toronto. I'd already informed Marilyn and Jack Kane of my decision and they were dancing on air. The Snowback was back.

Jack convinced the CBC to pay me $200 per show on *Music Makers*. I'd never make ends meet on that measly sum, but it was better than nothing. Fortunately, I was also offered a job on Jack Duffy's show, *Here's Duffy*, again for $200 per. So, I had two full-time jobs at half the money I'd earned in New York.

Bill Davis was the director of *Here's Duffy*. He had worked his way up from stagehand, to lighting grip, camera operator and, finally, directing. He was one of the few CBC directors who hadn't graduated from Lorne Greene's academy and he was better off for it because he had hands-on experience with all aspects of production. Bill was in his late 20s. He was my height with a bunch of tightly curled brown hair. He had a wonderful attitude and a real good way with actors.

I met with Davis, Duffy and Alan Mannings, a writer Norman Jewison had brought up from the U.S. Duffy, whom I had known for years, looked and sang like Frank Sinatra. Like Sinatra, he had sung with the Dorsey Band, but unlike Sinatra, he was also a truly great comic actor. Mannings was an inscrutable but charming guy, hiding behind a thick black beard and heavy black glasses.

"Alan has written some monologues for me," Jack Duffy said. "The jokes are pretty funny, but I'm not a stand-up joke teller. I'm an actor."

"Steve Allen solved that very same problem by hiring Don Knotts, Tom Poston and Louis Nye," I said.

"Can we get these guys?" Alan Mannings asked sarcastically.

"I doubt it, Alan, but we might form a screw-up group with Jack and some other actors that the announcer could interview every week."

"That sounds good," Duffy said.

"A family of bullfighters, chefs, acrobats, jugglers or ballet dancers."

"We could definitely write that funny," Mannings added.

"But they're really bad at what they do and they don't know it. Complete screw-ups!" Duffy said.

"Total confidence, but no talent," I said.

"Can you get it ready for next week?" Bill Davis said.

"I don't see why not," Mannings replied.

"I'll bring in Jill Foster, Alfie Scopp and a couple of other funny guys," I said.

"I'm laughing already," said Bill.

So the clumsy family was born and they were a big hit — the bull-fighting family was hilarious. However, while Alan Mannings was terrific in meetings, when it came time to actually put pen to paper, he was nowhere to be found. I ended up doing all the writing myself.

I also had to get things going on Jack Kane's *Music Makers*. I met with Jack and his producer-director, Norman Sedawie, at Jack's house.

"I've been thinking," I said.

"Thank God," Jack said.

"Why not put Mickey Mouse Club hats on the whole band. Let them sing out M-I-C and Jack says, 'See ya real soon.' Then the band: K-E-Y. Then Jack: 'Why? Because we love you,' and everybody:

M-O-U-S-E. Then Jack and the band do a wonderful big-band jazz version of the Mickey Mouse Club theme. At the big finish they all toss their mouse hats in the air."

"That's the kind of fun we need," Sedawie said.

"You're telling me!" Jack agreed.

"We can also put Groucho Marx mustaches on everybody. Give the drummer, bass, guitar and piano a cigar and do 'Lydia the Tattooed Lady' between Jack and the band. It's not a song you have to sing, you can just talk it in tempo. Then we do a big-band version with jazz solos. I know Jack can arrange the hell out of that tune."

"We'll rock the place!" Jack said.

I was working my ass off on two shows for $400 a week and I was having a ball, but the money was going out fast and faster. The season was coming to an end and I wasn't sure what to do for the summer, when I got a phone call from my old pal Norman Jewison in New York.

"I'm directing a summer replacement for *The Garry Moore Show* starring Andy Williams," he said. "John Aylesworth is already on board and we want you, too — $700 per, plus a nice big furnished apartment on the Upper East Side of Manhattan."

"When do you want me there?"

"One week from this Monday."

"I will see you then!"

When I told Marilyn the news, she was furious. "You just got home and now you're going to be in New York all summer!"

"I didn't get any offers to stay home."

"I'll be alone again."

"And so will I. Look, they're getting me a nice apartment in a good section of town. Bring the girls and Tommy. We'll have a great time."

"I can't bring three babies to New York!"

"John and Jean are living in New York with their babies and love it. And Jack and Claire Kane will be there with their babies, too."

"I can't think of anything more depressing than living in New York."

"New York is full of people living happily."

"I won't go to the Excited States! No way! And that's that." She had become a stone wall again.

"Well," I sighed, "maybe you can bring Robyn down for a weekend."

"I'll have to think about that."

A week later I arrived a half-hour early for the first production meeting at the CBS offices on West 57th Street. Aylesworth, Kane and Jewison were already there — four Snowbacks, a half-hour early, or right on time, depending on where you were from. Perry Lafferty was the next to arrive, and Norman introduced him to Jack and me. Perry was in his late 30s or early 40s and bubbling with life. He was tall, with straight brown hair cut very short. Behind his glasses were darting eyes that seemed to take everything in at a glance. He dressed neatly and simply.

"You Canucks ready to roll?" he asked. We all smiled and nodded.

The rest of the staff started coming in: Dick Williams, Andy's brother, who would handle the singing group and who looked a lot like Andy, just a bit older. Peter Gennaro, the choreographer, a little Italian spark plug, with curly black hair, dancing brown eyes and nervous feet. Buddy Arnold, who had written with John on *Your Hit Parade*. He was in his early 50s with a dark, leathery complexion, overweight and seemed to have the troubles of the world on his shoulders. Bob Shearer, another writer, was a friend of Andy Williams. Bob used to be a tap dancer on Broadway and was hoping to direct television one day. He was about my age, blond and agile-looking. His face was very expressive — he seemed to be enjoying life.

Perry Lafferty was about to show everyone to their various offices when Andy Williams arrived and made a friendly point of meeting and talking to each of us.

An amazing thing happened that summer — everybody on the show involved themselves with every facet of the production. It was a thorough collaboration. Perry held the strings and, like a good producer, when things were going well, he let them happen. The four writers met with Dick Williams and Jack Kane to discuss the musical ideas. If anybody had a thought about some comedy, the writers' door was always open. Perry and Norman checked constantly with the writing and music people to see if they were happy with guest stars. A 22-year-old set designer named Gary Smith came on the show and became involved in everything we were planning. When John and I had an idea called "The Wonderful World of LPs," and we asked Gary to construct a wall and floor of real LPs, there was no problem. The next day Gary showed the design to everyone, while John and I explained the idea. Perry said, "I love it! We'll use it every week. Write it and build it!"

And that's how it went all summer. We were all working together and we were all heading up the ladder of success. Later, when I began producing my own shows, I always strived to replicate the positively charged atmosphere Perry created that summer.

Perry Lafferty became the producer of *The Danny Kaye Show* and the vice-president of CBS. Norman Jewison went on to direct Academy Award–winning movies. Gary Smith would produce *The Judy Garland Show* and the Tony Awards and win many Emmys. Bob Shearer directed *The Steve Allen Show* in Hollywood. Peter Gennaro choreographed hit Broadway musicals. Dick Williams had fabulous success with commercial jingles on radio and TV. Jack Kane continued his own show in Canada and did arrangements for Ethel Merman, Steve and Eydie, and Andy Williams.

John and I were about to happen very soon, too.

The guests on *The Andy Williams Show* in the summer of 1958 were about to step into success, as well — Dick Van Dyke three years from his own hit television show on CBS; Johnny Carson two years away from a huge career on *The Tonight Show* on NBC; Andy Griffith one year away from a wonderful trip to Mayberry; Steve Lawrence, starring on Broadway in *What Makes Sammy Run?*; movie actor Eddie Albert, starring in the hit situation country comedy *Green Acres* with Eva Gabor; and, of course, our star Andy, who went on to a big television career and a string of hit records — "Moon River," "Canadian Sunset," "The Most Wonderful Time of the Year" and many more. The show's reviews were terrific and it was such a pleasure working on it that the summer seemed to fly by.

When Marilyn did come down for a weekend with little Robyn, I wanted everything to be perfect — to show my wife what a wonderful town New York could be. They arrived late Saturday morning and we had a lovely time, shopping and eating out. As we ambled back to the apartment in the early evening, all the lights went out. Half of Manhattan had suffered a blackout. Naturally, my apartment was in the blacked-out half. The elevator didn't work and the three of us had to grope our way up five floors of pitch-dark stairs to the apartment, which was also in total darkness. Robyn was scared to death. Marilyn was in a rage — she blamed the city. Thank God the phone was working, because Marilyn insisted on flying back the next morning. I made the plane reservation and the short, dark weekend was over.

The summer was almost over, as well. Just one more show and this wonderful group of talented people would scatter to the four winds. A guest on the last show was an idol of mine and I was thrilled to meet him. His name was Johnny Mercer, one of the great songwriters of the 20th century. We wanted to do something special for Mr. Mercer, so all the writers, Jack Kane and Dick Williams got together and came up with a wonderful medley for Andy and Johnny. The premise was that Johnny Mercer had written at least one song for every letter in the alphabet. We started with "Atchison, Topeka and the Santa Fe" and kept right on singing until we got stuck on the letter Q. Johnny Mercer solved the problem and wrote a song on the spot: "Q is the cutest little letter, the cutest you can get. Q is the cutest little letter in the whole darn alphabet." We also wrestled with the letter X, but we made do by slightly changing a big Mercer hit to "Xcentuate the Positive" and finished with Andy and Johnny swinging along with "Zip-a-Dee-Doo-Dah." The alphabet medley was the hit of the show, and Williams and Mercer received a huge ovation from the studio audience.

It had been a really productive summer and people in the business were talking about the show, congratulating the whole staff for producing something more than a fill-in summer replacement. That was all very nice, but I was again out of work. You can't spend pats on the back.

"Are you going to continue with *Your Hit Parade?*" I asked John on our last day in the office.

"It was canceled and Norman is doing something with Harry Belafonte."

"Without you?"

"Harry has his own people."

Jack Kane walked into the office. "What are you guys doing?" he asked.

"Just reminiscing about when we had jobs," I said, and Jack laughed.

"It's not funny," John said.

"Take it easy, Johnny," Jack said. "I bring news from the Kremlin! They're putting on *Music Makers* every other week, with Norman Sedawie directing. Then I'll have another musical variety show the other weeks, with Stan Harris directing. The whole thing will be called *Music '60.* They want you two to write it all. If you're interested, Bob McGall in business affairs would like to meet when you get back to Toronto."

I phoned Marilyn with the good news.

"That's wonderful, sweetheart. You'll be here all winter."

"Seems like it, if Mr. McGall gives us a decent deal."

"I'm sure he will."

I was not so sure, but I sure was happy to be home. Oh, how I had missed my beautiful babies! I almost cried when I saw them. They had all grown so much and I had not been in on any of it.

"Our house is not dark and scary like the one in New York," Robyn said as I picked her up and kissed her.

"That's a relief, I forgot my candles."

"Oh, Daddy!" Robyn giggled.

Marilyn made a wonderful chicken dinner and we all sat around the dining room table. Melissa wasn't quite one, so she was in a high chair and she managed quite well, spilling a little bit here and there, but only a little bit. After dinner we watched some television, and Tommy took Melissa upstairs to bed. A little later I told Robyn and Marney if they went up and got ready for bed, I'd come and tell them a bedtime story. It was domestic bliss.

"We're in bed, *Daddy*!" Robyn called down. I went upstairs, tucked them in and told them a goofy story I made up as I went along.

"There was this cute little dog who was owned by two little girls named . . . ?"

"Marney and Robyn," Robyn said, and Marney laughed.

"This was a very special dog. You see, he could talk, but only Robyn and Marney could hear him. 'There's something in the attic I don't like,' the dog said. 'Listen!' And they heard a *tap, tap, tap, tap*."

"What is it?" Marney asked.

"Nobody knew, but it went on tapping in the attic in the dark. *Tap, tap, tap, tap*."

"That's scary," Robyn said.

"It *was* scary. And then all the lights went out and the strange tapping went on. 'Listen,' the dog said. 'It's coming down the stairs. *Tap, tap, tap, tap* and getting louder. Shh, don't make a noise, it might get us!'"

"Ohhh, I'm afraid!" Robyn said.

"Me, too," Marney chimed in.

"'It's coming into the room. *Tap, tap, tap, tap.* I'm going to shine my flashlight on whatever is making the strange tapping. Ready?'" Robyn and Marney both squealed. "The light went on, and there it was — the tapping thing."

"What was it?"

"A mouse with a wooden leg."

Robyn and Marney both laughed and hit me with a pillow.

"You tricked us!" Robyn shouted.

"What's going on up here?" Marilyn said from the doorway.

"Daddy scared us, then tricked us!" Robyn said.

"Tell us another story!" Marney pleaded.

"Tomorrow night," I promised, then tucked them back into bed and turned out the light. "Night-night."

"Could that dog really talk, Daddy?" Robyn said.

"You heard him."

"That was *you*."

"Come on now, off to sleep," Marilyn said. "We'll see you in the morning."

A little later, in our bed, I said, "It's been so long since we've had sex, I had almost forgotten how."

"You did just fine," Marilyn said. "You haven't forgotten a thing."

"And no more pregnancies," I said.

"No more pregnancies," she said, "though I know you want a boy."

"That is not true! I'm the only man in this house and that's the way it's going to be."

"Unless Tommy gets married," Marilyn said, and we both laughed.

The next morning Robyn, Marney and I played hide-and-seek all over the house and in the backyard. The two girls had so much energy it was scary, as though they were some kind of beautiful mutants. A couple of hours of hiding and seeking and I was zonked out, but they were still raring to go.

"Come on, Daddy, it's your turn to hide," Robyn said.

"Daddy needs a breather."

"Tell us a story," Marney said.

"Tonight, before bed."

"Promise?"

"Promise."

"Another story about Sam?" Robyn asked.

"Who is Sam?"

"The dog who talks to us."

"Oh, you've named him Sam."

"He told us his name, didn't he, Marney?"

"Yep!"

"Sam is a good name for him," I said, and they both clapped their hands.

I was getting to know my kids and it was wonderful. They were *my* kids and I was *their* daddy — I felt an overwhelming sensation of love and happiness. Somehow I had to arrange my life so I wouldn't be parted from the girls again.

"Will you tell us a story about Sam tonight?" Robyn asked.

"*Every* night," Marney said.

"Every night I'm home."

"Promise?"

"Promise."

Now I would have two shows to write at the CBC and a story to write about Sam every night. As much as I loved my work, the Sam stories were my greatest joy.

"GOOD MORNING, GENTLEMEN," Bob McGall said from behind his large oak desk. "Take a seat." John and I pulled up chairs across from him. "I see you're early. You didn't lose a Canadian tradition in New York."

"Not a chance," I said.

"Okay," he said, "let's get down to brass tacks. What kind of money are you boys looking for?"

"A thousand a show," John said firmly.

"Between you?"

"Each!" we both said.

"No, goddarn it! You're not going to make more money than me!"

"Our jobs aren't really comparable, Bob," I said.

"You get paid for 52 weeks," John added, "and we get paid for 30."

"Eight hundred," Bob said.

"Nine," John said.

"Eight-fifty."

"Deal," I said, and held out my hand to shake on it.

Bob shook hands with both of us. "The contracts will be ready in a day or two."

We smiled our way over to the television building to meet with directors Stan Harris and Norman Sedawie. Stan, like Bill Davis, had also worked his way up the TV ladder to be the boss of a big one-hour show. He was a very large, outgoing man, well dressed, hair parted to one side and with a heavy five o'clock shadow at 11 a.m.

"How'd it go with Bob McGall?" Stan asked.

"We got the job," I said.

We had one other writer to help us put together an hour show every week. Saul Ilson was from Montreal, a few years younger than John and me, with short brown hair and a constant happy grin across his face. Although he had no television experience, he had written a stage musical that had been produced and he was bubbling over with ideas. I liked him immediately. We worked in an apartment across the street from the Kremlin, where we wrote without any disturbances. It was swell.

We did some interesting things on *Music '60*. Saul wrote a wonderful parody of a Cole Porter song, but the CBC couldn't get Porter's music publisher to okay it. I called Bill Harbach in New York who gave us Cole Porter's private phone number. We called Porter, and Saul read him the new lyric. "A darn good parody," Porter said. "Go ahead and use it. I'll call my publisher and tell him to clear it. But next time, write your own damn song. Good luck." Cole Porter's publishers were furious that we had called him directly, but what could they do? Cole had spoken.

We had a lot of fun with the show and it came across in the finished product. We had Ella Fitzgerald trying to teach an opera singer how to scat. In another bit, Jonathan Winters was hilarious — the director panned across people in the audience and Jonathan would tell us what they were thinking. We got to know Jonathan very well, not realizing we'd be working with him again.

Saul, John and I worked hard to feature guests like Cab Calloway, the great trombone players Kay Winding and J.J. Johnson, Buddy Rich and the Four Brothers, in well-thought-out presentations. We always brought the guest artists into the show with some special material, instead of the usual "Our next guest is . . ." or "Please welcome my good friend . . ." or "Here they are. . . ." We tried to give each show a theme, so that all the acts would hang together in a cohesive whole.

About halfway through the series, just after Christmas, we were working in our little office apartment when the phone rang.

"Frankie?" a familiar voice said. "It's Nick, Nick Vanoff, and I need your help."

"What the heck's going on?"

"I'm producing and directing a big special with Bing Crosby and Perry Como."

"That *is* big."

"The writers they gave me are no good. I need you and Johnny."

"When?"

"Now!"

"We're in the middle of a series, Nick."

"Just a couple of weeks. I'll send you plane tickets, rent you a suite in Beverly Hills and pay you $5,000 each. Okeydokey?"

"Just a sec, Nick." I told John what Nick had said.

"Go!" Saul Ilson said. "We're written ahead two shows and I can take care of rewrites or I can call you."

"I think we can make it, Nick," I said into the phone.

"Your tickets will be at the airport tomorrow morning and I'll meet you in L.A. at the Beverly Wilshire Hotel. Okeydokey?"

While I was packing, Marilyn said, "You're not going to be here New Year's Eve?"

"Five thousand dollars, babe. We can pay off part of the mortgage."

"It's just not fair."

"You go where the work is."

"You sound like a farmworker or a berry picker."

"Come on, sweetheart, it's Crosby and Como!"

"Oh, I know it's a big deal, but I can't help it if I miss you."

"You could come with me, you know. Beverly Hills, sunshine, movie stars, shopping!"

"Not a chance, mister!"

An hour after we landed in Los Angeles, Nick Vanoff had us in a small prop plane, headed for Palm Springs. We had to fly low over the coastal mountain range and, believe me, it was bumpy. Our drinks flew off our tables. John grabbed a sick bag and started throwing up.

"Those mountains are awfully close!" I said.

"Relax," Nick said. "We'll be landing in a few minutes."

"Or crashing!" John groaned, and went back to his bag.

"Welcome to Palm Springs," the stewardess said. "The weather is clear and the temperature is 96."

"Ninety-six!" I said.

"We're in the desert, guys," Nick explained. "It's a dry heat."

When we stepped off the plane, the dry heat, as Nick called it, smacked us in the face like a flatiron. I wondered what a wet heat would have been like. To make matters worse, John and I were wearing heavy Canadian winter tweed suits. We worked up a full sweat just walking from the tarmac to the air-conditioned limo that would take us to Bing Crosby's country club.

WE HAD JUST COOLED OFF when we arrived at the club and had to walk the 70 or 80 yards to the entrance. We were dripping sweat again by the time we were at the door. Maybe it was a dry heat, but it sure was wet on me.

"Jesus, it's hot!" John said.

"I told you, it's the desert," Nick reminded us. "You'll be fine once we get inside."

We opened the door, stepped into the clubhouse and the sweat on my body started to freeze.

"May I help you, gentlemen?" a man with a clipboard asked us.

"We have an appointment to meet Mr. Crosby in the dining lounge," Nick said.

"Oh yes, Mr. Vanoff and party." He led us down a hall past a galaxy of framed photos of movie stars playing golf — Bob Hope, Cary Grant, Joan Crawford, Spencer Tracy, William Powell. I'm not kidding. They were all there, frolicking on the golf course.

"Mr. Vanoff," a voice called as we were about to enter a dining room that belonged in the Waldorf Astoria, not in a golf club. A blond, movie-star-handsome young man waved us over to a large television set. "You and your party are here to lunch with Mr. Crosby?"

"Correct."

"Well, I was just checking the golf course TV." He clicked a switch and there was Bing. "Mr. Crosby is just teeing off on 18. He should be here in about 20 minutes."

"Do you have a camera on every tee?" Nick asked.

"And every green," movie-star-handsome said. "Let me show you to your table and you can relax with a drink while you wait. Follow me."

Nick and his party, who I presumed was us, followed the young man, who seated us at a table. We ordered drinks and started looking around.

"There's Rosalind Russell over there," Nick whispered, and nodded toward an attractive brunette woman.

"Wow!" John said. "Loved her in *Front Page* with Gary Grant."

"And *His Girl Friday* with Cary Grant," I added, gawking.

"Look who is coming in," John whispered. "Ray Milland!"

"*Dial M for Murder*," Nick said, "and *The Lost Weekend*, Academy Award."

Milland walked in with a woman and sat down at the next table.

"Imagine, Ray Milland sitting right beside us," John whispered. Ray Milland took off his golf hat. *"He's bald!"* John yelled, and for a moment all talking stopped. All eyes were on John. "I'm . . . I'm . . . terribly sorry!" John stuttered to Ray Milland's table.

"That's okay," the woman said. "Somebody had to tell him."

The whole dining room burst into laughter — even Ray Milland. The funny woman had saved John's Canadian bacon.

A few minutes later Bing Crosby was walking across the room toward us.

"Here comes Bing," Nick whispered. "He is also bald, Johnny, so let's keep his little secret. Okeydokey?"

"Well, well, well, Nick and the scriveners are here," Bing said in his soft, singsong voice.

Nick introduced us. As we had our lunch, Bing laid down a few rules. "My last two specials had themes like glass and wood and I was sort of the second banana. I'm a crooner, not a carpenter or a glass-blower, so let's keep things straight ahead and simple."

"Right," Nick said.

"And we must remember that the pairing of Crosby and Como is very special, like Merman and Martin," John said. "People have never heard you two sing together."

"Music lovers all over the world will literally want to stick their microphones into the proceedings," I added.

"And we will see to that!" Nick enthused. "Fifty or more micro-phones will pop in over your and Perry's heads and we go on from there, okeydokey?"

"Okeydamndokey!" Bing said.

"It'll be a Crosby-Como crooning contest!" I added.

"I'll bring my pipes along and proudly participate!" Crosby said.

As we rode back to the Palm Springs airport, Nick said, "We got the old man geared up. Good job, guys. Now you can start working on some patter to get us into the medley and start putting a medley together. Okeydokey?"

We landed at Burbank airport after another teeth-rattling, roller-coaster ride over the coast range. On the way back to the hotel, Nick said he had a big surprise for us: "We're all invited to Frank Sinatra's New Year's Eve party tomorrow night."

"You are kidding, right?" I said.

"I'm not kidding, Frankie. Sinatra's New Year's Eve party, and you're both invited."

"Thank you, Nick, that's fabulous!" I said.

"Wow!" John exclaimed.

"I can't pick you up, so I'll give you the directions. The party starts at 10."

"Ten o'clock!" John said as we entered our luxury suite at the Beverly Wilshire Hotel. "What kind of time is that to start a party?"

"It's New Year's Eve, John. The New Year is at 12 o'clock. Get it?"

"Nobody in Toronto would start a party at 10 o'clock at night."

"Why don't you just tell Mr. Sinatra that delightful Canadian custom?"

The next day we woke up at noon, and even though we were still very tired from our trip, John and I walked around Beverly Hills, exploring Rodeo Drive — the fancy boutiques, the jewelry, the restaurants and the gorgeous women everywhere you looked. We walked the whole length of Rodeo Drive to Santa Monica Boulevard, then past some big, beautiful homes up to Sunset Boulevard.

"Look." I pointed. "The Beverly Hills Hotel."

"The Polo Lounge," John said. "Let's go in and have a drink."

The place was jam-packed. It was New Year's Eve day and folks were getting fueled up for the evening. We found an empty stool at the bar. John sat down and I stood behind him.

"What can I get you?" one of the bartenders asked.

"They're famous for their banana daiquiris," I whispered to John.

"Two banana daiquiris," John said.

We watched him make the drinks in a blender — vodka, cream, a few kinds of liqueur and a banana. It was delicious and expensive: $27 with tip. We only had the one drink each and then started walking back to our hotel. About halfway there, our steps started to drag. We were still in our heavy tweed suits.

"I wish this was New York," John said. "We could hail a cab."

"Let's sit down on these steps and rest a bit."

We settled down on some red brick steps in front of the gate to a huge house that looked like it had been brought over, brick by brick, from the set of *Gone with the Wind*. We hadn't been sitting there more than 10 minutes when a Beverly Hills Police car pulled up. There were two officers inside and one got out and stood directly in front of us.

"What do you think you're doing?" he asked menacingly.

"Just sitting here," John said.

"Do you live here?" he asked, pointing at the plantation house behind us.

"No, we don't," I answered.

"This is a private residence and you're trespassing."

"On the steps?" John asked.

"What are you doing in this area?"

"We're staying at the Beverly Wilshire Hotel," I said.

"Then I suggest, if it's true, that you get off these private steps and move on down to where you say you are staying."

"We *are* staying there."

"Then move it!"

We got up and started walking. The police car moved right along with us. When we arrived at our hotel, the car stopped and one of the cops walked into the lobby behind us. He watched us get our room key at the front desk. Then he waved goodbye to us as we got in the elevator.

"I hate to think what would have happened if we *weren't* staying here," I said as the elevator rose.

"We'd be in jail and miss the Sinatra party."

It was late afternoon, and we were both tired and sweaty from our long walk. It was past 8 p.m., Toronto time. We were still getting used to the three-hour time difference.

"Let's have a nap," John suggested, "and we'll be well rested to talk to Frank and the gang."

"Frank and the gang?" I said. "What the hell are you — a Rat Pack member all of a sudden?"

"I was just —" John started to say when there was a light rap on the door. I opened it and two very sexy-looking ladies stepped into the room.

"Surprise!" one of them said.

"What's the surprise?" I asked.

"*We* are!" the other lady said. "We are a gift from a friend of yours.

We can't say who, but he paid us $200 each and here we are, just for you."

"Four hundred dollars? That's an expensive surprise," John said.

"I think you'll find out we're worth it. And it's not your money, Mr. Barster."

"Barster?" I said. "I'm Peppiatt and he's Aylesworth. No Barster, ladies."

"Fuck!" one lady said. "We have the wrong goddamned suite! Happy New Year, boys — see you around." They opened the door and slipped out into the hall.

"Let's have that nap you suggested before the Dolly sisters dropped in," I said.

We loosened our ties, stretched out on our beds and nodded right off. The little nap to get us rested for the party lasted about 10 hours. When I woke up, the sun was streaking through the window.

"Shit!" I yelled, and John woke up.

"What happened?"

"We missed the Sinatra party!"

"It's only six-thirty — maybe it's still going on."

"I'm sure Frank and the gang would welcome us with open arms — two complete saps arriving eight and a half hours late."

The phone rang, and I picked it up.

"What the hell happened to you guys?" said Nick.

"We took a nap and just woke up," I said.

"You missed *some* party. I'm just getting home. Dean Martin, Shirley MacLaine, Joey Bishop, Sammy Davis, Peter Lawford and lots of beautiful girls. Some guy named Zeke Barster brought in two doozies."

"Barster?"

"Yeah, you know him?"

"Not to my knowledge."

"Okay, guys, happy New Year and I'll see you Monday."

"How was the party?" John asked me.

"Sinatra and the whole gang were there and apparently our $400 surprises showed up, too."

"You're kidding."

"Along with the fabled Mr. Barster."

"I'll be damned!"

We phoned and wished our wives and children a happy New Year and told them about the Sinatra party mix-up. I had never heard Marilyn laugh so loud.

"What'll we do now?" John asked.

"Let's work," I said, and we did for three straight days. We finished a good first draft of the medley scene with the 50 microphones. Nick was thrilled with the spot, suggested a couple of changes and it was ready to take to the musical director. Perry Como arrived, and he and Bing hit it off right away. They both loved the medley, and John and I started filling in the rest of the show. Three days before the taping, the CBC called and said they needed one of us to come back and fix some problem. We flipped a coin. I lost and took a plane back to Toronto that afternoon.

Saul Ilson and I solved the problem they were having with the *Music '60* show, and by Monday morning, John, Saul and I were back at work in the little apartment/office. John said the taping had gone well and he brought thanks from Bing, Perry and Nick.

That morning Nick called us at our office.

"Let Johnny listen to this, Frankie," Nick began. I held the phone so we could both hear him. "Mr. Como has fired his whole production staff and he wants me to produce *Perry Como's Kraft Music Hall*, starting in September — 30 shows on NBC, Wednesdays at nine."

"Congratulations!" we both said.

"Perry also told me to bring along the two Canucks. He thinks you're terrific writers and he loves your Laurel and Hardy."

"Is that a firm offer?" John asked.

"You can take it to the bank."

"Open an account and just tell us when you want us to be there."

"I'll give you all the details next week. We've got a deal. Talk to you soon. Okeydokey?"

It was sure okeydokey — and then some.

✦

WHITE CHRISTMAS WITH PERRY COMO

THIS TIME I DID NOT ask Marilyn. I *told* her. "We have to move to New York."

"You didn't even ask for my opinion!" she wailed.

"About what?" I shouted. "To have a job or not have a job?"

"You can work in Toronto."

"Doing what — looking for work?"

"You just finished doing a successful show here."

"Yes, and it's canceled because it's too expensive. The Kremlin has already told us they aren't sure there'll be anything for us in September."

"They'll work that out."

"I don't intend to wait for them to do that. We are responsible for three children, Marilyn."

"We can't bring up our kids in New York!"

"You sound like we're moving to Nazi Germany, for chrissake!"

"What about *my* career?"

Her career? Since we became engaged she'd had one booking as a guest on a television show. It paid less than a hundred dollars. That was not a career! Granted, she'd had three babies in four years, which kept her more than busy, but in all those years she'd never mentioned her career. Now, suddenly, she was worried about *her* career! But even before we were married, Marilyn's career had only afforded her a tiny furnished room, and not in the best part of town. I bit my tongue. I wasn't going to throw all that at her. Finally, I said, "You can sing in America as well as Canada, sweetheart."

"I tried that once. No thanks!"

"Well, I'm asking you to try it again with your husband and our children. I'm not asking you to live in Manhattan. There are plenty of lovely suburbs all around the·city."

"You'd have to commute."

"What do you think I do here from Downsview?"

"Yes, I guess you do."

In all our many loud fights on this subject, this was the first time she had ever conceded one point to me. "Look, sweetheart," I said softly, "Nick Vanoff said they would rent us a house for the winter in a nice town in Westchester County."

"Close to New York?"

"About 30 or 40 miles away, and while we're living there you'll have a chance to look around for a house to buy."

"Can we afford that?"

"I'll be making $2,000 a week! Let's try it."

"All right, on one condition."

"Name it."

"If you run out of jobs, we come back home."

"It's a deal."

Thank God, she had finally agreed to give it a shot. Our four-year battle was over at last. It had taken its toll on our marriage, but now I felt some hope again.

"So, you're going to be gone for three years?" my mother asked when I phoned her that evening.

"Only if they pick up the option, Mom."

"Oh, they'll pick it up."

"You two can visit us and we'd come here for the whole summer, unless we buy a house down there."

"Another house?" my father said. "That takes money!"

"Dad, I'll be making 2,000 a week."

"Two thousand dollars?"

"That's right."

"Look," my dad went on, "you don't write the songs. You don't lead the band. You don't play the piano. Perry talks just fine on his own. So what do you do for all that money — cut his hair?"

"Not yet, Dad" was all I said. I had once tried to explain to him what exactly I did for a living, but he wasn't interested. The more successful I became, the less interested he seemed to be. He still hadn't got over his disappointment at my not becoming a lawyer, and now, on top of that, he seemed to have developed a bad case of envy.

"Why can't I get a job like that?"

"Leave it, Frank!" my mother said. "Just leave it!"

"Kids today, they make money without selling a damn thing!" he muttered.

The Toronto *Evening Telegram* featured a half-page cartoon of Perry Como with his arm around each of us. Underneath the drawing was a really nice story about our move, with the headline "A Trip to the Big Time." I don't believe our old nemesis, the TV critic Ron Poulton, was at the paper anymore.

WHEN WE ARRIVED AT OUR beautiful new house on Foxmeadow Road in Scarsdale, I was bowled over by the manicured gardens, spacious living room and dining room, completely equipped kitchen, four bedrooms, four bathrooms and a huge sunken music room with a grand piano and French doors leading out to a large patio and backyard. The kids and Tommy tore through the place like they'd been released into Never Never Land. Nervously, I glanced over at Marilyn. She was actually smiling! *Phew!*

The next morning I met the creative core of *Perry Como's Kraft Music Hall* at an Italian restaurant on 38th Street. "Over here!" Nick

Vanoff waved to me. He was seated with John and three other men. "This is the other Canuck, Frank Peppiatt," he said to them. "You've met Dwight Hemion, when he was director of *The Steve Lawrence and Eydie Gormé Summer Show*, and this is our choral director and arranger, Ray Charles, not to be confused with the brilliant blind singer/piano player of the same name, and this is our head writer, the esteemed Goodman Ace, whom everybody calls Goody."

Ray was a cheerful, professorial-looking man with dark hair, glasses, sharp features and a lovely singsong voice, while Goody was in his early 60s, dour-looking and tall, with a very white crew cut. He was chewing on an unlit cigar and giving John and me the once-over — twice.

"You fellows don't mind writing with other people?" he asked.

"As long as the other people are writers," I answered.

Goody smiled and the others laughed. "You'll do," he said.

"What about me?" John asked.

"Do you mind writing with other writers?"

"No, as long as the other writers are people."

"So, the comedy-writing gorilla is out?" Goody came right back.

"Only if *he* wants to be," John said, and Goody smiled again.

The Perry Como office was on Park Avenue at 54th Street and Goody's office was just three blocks away. Goody told us we'd be writing at his office every morning, and then John and I would work every afternoon and Saturday morning with Nick, Dwight Hemion and Gary Smith, the set designer we'd worked with on *Andy Williams*, in the production office. We didn't mind the extra hours — it allowed us to be involved in all aspects of the show.

On our first day at work in Goody's office we met the other two writers, Jay Burton and Selma Diamond. Selma had dyed red hair, a penetrating New York three-pack-a-day cigarette voice, snapping green eyes and an opinionated attitude. She looked to be in her early 50s and wasn't too happy about it. Jay was about the same age, a seemingly carefree guy with a pudgy pink face, deep-set brown eyes and a joke machine for a mouth.

We talked about the show for a couple of hours. Goody had written for Perry Como before, so he knew the type of humor he liked. Around noon, his secretary took orders for lunch, and after we ate, Selma and Jay started playing gin rummy while Goody got on the phone with his stockbroker.

"I guess the meeting's over," I whispered to John. He nodded and we got up to leave.

"See you tomorrow at 10," Goody said, and went back to the phone.

We walked over to the Como offices on Park Avenue, a large, lavish suite with thick carpeting, nice soft lighting and tasteful furnishings. We had come a long way in a few years from the folding chairs at the CBC. It was a pleasure to work in the Como offices. We usually met with Nick, Dwight and Gary in the boardroom. The five of us came up with most of the creative production ideas on Saturdays because there would be no interruptions then. We'd figure out a rundown for the upcoming show, kick around ideas for an opening production number and decide on sets and costumes. Then we'd work out an idea for a medley with Perry and the week's guest. For instance, Dennis Weaver from *Gunsmoke* was going to be on the show. I remembered having read somewhere that his singing was so bad he limited his vocalizing to the bathtub. So I suggested that when Perry introduced Dennis Weaver and asked him to sing, Dennis would say no, because he only sang in the tub. Then two stagehands would roll a couple of bathtubs onto the set. Perry would get into one, Dennis in the other, and off they'd go into the big medley. Then, for the last song, we would roll in all 12 of the Ray Charles Singers in bathtubs. Big ending! We tried very hard in those meetings to get a specific idea and use it in every aspect of the show, scenically, sonically and comically.

The following Monday morning, back at Goody's office, the five of us would write the humor. Our first day there, the secretary overheard

John and me explaining the bathtub business to Goody. She laughed and said, "That's so funny, it'll write itself!"

Goody snapped back, "But will it *rewrite* itself?" We wrote and rewrote and rewrote our sketches till Goody couldn't find one syllable out of place. It was a great lesson and I never forgot it.

Things were going well on the show, but not so well on Foxmeadow Road in Scarsdale. Marilyn was having trouble adjusting to our new life. She'd often be well into her cups when I got home in the evening. Obviously she was unhappy, but I couldn't figure out why. Finally, one evening in November, she said, "You should be able to get me into the Ray Charles Singers."

"Sure, sweetheart, I could get you an audition."

"An audition!" she shouted. "I'm a professional. I've made a living singing with big bands and on network television shows."

"I know that, but Ray has never heard you sing."

"I've got two recordings with Art Hallman's band. Play those for him and we'll see. Audition my eye!"

I played the recordings for Ray Charles and he thought she was terrific.

"Most of the choral work," Ray said, "is to back up Perry and it is all harmony. Can your wife sight-read?"

"I don't really know," I said in all honesty. "I suppose so."

"It's not a matter of taking the music home and learning it, Frank. It's, like, here's the music, sing it right now, in harmony. Understand?"

"Yes, and I'll explain that to her."

"Take this with you," he said, handing me some music sheets. "It's a chorus part from last week's show."

"Thanks, Ray," I said. "Whatever you write, they sing it right then? Right?"

"Right."

I went home and told Marilyn that Ray Charles really liked her voice. I was very excited for her.

"That's super!" she said. "Now, what's next?"

"Read this." I handed her the sheet music Ray had given me.

"I can't read music," Marilyn said dismissively.

I was astounded. "You're kidding? Ray says you have to sight-read from the word go."

"I can't do that."

"You could learn. Come in to New York and take lessons. Tommy has the girls all settled in now, so you have the time. Very soon you'll have a whole new career. You'll get an agent, you'll go to Broadway auditions. Who knows where that will lead?"

"I'm not going to go through all that just to be a backup singer."

"Marilyn, the Ray Charles Singers *are* backup singers! You wanted to sing with them."

"I'm not going to take lessons like some high school kid."

"Well, it's up to you. Learn to sight-read and you've got a job on television."

"I'm too old."

"You're in your mid-30s, for chrissake. You look teriffic."

"I can't do it and I won't do it!"

"Look, I know it's not easy."

"It's never been easy, Frank. I don't get jobs just handed to me, like you do."

I was stunned. Handed to me? That really hurt. I knew she had never been all that interested in what I did, exactly. But I didn't know she had not even noticed how hard I had been working all these years. It was as though she didn't really know me. She sounded just like my father. She didn't know or care what I did, but she was envious of me. Not only that, Ray Charles was "handing" her a good job on a hit show. All she had to do was learn to sight-read, but she was too stubborn to try.

At least the Como show was going along smoothly and I was loving every minute of it. We had some great guests on the first few shows

— Sid Caesar, Jack Parr, Lena Horne, Harry Belafonte and Jimmy Durante. John and I came up with an interesting way to present Ethel Merman. She and Perry were about to sing a duet, when Ethel explained that she would have to leave early to get to the Broadway theater for her eight o'clock curtain. Perry said, "Go ahead, Ethel, but keep on singing." They started the duet, and after a couple of minutes, Ethel said she had to go. One camera followed her as she sang and walked up the aisle of the theater, while another camera stayed on Perry, singing onstage and in harmony with Ethel. The first camera followed her, singing, as she got into a taxi, while Perry continued onstage. She rolled down the taxi window and she and Perry sang back and forth, from the cab to the stage, all the way to her theater. Outside the Broadway theater, the Ray Charles Singers were waiting, dressed like theatergoers. The singers joined Ethel for a big ending to what had started as a simple duet on the Como stage. Ideas like that may have been the reason shows just got handed to me.

As the weeks went by, Goody Ace and Jay Burton became our good friends, but we couldn't win over Selma Diamond until my daughter Robyn got into the act. Robyn was in kindergarten, learning American history. That November of 1960 John F. Kennedy was elected president, and one day the teacher asked Robyn who George Washington was. She answered, "He was the first Kennedy." I told that story to the writers in the office and Selma laughed and said, "That's so sweet and funny! Can I use it on *The Tonight Show*?" Jack Parr liked Selma's sense of humor and booked her on the show every once in a while.

"If you give Robyn credit."

Selma told the story on the next *Tonight Show*, and Jack Parr and the audience loved it. Jack said, "Hire the little girl, Selma."

Every time I heard Robyn say something humorous or just plain cute, I'd give it to Selma and she was thrilled. The biggest laugh my daughter's stand-up material received concerned the word Marilyn used for the three girls' private parts. They all called it their *Betsy*. One day I was in the shower and as I stepped out, Robyn walked into the bathroom. She took one look at me, burst into tears and ran out. I heard Marilyn call to her. "What's the matter, sweetheart?"

Robyn shrieked, "Daddy's Betsy is falling out!"

Everybody in the office laughed when I told the story, and Selma got up and kissed me on the cheek. "Thank you, Frank," she said.

"Thank Robyn — I'm just her agent."

Perry's Christmas show was very special for everybody. All the staff's children were invited onstage to listen to Perry tell the story of the season, backed up by Christmas carols, the manger, Mary and Joseph, the wise men and the shepherds. It was always the most watched Como show of the year. Melissa was a little too young to be on the stage, so she sat in the audience with Marilyn and my parents, who were visiting for the holidays, while Robyn and Marney gathered onstage with Perry and the other kids. All my girls were adorable, but at three, Marney looked cuddly and sweet as a cherub. Just before the Christmas scene began, Perry lifted her up onto his knee and that's where she sat for the whole segment. Marney was thrilled; Robyn was not and I don't think Marilyn was, either. The next day a picture of Marney on Perry Como's knee appeared on the cover of *Women's Wear Daily*. Today, Marney has her own children and that magazine cover is still with her.

In 1961 Roger Maris broke Babe Ruth's home-run record, hitting 61 in the season. Mickey Mantle hit 54. The two ballplayers were the talk of America.

"You're a baseball fan, right, Frank?" Goody asked me one day.

"A big fan. I read every box score, every day."

"Thank God somebody around here does," Goody said. "A car will pick you up downstairs in one hour and take you to Yankee Stadium, where you will talk to Mantle and Maris about their appearance on the show next week, okay?"

"More than okay," I said, astounded. "Wow. You're not kidding?"

At Yankee Stadium I showed my pass to the clubhouse attendant. "I'm here to talk to Mr. Mantle and Mr. Maris about their appearance on Perry Como's show." I expected the attendant to turn me away and I'd find out it was all a practical joke. It was just too good to be true.

"Frank Peppiatt, right?"

"That's right."

"The boys are expecting you. Go ahead in."

I walked inside the Yankees' dressing room, still wondering when I'd be kicked out. They were all there in various stages of undress — second baseman Bobby Richardson, shortstop Tony Kubek, third baseman Clete Boyer. Unbelievable! I turned a corner and nearly ran into Yogi Berra.

"You lookin' for Rog and the Mick?"

"Yeah, I'm —"

"I know, Perry Como. Keep walking. You'll run into them. You don't look like Perry Como."

"Yogi, I'm not — Oh, never mind."

I introduced myself to Roger and Mickey, sat down between them, asked a few questions and made notes. Boy, they were so darn nice to me. I was in baseball heaven.

When I got back to Goody's office after 12, John was gone, and Jay and Selma were playing gin rummy. "Thanks, Goody. That was a wonderful experience."

"I thought you might enjoy it. Jay and Selma probably don't even know who you went to see."

"Neither does John," I added.

Goody and I wrote the talk between Mickey, Roger and Perry at his desk while the gin game continued in the corner. We decided that the ballplayers would dress formally in white tie and tails. Then, at the end of their scene with Perry, they'd turn to go and we'd see their uniform numbers tacked onto the back of their tuxedos. The scene worked well and when Mick and Roger turned around, there was a huge roar of laughter and applause. As Goody and I had finished writing that piece, Jay Burton shouted, "Gin!" and Selma threw her cards at him, which is how their games ended every day. Selma Diamond lost a lot of gin games, but a few years later she won a leading role in the situation comedy *Night Court*, starring Harry Anderson and John Larroquette. For all eight years she appeared, she was very funny in it.

As the season progressed, we learned a lot more about Jay. He had started out as a press agent in the '40s, selling jokes to columnists like Walter Winchell, but his real ambition was to be a comedy writer on radio. He sent jokes in to all the shows, but no one bit. One week Jay was in Los Angeles on a press junket and he heard that Bob Hope was on location nearby making a movie with Jane Russell called *The Paleface*. Jay went to watch the filming, but he couldn't get past the rope that held back all the gawkers. He noticed a lady he knew who was a dresser on the movie and she let him watch from the wardrobe truck, where he found a rack of Indian costumes. He put one on, added some war paint and joined all the other costumed men dancing around Bob Hope. Whenever Jay got close to Bob, he'd stop and tell him a joke: "These girls are wearing their skirts so short, they'll have four cheeks to powder instead of two."

"Cut! Cut!" the director finally hollered. "Get that guy the hell out of here. He's ruining the scene!" Two big, tough-looking guys approached Jay.

"Leave him alone," Bob Hope said. "Those are good jokes!"

Bob hired Jay on the spot and Jay wrote on Hope's radio show for many years. It took a lot of nerve to do what he did, but I completely understood the strong comedy-writer hunger that drove him to do it.

BEFORE THE END OF THE first Como season, our options were picked up for the next two years, with a nice raise. This gave Marilyn a new mission — finding a house to buy. She went out every day with various real estate agents and looked all over Westchester County. She was keeping busy and that was good.

"I've found the perfect house for us!" Marilyn announced one day when she was picking me up at the Scarsdale station.

"Where?" I asked.

"In a sweet little village on the Hudson River called Dobbs Ferry. It's on three acres of land and it's over 200 years old — a coach house that some of George Washington's troops stayed in, they say."

"Who says?"

"The real estate agent. Why would he lie?"

I could have given her about 200 reasons, but I held my tongue. Her depression over her singing career had steadily worsened and she blamed me for all of it. I had introduced her to Andy Williams' brother Dick, who used singers every day in his thriving radio and television jingle business. Like Ray Charles, Dick Williams thought Marilyn's voice was very good and said he could certainly use her, but only if she learned to read music. Again, Marilyn refused, which only deepened her depression. She began threatening to go back to Canada and take the girls with her. So I was relieved to see her excited about something — anything.

"We can look at it tomorrow, darling," she said.

"I have to work. Make it Sunday."

"That's two days away. Somebody will snap it up!"

"I'm sure there are other 200-year-old houses that George Washington slept in."

"Oh you, always making a joke! We'll go first thing Sunday morning."

"It's a date."

We pulled up in front of the coach house two days later.

"Well, what do you think?" Marilyn asked.

"It sure looks old," I replied.

"It needs some work," Marilyn said. "It's a fixer-upper. I know just what to do with it."

I knew just what to do with it, too, but I kept quiet. She was smiling and animated. After all, if it was what she wanted, it was fine with me. I just couldn't figure out *why* she wanted it.

The real estate agent arrived and accompanied us toward the front door. To the left of the entrance, there was a crumbling greenhouse with smashed panes of glass and a large, overgrown area that was probably once a garden. The interior of the house was chilly and drafty, but the rooms were enormous. The living room alone was 1,600 square feet, with a walk-in fireplace where George and Martha Washington probably danced the quadrille.

"Can we have a look at the basement?" I asked.

The agent spoke up. "You can't get to the basement from here. You have to go outside. It's a coach house, you know."

Whatever being a coach house had to do with that, I had no idea.

"That's an easy fix," Marilyn said, and the real estate guy nodded.

"There are two staircases to the upper story," Mr. Real Estate said.

"And none to the basement?" I asked.

"It's a coach house," we all said together.

There were two bathrooms upstairs and three bedrooms. "This will be our bedroom," Marilyn explained. "It has its own bathroom. The middle bedroom will be for Tommy and she will share a bathroom with the kids."

"Will the kids all sleep in the same room?" I asked.

"It's a huge room — plenty of space for three beds," she said. "They'll love it!"

"Can we have a look at it?" I asked.

"Not right now," Mr. Real Estate said. "We don't want to disturb the wasp nest."

"What do we do, wait till they're asleep?"

"That's funny," Mr. Real Estate said without cracking a smile.

"My husband is a comedy writer," Marilyn said, rolling her eyes.

"How is the house heated?" I asked.

"Oil — oil furnace."

"In the basement?"

"Of course."

"And if something goes wrong with it in the winter?"

"You have to go outside, around the house and go in the cellar door."

"Because it's a coach house," I said.

"That's right."

"There's so much we can do with this place!" Marilyn enthused.

"I hope so," I said.

"You two talk it over and let me know. The owner is anxious to sell."

"I'll bet he is."

"*She*," Mr. Real Estate corrected me.

"She's a sweet old lady, Frank. You'll love her," Marilyn said.

"What's the asking price?"

"Sixty-thousand, firm."

"Okay," I said, and shook his hand. "We'll get back to you."

"Isn't it fabulous!" Marilyn said on the way home.

"I think you see more in it than I do."

"You'll love it when I start redoing things."

"Sixty-thousand, a firm sixty-thousand."

"It's a steal!"

"From who?"

"I've seen hundreds of houses and they're all boring." Marilyn said. "This is the house I want to live in. It has character."

"I'll give it that," I said.

"Look, Frank, I didn't want to move down here, but I went along with your wishes. Now the least you can do is go along with mine."

What the hell, I thought. *She'll be spending most of her time in the place and I'll be in New York.*

"Okay, let's buy it."

"Oh, thank you! *Thank* you! I can't wait to get started. Thank you, darling."

"Start with the wasp nest," I said with a smile.

Chapter 12

✦

LOSS

Now we owned a small house and mortgage in Toronto and a gargantuan 200-year-old coach house in Westchester County with a very large 30-year mortgage. Luckily, we were just then notified by the Province of Ontario that they were condemning our house in Downsview to build a freeway and they would refund all the cash we had spent on it. I breathed a massive sigh of relief. Though the refund didn't amount to much money, at least now there would be only one mortgage.

"It's fantastic!" Marilyn said. "We can use the Canadian money to fix up our house here."

"We'll need more than that to fix up this coach house," I said.

While we were in Toronto closing down our Downsview house, I went to see Jack Kane. It had been many months, and we had a lot of catching up to do. I also needed to get his advice about Marilyn and her singing career.

We gave each other a hug.

"How's it going, Mr. Music Maker?" I asked.

"Not so good, Frankie."

"What's the problem?"

"The doctor says I'm going to die."

"What the hell are you saying, Jack?"

"I've got advanced cancer of the thorax." Tears welled up in his eyes.

"Can't they operate or something?"

"Too far!"

"You better stop doing the show and relax a little."

"No way, I'm gonna keep going until they *carry* me off the god-damned bandstand!"

Jack, my dearest friend, with cancer. Jesus, he was only 33, with two children and another on the way. What could I do? Not a damn thing. I felt helpless and very, very sad. I cried in my car all the way home.

"That's not possible," Marilyn said when I told her the news. "Jack's a young man."

"Cancer doesn't seem to pick and choose," I said. "He's got such a wonderful career ahead of him. Damn! Damn! It's just not fair!"

I saw Jack every day for the next few weeks. We worked on ideas and material for his show, which was going on again in the fall. I don't know if we came up with anything good, but I treasured every minute of my time with him.

MARILYN AND I HAD THREE weeks to get out of the Downsview house before the walls came tumbling down. We loaded the kids in the car and headed for Dobbs Ferry, followed by a moving van packed with all our worldly goods. The 200-year-old coach house was still there. The wasp nest was gone, thank God, but everything else was the same — the falling-down greenhouse, no stairs to the basement, the enormous living room and dining room that made our Toronto furniture look like dollhouse tables and chairs. I decided not to complain. It *was* our new home and we had to make the best of it. *So shut up and live,* I said to myself. *Don't be such a pain in the ass.*

While we were unpacking, a couple who lived across the back lane dropped in to welcome us. "We're the Vosses. I'm Fred and this is my wife, Corky." Corky was a stay-at-home mother of two and Fred was an architect who designed hospitals. "You've got *some* work to do here," Fred said, gesturing around the monster living room.

That worried me. The guy was an architect and *he* saw trouble. "You have to go outside to get to the basement," I said.

"It's a coach house," Fred reminded me.

"Of course, I keep forgetting that tradition."

Fred pointed to a corner of the room and said, "Right in that corner you could put a circular staircase to the basement."

"What a wonderful idea!" Marilyn exclaimed, and I thought, *Thanks for spending my money, Freddie.*

Shortly after we moved into the coach house, I began my second year with Perry Como. I still loved the work, but that entire year went by in a blur. Robyn was six and in first grade, Marney was four, Melissa three, and they were all completely under Tommy's care. Marilyn had become a full-time construction engineer. Every morning she'd put on a pair of big, baggy overalls and work boots and take up her post as crew boss over the army of workers who were fixing up our fixer-upper. She was as happy as I had ever seen her. She reminded me of my father, who worked every weekend at his bench in the basement, making storm windows, repairing furniture, sawing and drilling and banging and loving it. Like my father, Marilyn could not understand why I wasn't joining in on all the home-improvement fun. My father sure would have. I thought about the old Freudian canard: we marry either our mothers or our fathers. Well, it was becoming clear — I had married my father.

One night when I got home there was a large hole in the floor of the living room.

"What's with the hole?" I asked Marilyn.

"That's where the circular staircase is going to go."

The circular staircase was assembled in the living room and turned out to be too big to fit the hole. Men were on the roof fixing leaks in the tiles and a stonemason was repairing the flagstone terrace.

"They have to widen the hole and they'll have the staircase installed tomorrow."

"That's good," I said, "but our money is going out as fast as I earn it."

"But, Frank, sweetheart, the more we fix up, the more the value of the house goes up."

"Are we planning to sell?"

"Hell no, I love this place."

"Then it doesn't mean a damn if the value goes up."

"There's not much more to do. We'll be fine."

"Don't tell me. Tell the bank."

"You always think the glass is half-empty."

"Half-empty, I'd be thrilled with," I said.

Marilyn turned away from me. "Will you call the kids? It's dinnertime."

That's the way it was going. Marilyn would not learn to read music, but she did learn to change the subject and spend money on this edifice we had purchased. And to top it all, Jack Kane's impending death was eating at my heart.

The nights were starting to get chilly, so we tried to turn on our oil furnace. It wouldn't turn on. We called a furnace guy and he said we needed a new furnace. Why didn't I think of that? The nice little old lady had stiffed us with a fake furnace. While the new furnace was being installed, I thought it would be a good idea to warm up the place with a roaring fire in the giant fireplace. I had logs delivered the next day and that evening we all sat around the fireplace to enjoy the warmth.

"This is so cozy," Marilyn said.

The flames danced around in the fireplace but the smoke didn't go up the chimney. It came into the living room. The smoke was pouring in and we were all coughing.

"Do something!" Marilyn shouted, and she herded the kids to the front door.

I filled a bucket full of water and doused the fire. *No fireside chat tonight,* I thought. It turned out the chimney needed to be swept and peaked, whatever that meant. Actually, it just meant lots more money. The glass was now definitely less than half-full.

Our first Christmas in the coach house turned out to be really merry. The circular staircase was installed, the new oil furnace was keeping out the cold, the fireplace was crackling with the smoke going up, not out, and the whole property was covered with snow — it was a white Christmas. I was beginning to think everything would work out, after all, until I phoned Jack to wish him a happy New Year. He sounded weak and low. I didn't comment on it, of course, but it was upsetting.

In March 1961, Jack Kane died. He was only 33. My best friend ever. I could hardly believe it. I felt like part of *me* had died. I cried in the car again. Marilyn and I flew to Toronto for Jack's funeral. Hundreds of people were there, including all the singers, technicians and musicians who had worked with him. It was tough saying goodbye.

We stayed with my parents while we were in Toronto. My father didn't look at all well. "Frankie," my mother said, "come down to the basement. I want to show you something."

I followed her down the stairs and when she turned around she was crying. "Mom, what's wrong?"

"Your father didn't want me to tell you but he has incurable cancer. The doctor says it's all through his system — pancreas, liver, everywhere."

"Oh my God! Are you sure there's nothing they can do?"

"They said it was hopeless. I can't go on without your father."

"Now stop that kind of talk," I said, hugging her and joining in the sobbing.

My father died in June. He was 58. I loved him and I know he loved me. We just had a problem showing it and sharing it. I felt I had to get my mother away from the house where everything reminded her of my dad. We sold the place for over $100,000, and I moved her to a lovely apartment three blocks from her brother Duncan's house and close to all her sisters. She had enough money, but she didn't have my dad, and she missed him every single second. Her inconsolable grief tore me apart, just as my father's death had. She never really recovered. So, in one year I lost my father and my two best friends — my mother and Jack Kane.

DURING THE LAST MONTH OF the second *Perry Como* season, John and Jean were divorced. I only found out about it when he told me he was marrying a production assistant in the office, Nancy Eberle, the daughter of Ray Eberle, a former singer with the Glenn Miller Orchestra. I never knew the details. As usual, John simply didn't discuss personal things, so I kept to myself all the weight I had taken onto my shoulders the past six months. As for Marilyn, she was too busy with her construction project to provide much sympathy, though I may well have been beyond consolation. I sucked it up and held it all in.

In the third season of *Perry Como's Kraft Music Hall*, CBS put on two new shows opposite us: *The Beverly Hillbillies* and *The Dick Van Dyke Show*. Both shows were huge hits, and suddenly Perry was no longer the Kraft Cheese Whiz. We tried our best to find ideas to juice up our ratings. We did one show in Cuba at Guantanamo Bay during the missile crisis. We did another at Perry's golf course with Gary Player, Jack Nicklaus and Arnold Palmer. We booked big rock-and-roll acts, even though they didn't mix well with Como's laid-back style.

But nothing seemed to work. Perry gave up and started booking guest stars from his era, like Alice Faye and Eleanor Powell, the greatest female tap dancer ever, who arrived on the set with her own dance mat. I admit I liked these older stars, too, but they didn't bring in new viewers. We limped through that season.

On the last show, Perry wanted to bring members of his staff

onstage and introduce them. We were waiting backstage to be introduced by Perry, just to take a bow. But Perry had planned a surprise
for us. The dancers slapped derby hats on us, put a tiny mustache on
me, wrestled me into a fat suit and pushed us onstage. He had always
loved the Laurel and Hardy routines John and I did.

"Two of my writers," Perry said, "Stan and Ollie."

"Say hello to Perry, Stanley," I said.

"Hello to Perry, Stanley. I thought his name was Perry Como,
Ollie."

"Now stop that and tell Mr. Como who your favorite singer is."

"Andy Williams."

Perry and the audience broke up.

"This is another fine mess you've got us into, Stanley. I *know* my
favorite singer is our boss, Mr. Perry Como. So there!"

"Yesterday you said it was Bing Crosby."

"Well, I never!" I said, making John cry like Stan Laurel, as I
pushed him off the stage.

"And believe it or not," Perry announced, laughing, "they're good
writers, too!"

There was big applause for us. It was a nice way to end our years
with Perry Como.

We were all wondering about next year and what we would do.
Nick wanted to form a production company called Five Incorporated,
with Dwight Hemion, Gary Smith, John and me. It sounded like a
damn good idea, but John was against it. His new wife, Nancy, had
been involved with Nick before she had met John and she didn't want
her husband working with Nick on a permanent basis. Nick was furious with me when John and I pulled out. I was torn, but John and I had
been partners through a heck of a lot over 10 years. My loyalties lay with
him. It was a while before Nick spoke to me again, and I felt terrible
about it because he was the man who had really got our careers going.

Anyway, we were out of work again. No Perry Como, no Five Incorporated, no Nick Vanoff and no job. Another fine mess you've gotten us into, Stanley.

Our fortunes would soon change, though, courtesy of Jimmy Dean.

Dean, who had a smash hit recording, "Big Bad John," had occasionally filled in as host on *The Tonight Show* and had done an excellent job. ABC signed him to star in his own hour-long variety show, produced by Bob Banner, who was also responsible for *The Garry Moore Show* and *Candid Camera*. Banner offered John and me the head writing job on *The Jimmy Dean Show* at $2,600 per for 26 weeks. We snapped it up. Bob assured us we would love Jimmy and find him easy to write for. Bob, however, wouldn't be doing the writing, so that was easy for him to say. Anyway, we interviewed several writers and chose six to join the writing staff. One of them was a six-foot-seven Irishman, Harvard graduate and Olympic hurdler named Pat McCormick. He was very funny in an outrageous way — naturally, John and I took to him right off the bat.

Jimmy Dean and Bob Banner were both from Texas, so Bob thought it would be a wonderful idea if all the writers wore cowboy boots when they first met Jimmy. Bob said he'd give a signal and we'd all cross our legs, revealing the boots. I did not quite get it, but Jimmy Dean thought it was hilarious, and that was all that mattered.

"Now, *I'm* gonna show y'all something you'll never forget," Jimmy announced after Bob had introduced him to everybody. Jimmy went into a closet and closed the door. A few seconds later he emerged, standing proudly with his testicles hanging out over the top of his pants. "I'm like the rich giraffe at the bar. The highballs are on me," Jimmy shouted, and roared with laughter. Bob laughed and some of the writers tittered politely.

But Pat McCormick had something to add: "He lost his dick in a cockfight!"

Now, *everyone* in the room roared with laughter. Everyone except Jimmy Dean and Bob Banner. Bob tapped me on the shoulder. "What's the matter, Frank? Didn't you think Jimmy's joke was funny?"

"Sure I did, Bob. It's just perfect for the first show."

The Flintsones was also a big ABC hit show that year, so John came up with the idea of featuring Fred Flintstone as the guest on our first show. We wrote a sketch and a duet for Jimmy and Fred. The song was "Yabba Dabba Doo," the catchphrase on *The Flintstones*. We sent the sketch and the music to Hollywood so they could get to work on the animation, which took care of at least six or seven minutes.

The Jimmy Dean Show was very badly organized, because Bob Banner felt he had to micromanage every detail. Since he was also producing two other shows, we wasted tons of good writing time waiting for Bob to come in and okay every little thing. Mr. Banner would show up late in the afternoon and call the whole staff in for a meeting. To quell our hunger for dinner, Bob always ordered apples and clam chowder for everyone, whether you liked apples and clam chowder or not.

Once, Bob mentioned that we needed a running segment like *The Garry Moore Show*'s "That Wonderful Year."

Pat McCormick suggested "That Wonderful Month."

"No, that's too similar," Bob said in all seriousness. The rest of us in the room were turning blue, trying not to laugh out loud. Then Bob announced that he was having a big robot built to work with Jimmy on the show.

"What would be the comedy basis for that?" I asked.

"Well, just Jimmy with a robot sidekick is your basic comedy right there," Bob said, and all the writers looked very confused.

"Will the robot talk?" John asked.

"Oh, yes," Bob said. "We'll put a midget inside the robot with a microphone."

"Oh," John said.

"Robby the Robot will be finished in a couple of weeks and that'll give the writers time to come up with some really funny scenes for Jimmy and Robby!"

Nevertheless, the first show went well, even though it was under-rehearsed because so much time had been wasted by our apple-and-clam-chowder festivals. The *Flintstones* segment was a big hit — it was already on film and couldn't be changed or mulled over by Mr. Banner.

We received a great deal of mail after the first show, and Bob Banner's assistant producer, Julio DeBenedetto, had the receptionist read it all and separate the good letters from the bad. I never figured out why Julio did this, but it sure as hell kicked him in the ass. Jimmy Dean came in around noon, just as the receptionist was finishing the letter sorting. He saw the two piles of letters on her desk and said, "Fan mail, great!" He grabbed one pile of letters and went into his office.

As luck would *not* have it, he had grabbed the wrong pile. A half-hour later he was in tears in his office. Julio was in there, trying to explain to Jimmy how the letters had been divided. "Why the hell would you do that?" Jimmy demanded. Julio did not have an answer. I don't think Jimmy believed him, anyway. I almost felt sorry for the guy.

After that, Jimmy became very unsure of himself, which made him even more difficult to work with. That evening the apple-and-clam-chowder meeting went on for hours as we tried to resolve the fan-mail fiasco.

Finally, to change the subject, Pat McCormick asked Bob Banner, "How's Robby the Robot doing?"

"Looking good. He's going to be hilarious," Bob said.

"Maybe he'll fall in love with the coffee machine," Pat said.

"Pat, that is just the kind of joke I do *not* want for Robby!" Bob said. "We have to make him seem human."

"But he's a robot with a midget inside!" John said.

"That's correct!" Bob snapped, and that was the end of it.

Jim Henson, the Muppets creator, was also at the meeting to show us a new dog puppet named Rowlf. The puppet was adorable. Rowlf made the cut, and Jimmy did a very amusing spot with the puppet every week. It was fun to write those, and the audience loved them. Rowlf was not a robot — just a normal talking dog.

Besides the testicle routine, Jimmy had another habit that bothered me. Just as we were having an orchestra rehearsal for the third show, Jimmy walked in after watching *his* Yankees get beaten by Sandy Koufax and the L.A. Dodgers.

"How was the game?" Peter Matz, our orchestra conductor, asked.

"Ah didn't mind the Yanks losin'," Jimmy said, "but ah didn't like 'em bein' beat by a *Jew*!"

The huge rehearsal hall went dead silent. Most of band members were Jewish, as was the conductor. Peter Matz let Jimmy know he was less than thrilled with his remark. "Ready to rehearse, Mr. Taste?" Peter snapped.

"Let's go!" Jimmy said, entirely unaware that his remark had pissed off everybody in the room.

I WAS NOT FEELING AT all well. The show was getting me down and my home was still a permanent construction site. The doctor told me I had developed a peptic ulcer. He put me on a diet and said I had to relax and not worry so much. Easy for him to say. By the way, apples and clam chowder were not on the diet. The next day at the studio, John and I were sitting in the bleachers, watching the rehearsal.

"I want out of this, John," I said.

"We've got 23 shows to go."

"Not for me. It's making me sick."

"We'll be dumping over a hundred thousand bucks."

"We'll find something else."

"Sure we will. I wasn't looking forward to the next 23 shows, either. I will miss the apples and clams, though."

We met with Bob Banner and told him we were leaving. I said I was sick with a peptic ulcer and just couldn't continue. He agreed to let us go, as long as it wasn't in the newspaper that we had quit. He wanted to announce that a serious illness had caused him to graciously release us from our contract, and we agreed. As John and I were leaving the building for the last time, a truck pulled up and two husky drivers started unloading a large robot.

"So long, Robby," I said.

The Jimmy Dean Show lasted two more years. Pat McCormick stayed on. He told me that Jimmy never tired of pulling the testicle bit. Eventually, Jimmy Dean gave up on his balls, named a sausage after himself and made a fortune.

Chapter 13

✦

JUDY! JUDY! JUDY!

"I know you're not feeling well," Marilyn said, "but you and John are throwing away $100,000!"

"One hundred and fifteen thousand, to be exact."

"That's not funny, Frank. That money could have gone into the house."

"The house is fine."

"The hell it is! There's lots more to do."

"We've put every spare dime, and then some, into this house for more than two years! Whatever is left to do can wait."

"No, it can't! We might as well sell the house and I'll take the kids back to Canada."

"Is that a threat?"

"Take it whatever way you want!"

That really scared me. "What the hell are you getting at?"

"I'm not getting at anything! I'm already there!"

"Will you stop arguing!" Robyn cried from the doorway.

My beautiful eight-year-old was upset and it was my fault. Marilyn had a point — I had thrown away a lot of money. But she didn't seem the least bit worried about my health. The peptic ulcer was already subsiding, even though it had been only a few hours since I'd walked off *The Jimmy Dean Show*. It was an expensive cure but to me it was worth it. I'd get another job, I just *knew* it.

Marilyn left to have a drink — or three — with our neighbor Corky Voss, which is how many of our fights ended these days. I watched her storm across the backyard in her overalls and work boots. Now that there was no more money coming in, she'd lose her job as construction-crew straw boss.

I settled down in the kitchen and had a drink or two myself. I knew it wasn't good for my $50,000 ulcer, but at that moment it was good for me. I was pouring my third drink when the phone rang. It was Norman Jewison, calling from Los Angeles. "I read about your health and *The Jimmy Dean Show*."

"I'm feeling much better now, Norm. That press release was just so Bob Banner wouldn't have people read that somebody had quit on him."

"So you can still work?"

"For sure."

Norman explained that he had been hired by Judy Garland to find a new staff for her show on CBS because the first 13 weeks hadn't gone well. "I'm making Gary Smith the new producer and I'd like you and John to be the head writers."

"We'd like that, too, Norman."

I hung up and walked over to Corky Voss's place with the Judy Garland news.

"Judy Garland — wow!" Corky said.

"I'm not moving to Los Angeles!" Marilyn growled.

"It'll be so much fun!" Corky said.

"Then *you* go with him!" Marilyn shouted.

"I'm not asking you to move, Marilyn," I said. I knew that was hopeless. Besides, I wasn't too anxious to have her around anymore. "With the Judy Garland money, you can bring your crew back and do more fixing-upping."

"I'll drink to that!" Marilyn said, and we did.

I was not a happy drunk.

The next day John and I made the deal with Judy Garland's manager. I informed Marilyn of the details: she would get my full salary, $2,222.50 per week, and I would live in Los Angeles on the expense money the show would be paying me.

"I'm back in business!" Marilyn exclaimed happily.

JOHN AND NANCY RENTED A house on the beach in Santa Monica and I checked into the good old Chateau Marmont Hotel on Sunset Boulevard.

Judy was taping some songs at CBS the day we arrived and met Gary Smith and Norman Jewison at the studio. That year CBS had also signed Danny Kaye and they built him a bungalow on the roof of Television City on the corner of Fairfax and Beverly Drive. For Judy, they provided a state-of-the-art trailer, with a yellow brick road painted all the way from it to the studio door. Some big doing. Norman led us up the yellow brick road to her trailer and we met the legendary Judy Garland.

"They tell me," Judy said, "that as well as being good writers, you guys are very friendly with my favorite comedians, Stan and Ollie."

I whispered to John, "Same as Como." John nodded and slipped into Stan Laurel. As Oliver Hardy, I said, "Why don't you say hello to Judy, Stanley."

"Hello, Judy Stanley," John said. "I thought her name was Judy Garland."

"Will you stop that and tell Miss Garland who your favorite singer is."

"Barbara Streisand."

"Now, this is another fine mess!" I said as Oliver.

John started blubbering like Stanley.

Norman, Gary and Judy were all laughing.

"There, there, Stanley," Judy said, patting John on the back. "Barbara Streisand is *my* favorite, too. So there, Ollie!"

"Well, I never!" I huffed and puffed.

Judy was one swell lady and she made us feel at home right away.

"I'm having people over Sunday night to watch the show," she said, "and I'd like you guys to join us, okay?" We both nodded happily. "Sevenish."

Sevenish to us meant seven, and being Canadian, quite a few minutes earlier even. It was a balmy Los Angeles October evening and we were sweating in our Canadian winter tweeds when we arrived at Judy's house. A maid opened the door. "You guys here with the ice?" she asked brusquely, buttoning up the collar of her uniform.

"We didn't know we were supposed to bring ice," John said.

"He's kidding," I said. "We're here to watch the show and stuff."

"Oh," the maid said, "I'm terribly sorry, go right on into the living room!"

We walked into a spacious living room and there sprawled on a couch was Glenn Ford, movie star and Judy's current man, reading what looked like a script.

"It's Glenn Ford," John whispered.

"He was born in Canada," I whispered back.

"Good evening, Mr. Ford," John said, and Glenn Ford looked up. "We're both from Canada, too, Mr. Ford."

Glenn didn't say a word; he just glanced at us as though we were there to fix the plumbing or something, and went back to reading his script.

A bartender showed up and started arranging the bar with various bottles and glasses.

"I guess sevenish doesn't mean seven," John said quietly.

"Is it too early to get a drink?" I asked the bartender.

"Are you guests?" he said.

"Yes, Miss Garland invited us," John said.

"You're early!"

"We know," we both said. I added, "We'll have a double gin and tonic."

"The ice isn't here yet."

"We know that, too," we both said.

We sat in the corner sipping warm double gin and tonics, watching Glenn Ford read and feeling so very out of place.

Around eight o'clock people started arriving. "I guess sevenish means eight," John said.

"Then why didn't she say eightish?"

"That means nine."

After Judy made her entrance, she introduced us to everybody — Peter Lawford and his wife; Roddy McDowell; her two daughters Liza and Lorna; Mickey Rooney and Glenn Ford, whom we'd already met, sort of. The ice had arrived and we had a cold drink for a change.

"I'd really like to talk to Mickey Rooney," I said to John.

"Me, too. Let's sidle over there and see what we can do."

I wasn't an expert sidler, but I did my best. Mickey was just turning away from the bar with a new drink when the two Snowbacks intercepted him. "It's really a pleasure meeting you, Mr. Rooney," John said.

"Mickey, please, Mickey," he said. "So you two are the new writers." We told him how much we enjoyed his movies, the *Andy Hardy* series and all the musicals with Judy. "You know," he said seriously, "Judy and I both have a lot of trouble sleeping, and I blame those movies." He told us that back in the '30s and '40s, when he and Judy were huge moneymaking stars for MGM and keeping the studio above water financially, Mr. Mayer, the studio head, had an ambulance pick them up at the end of every shooting day. He and Judy would be taken to a clinic, where they had a lovely dinner. Then they were both injected with a needle that put them right to sleep until 5 a.m. In the morning, they were given breakfast and taken to the studio for makeup and costumes. By 7 a.m. they were ready to film the first take of the day. Nobody was late, nobody was tired. The two stars were bright-eyed and bushy-tailed, just the way Mr. Mayer wanted them. They were his stars and he kept them in line. However, when the movie was completed, they were given three or four weeks off with no nightly needles.

"I don't know about Judy," Mickey said, "but I had terrible problems getting to sleep during those off weeks."

"And the whole thing would start again with the next movie?" I asked.

"That's right, and I kind of looked forward to all that sleep."

"And Judy has a problem, too?" John asked.

"Sure she does. Just ask her."

John and I weren't about to ask her. A few weeks later we learned Judy had broken up with Glenn Ford. The reason: he had called her late one night and wakened her — an unforgiveable transgression. We weren't sorry to see the back of him. You see, Glenn, you stiff somebody and you get stiffed right back.

As John and I moved into our new offices, the old staff were moving out, including my old writing pals from *The Steve Allen Show*, Arne Sultan and Marvin Worth.

"Judy has hired the Snowbacks," Arne said.

"Good luck, guys, you're gonna need it," Marvin added, and they went out the door.

My next surprise walked into our office five minutes later. It was my old nemesis from Steve and Eydie's show and the Janis Paige fiasco, Johnny Bradford.

"I worked with Frank on *The Steve Lawrence and Eydie Gormé Summer Show*," he told John. "I always knew he would make it."

Sure, I thought, *he wanted me to make tracks back to Toronto*.

"I brought you guys a freshly baked loaf of bread from the farmer's market behind CBS. We'll have to have lunch there."

One lousy loaf of bread. What did he expect — I'd take half a loaf back to the hotel and John would take the other half to the beach? Big deal.

Johnny Bradford sat down and made himself comfortable. "So, what are we working on today?" he asked.

"We thought you'd been let go with Arne and Marvin," I said.

"No one told *me* that."

"I think you'll find out when you don't get your paycheck," I said.

"We'll see about that," he said, then tossed me the gift loaf and left.

That afternoon Gary Smith was introducing us to the rest of the staff. "I didn't know Johnny Bradford was still with the show," I said.

"He's not. Norman let him go."

"Somebody better tell him."

"Hi, guys, welcome to the show," a familiar voice said, and I wheeled around toward its source. The voice was familiar because it belonged to Mel Tormé, "the Velvet Fog." Mel wrote all the chorus music for the show and was sort of the music coordinator. He had always been one of my favorite singers *and* he wrote "The Christmas Song" with Johnny Bradford's brother.

"Mel and I and Judy have a favor to ask you two," Gary Smith said. "We have a show with Mickey Rooney and some other guests to go on the air in two weeks."

"What's the favor?" I asked, and Mel spoke up.

"Twelve minutes are unusable and we have to tape something to fill in the time."

"And you want us to write something?" John asked.

"Yes," Gary said, "and . . . for no money."

"The no money doesn't bother us, it's the new idea that's the problem," John said.

"Wait a minute," I said, standing up and moving around the office. "We can use the whole studio?"

"Yes, of course," Gary said.

"Judy and Mickey have made a bunch of movies together, right?"

"Right," Mel said, smelling an idea.

"We take a prop from each movie, an old car, a beat-up piano, a front stoop, a hay wagon, whatever."

Mel stood up. "And as they talk and move around the studio, each prop has a story and reminds them of a song from the picture!"

"You took the words right out of my mouth!" John said. "And a different hat for Mickey in every scene."

"It's perfect!" Gary shouted.

Judy loved the idea and suggested that in each scene she could refer to Mickey by his character's name in that movie. Judy and Mickey were absolutely wonderful in the number and they thanked us for giving them something so familiar and nostalgic.

"I told Judy you guys did it for nothing," Mel informed us. "She thinks you're the bee's knees."

We were glad the material worked out because we could have just as easily been the bee's bum. As for the no-money part, I didn't care. Had we been paid, it all would have been gobbled up by Marilyn and the 200-year-old coach house.

Next, we started working on a show we *would* get paid for. The guest was a new comedian who had a hit comedy album. His name was Bob Newhart, a laid-back comic, but very, very funny. We knew he would do a monologue from the album but we needed a spot for Bob and Judy. Since Bob didn't sing, it had to be a comedy spot. We finally decided what to do and drove out to Judy's house. We explained that we'd like her to be an ordinary housewife, maybe her hair in curlers, and Bob would be her husband. "The two of you are sitting on a sofa, watching television," I said. "You're watching *The Judy Garland Show* . . ."

"And I can make fun of myself!" Judy said. "I love it!"

"Bob asks you why they have all the little lights rimming Judy's stage . . ." I said.

"So she won't fall off!" Judy broke in, laughing.

She was so smart, always right in step with what I was thinking — or even a step ahead. Judy and Bob aced the sketch and got big laughs.

Another time, Rich Little, an impressionist we'd known in Toronto, sent us a tape of some of his work. When we played the tape for Mel Tormé, he went nuts. "I've never heard anybody that good. We've got to get him on the show." Then we played tape for Gary Smith, who said, "We'll tape him on November tenth. Tell him to be here on the eighth."

We called Rich in Ottawa and he was thrilled. Then his manager got on the phone and we told him the terms of the deal. "The plane, hotel and fee are all fine," the manager said, "but what's the date of the taping?"

"November tenth."

"Oh, we can't make it that night. We're booked in Brockville."

"Gimme that fuckin' phone!" we heard Rich Little scream. "Tell Judy Garland we accept. I'll be there on the eighth and I'll tape on the tenth."

"What about me?" the manager yelled.

"*You* play goddamned Brockville!"

Mel, John and I wrote a parody of Judy's big hit "The Man That Got Away," as a duet for her and Rich. Rich worked flawless impressions of John Wayne, Humphrey Bogart, Jack Benny, James Mason, James Stewart and Jimmy Cagney into the song. Judy said she didn't want to rehearse with Rich — she wanted to react spontaneously on the actual show — so Mel Tormé rehearsed with Rich. When it came to showtime, the amazement on Judy's face was very real; when Rich did James Mason, with whom she had just finished a movie, she couldn't believe it.

The Judy Garland Show was a big springboard for Rich Little. Overnight, he went from playing places like Brockville to appearing on great variety shows such as *The Hollywood Palace, The Ed Sullivan*

Show, Kraft Music Hall, as well as a situation comedy and his own variety show on NBC, plus big, big nightclub bookings all over the world. Whatever happened to his manager, I never heard. I wonder how he did in Brockville.

ON NOVEMBER 22, 1963, PRESIDENT John F. Kennedy was murdered in Dallas. The president was a close friend of Judy's and his assassination hit her hard. She canceled her show that week and wanted to do a program of upbeat nationalistic songs like "When Johnny Comes Marching Home" and "It's a Grand Old Flag." She hoped to help lift the spirit of the American people with her music, even though she herself was depressed about the tragedy. But Kennedy's assassination took a heavy toll on Judy's spirits. Now she didn't have the energy to do her show. CBS was not pleased.

"It's like doing a goddamned movie every week!" she declared at a production meeting. "Everybody says to me, 'Hey, Judy, your last show was good. We start rehearsing for the next one on Monday, see ya!'"

Judy was not used to the demands of television. At MGM she'd make two or three movies a year, and that was it. But 26 one-hour shows in a row overwhelmed her. To add to the tension, the show's ratings weren't good. CBS had scheduled *The Judy Garland Show* opposite NBC's monster hit, *Bonanza*. They might as well have buried her alive.

After the last show, Judy threw a big party for everyone on the staff. "Fuck CBS!" she shouted to one and all. She asked John and me to do a final Stan and Ollie routine and kissed us both on the cheek. The next day she was off to England to make a movie.

I will always treasure the time I spent with her. Judy Garland was special.

Chapter 14

◆

HULLABALOO AND SINATRA TOO

It was 1964, winter was turning into spring and I was back in the 200-year-old coach house with Marilyn, Tommy and the kids. The six months I had spent on *The Judy Garland Show* in California had cured my ulcer and calmed my mind. I had worked long hours and spent my off-time in my Chateau Marmont room, watching sports and reading. It was just what the doctor had ordered. I was ready to settle back into family life. But was family life ready for me?

"I've got my own bedroom, Daddy!" Robyn exclaimed as she grabbed my hand and led me up the stairs. Marilyn and her crew had magically — to me, anyway — made the one huge children's bedroom into two beautiful normal-sized rooms.

Marney and Melissa dragged me into their new bedroom. "You can tell us Dog Sam stories right here," Marney said.

"No, he'll tell them in *my* room!" Robyn insisted.

"There are *two* of us," Melissa said, holding two fingers under Robyn's nose.

"We'll work it out," I said.

"There's another new room right out here," Marilyn said, proudly leading me to what used to be a large, empty space at the top of the stairs. It was now a new bedroom and bath. "For your mother, when she visits."

"Wow!" I said. "You add any more rooms and this could be a hotel."

"We don't want strange people coming in and out," Robyn said.

"Your father's only kidding, sweetheart," Marilyn said.

"You've done a wonderful job, kiddo. Congratulations," I told Marilyn.

"Thanks. Are you going to be able to stay home and enjoy the place?"

"Yes," I said, and I meant it. I knelt down and hugged my three girls. I was giddy with happiness.

Gary Smith had asked John and me to write a major presentation to sell NBC a rock-and-roll show called *Hullabaloo*. Our agent, the sartorially splendid Lester Gottlieb, had got us a sweet $25,000 fee. I knew just what to do with my share. "I'm going to give you kids an early birthday present."

"Where is it?" Melissa wanted to know.

"I'm going to rip out that broken-down greenhouse and put in a swimming pool."

"I didn't know you knew how to do that, Daddy," Marney said.

"He doesn't," Marilyn laughed. "If he's serious, I know just who to call and get it started."

"I knew you would and I *am* serious. Go to it!"

The kids yelled with glee and jumped all over me. Then Melissa suddenly started to cry.

"What's the matter, Meliss?" I asked.

"I can't swim!" she sobbed.

I held her. "Neither can I," I lied, brushing her tears away. "You and I will learn together."

She looked up at me and smiled.

JOHN AND I HAD TO get started on the presentation, but we had no place to work. Through Roger Gimbel, a producer friend of ours, we got a rent-controlled office on West 55th Street, just off Fifth Avenue.

It was one very large room with a small kitchen and bathroom for the ridiculously low price of $125 a month. We partially furnished the place and got down to work.

Elvis had just been deposed as the king of rock-and-roll by the Beatles. The Fab Four were on every radio station and singing out of all the jukeboxes and record shops in the country. Overnight, the Beatles' shaggy mops had replaced the Presley pompadour, love beads replaced neckties, and the business suit was a relic of the past. When we returned from California, it seemed that every New York talent agent (with the exception of Lester Gottlieb) was now sporting a scraggly beard and hair down below their ears. Barbershops were going bankrupt all over the Western world. New English groups were coming out every day, trying their best to emulate the Fab Four, and American pop music was dropping its Hs, trying to do the same. We were determined that *Hullabaloo* would be a vehicle for this movement.

In six weeks we submitted a 42-page proposal to NBC, who snapped it up. We went right into production with John and me as head writers. John, Dick Williams and I wrote the *Hullabaloo* theme, and our first show went on the air in January 1965. We featured musical stars like the Supremes, the Rolling Stones, the Mamas & the Papas, Tom Jones, the Four Seasons, the Everly Brothers, Marvin Gaye, Petula Clark, Sonny and Cher, and Herman's Hermits, many of them appearing on network prime-time TV for the first time. Some were so green they didn't realize they were expected to sing, not just lip sync as they did on non-prime-time shows like *American Bandstand*.

Hullabaloo was a huge hit with the under-30 demographic. Robyn and Marney were just old enough to appreciate the show, so I brought them to the set a few times, making them the envy of their schoolmates. I had to keep a close eye on them, though, for fear they'd get a contact high from the fumes wafting out of the dressing rooms.

In the early shows we tried using hip young comics, like Woody Allen, but the teen studio audience just screamed throughout his set. John and I were getting a firsthand education in what was "happening" and it was great fun.

Then, out of the blue, we were pulled back into our own era by Old Blue Eyes himself. He wanted us to come out to Los Angeles to write his TV special, titled *Frank Sinatra: A Man and His Music*. Excited by the prospect of working with this legend, we hired a writer to cover for us on *Hullabaloo* and prepared to meet Frank and write for him.

"I'll only be gone a couple of weeks," I told Marilyn as I packed my suitcase.

"Don't start making any new deals out in Lotusland," she said flatly, refusing to share in my excitement.

"One show with Frank Sinatra. Can you blame me?" It didn't even occur to me to ask her to accompany me to Los Angeles. While I was previously in California for many months doing *The Judy Garland Show*, the children and I had insisted that Marilyn bring them out for a visit. They stayed for six days, hardly leaving the Chateau Marmont Hotel — no Disneyland, no Malibu Beach, no Hollywood sign or shopping sprees. Marilyn was determined that no one should like it too much out there.

"I'll bet he can't read music," Marilyn snarled.

"I have no idea," I said, and continued packing.

"Ask him."

Sure, I was going to ask Sinatra: *Frank, my wife would like to know if you can read music.* I would be back on a plane to New York in about 11 seconds, possibly with a broken jaw. "Yeah, I'll ask him," I said drily.

"I'll bet he can't," she said seriously.

"If he can't, I'll quit his show."

"Don't be silly!" she snapped.

I'm *being silly?* I thought. Then I said, "No more new bedrooms while I'm gone. Okay?"

"There's no more room," she said, "and I'm busy with the drainage system on the back patio."

"Well, good luck with it."

"I don't need luck," she huffed. "I *know* what I'm doing!"

Just then, she once again reminded me strongly of my dad. It was not a fond remembrance.

IN LOS ANGELES, JOHN AND I were put up at the fancy Hotel Bel-Air, which was in a galaxy beyond the Chateau Marmont. Dwight Hemion, the producer of *A Man and His Music*, brought over Shelly Keller, the other writer on the show. He was a portly man with a large clown-like head of curly red hair and an open, friendly face. He introduced himself: "I'm the Earl of Essex, a man of parts. Do you know how hard it is to get parts for an Essex these days?" It was an old joke, but Shelly's delivery got a laugh out of me and I was instantly won over. Dwight explained to us that Frank was at the Paramount Pictures lot, making a movie called *Assault on a Queen*, written by Rod Serling, the creator of the popular *Twilight Zone* TV series.

Friends in New York had warned us that Sinatra was demanding and hard to get along with. Nervous, we went to meet him at noon the next day in his dressing room at Paramount. He could not have been nicer. He had lunch served for all of us, and not the usual dressing-room fast-food fare, either, but a gourmet meal with a formal waiter and a menu, white tablecloths, silverware and real cups and plates. Sinatra was in a great mood. He told us he was in love with an actress named Mia Farrow.

"We timed it just right," Shelly Keller whispered to me.

After lunch, Sinatra took us down to the studio and we watched a scene that took place in a lifeboat and featured Frank, Virna Lisi and Tony Franciosa.

"Let's rehearse the scene," the director said. "You first, Frank."

"I'm not going to do that first line," Frank said.

"Then I'll cut my line and go right to Virna," Tony Franciosa said.

"But then my line won't make any sense," Virna Lisi said.

"All we need are the last two lines," Frank said.

"Where's Rod Serling?" I whispered to Shelly.

"In England on another picture."

"But wouldn't he be upset to have his lines changed like that?"

"You guys are used to television, where the writer is always on the set so he can speak up if they make changes."

"Well, if you write it, you should protect it," John said.

"Doesn't happen in movies. It's a director's medium, or a star's — if he's big enough, like Sinatra."

"So you write the damn movie and take your chances?" I said.

"You catch on quickly." Shelly grinned.

"No wonder Rod Serling keeps coming back to television," I said.

"Right. He's in complete control of *The Twilight Zone*," Shelly said.

Later, we sat around the hotel room with Shelly and Dwight, talking about *A Man and His Music*. Dwight said Frank wanted the show to feature his latest album, *It Was a Very Good Year*, and Shelly suggested we insert a Sinatra standard that suited each of the years. "That makes a lot of sense," Dwight said.

"There are four sections. Right?" I asked.

"Right," Dwight said, "teens, 20s, 30s and older."

"Then why not use the seasons as a setting for each age group," I suggested.

"That would be wonderful!" Dwight exclaimed. "I'll get the set designer working on that right away. That'll take care of about 20 minutes. Thanks, guys!" He hurried off to run the idea by Frank.

The three of us went on discussing the rest of the show. Finally, Shelly said, "We're working well together already. Let's go to the bar and see if we drink well together."

We did and, as it turned out, we did.

Frank loved "The Very Good Years" idea and it was in the works. He said he planned to open the show with a concert section in front of the band. He wanted to talk about the early years and sing some of those songs. It took us about a week to come up with a script for the show. We wrote him a nostalgic, humorous monologue about how he had been this skinny kid with a bow tie and about 15 pounds of hair. Frank really liked the dialogue and didn't change a word. Rod Serling should have been so lucky.

The biggest thrill of my whole career didn't happen on the show, but in the rehearsal. Frank had taken a liking to John and me, and when it came time to rehearse the songs with the band, he sat on a high stool, facing the orchestra. Then he sat John and me down on either side of him. There we were, with Nelson Riddle conducting a 40-piece orchestra and Frank Sinatra sitting between us. *Wow!* and double *wow!* It was so damn exciting I came close to wetting my pants — Nelson Riddle's wonderful arrangement coming right at me and Frank singing full out beside me.

A couple of times Frank stopped the band. "Nelson," he said, "I think there's a wrong note in the trumpet section at bar 62."

Yes, Marilyn, he can read music. I will happily remember that afternoon as long as I live — maybe even longer.

The show received rave reviews and won the Emmy for best musical of the year. All three writers received special plaques from the Emmy committee, thanking us for our participation. It was some experience.

And when it was over, a plane ride brought us back into the world of the Kinks, the Lovin' Spoonful, Sam the Sham and the Pharoahs, Jay and the Americans, Freddy and the Dreamers, and on and on. Where are they now? I have no idea, but they each had their moment in the pop-music sun, until their record sales went south and they returned to wherever they returned to. The Beatles were the only group we didn't have on *Hullabaloo*. They were way too expensive. Their records are still selling today, but the Fab Four are now only two, and I, for one, miss their sound.

NBC gave *Hullabaloo* a second year, but all the groups were starting to sound the same. The English imports were dwindling and *Hullabaloo* fans were a couple of years older, which is all it takes to turn young eyes and ears in another direction. At the end of the second year, NBC canceled the show. On the last day, I changed the radio stations in my car back to sports, news, easy listening and jazz and drove home.

THE 200-YEAR-OLD COACH HOUSE HAD become very popular in the neighborhood because of the pool. Whoever Marilyn had hired to put it in had done an excellent job. I had fun, splashing with the kids. Melissa was developing into a strong swimmer.

"I'm going to bring in a truckload of crushed white stones," Marilyn said as we sat by the pool. "I'll spread them all around the rim of the pool to stop the kids from running."

"That'll do it," I said. *It'll also hurt their poor little feet like hell*, I thought.

"Do what?" she demanded menacingly.

"Stop them from running." I tried to stay calm.

"That's the idea!" she said loudly.

"I know!" I said, even louder.

"Don't you agree?" she screamed.

"Of course, but . . ."

"But what?"

"Nothing, never mind!"

And that was the beginning of yet another of our arguments over nothing. The kids were usually right there and it upset them badly. Was it me or was it Marilyn, or both of us? I had no idea, but it was happening more and more and more. Even though I was out of work,

I retreated every day into New York and the office to try to get some peace of mind. I hoped Marilyn and the children found some peace of mind, too, while I was away. John often met me there and we'd work on show proposals.

One afternoon, Hugh Horler, our old friend and boss at MacLaren Advertising, called and asked us to write and perform a series of 12 one-minute radio commercials for Esso gasoline in Canada. He and a partner had bought the agency and were doing well. We told Hugh we'd be pleased to do it and he offered us a very nice fee.

"So now *you're* going back to Toronto," Marilyn huffed as she watched me pack.

"For five days, to record some commercials we've written. Five thousand each."

"See, you *can* make a living in Toronto!"

"For one week, Marilyn, one week!"

"I hear Toronto's getting pretty big. Lots of work."

"Shoveling snow, maybe."

"You always put down where you were born!"

"That's not true!"

"Your old friends back home think it is!"

"What old friends?"

"All of them!"

"I don't know who you mean!" I shouted, then swallowed hard to calm myself. "Look, Marilyn, what I do know is, I'll see you all in a week and I'll bring home 5,000 bucks and some butter tarts." I closed my suitcase and was out the door.

"Big deal!" she shouted at my back.

In Toronto, we stayed at the Royal York Hotel and recorded at the old RCA studio on the top floor. The sponsor really liked our comedy commercials, and it was great seeing Hugh Horler. We had some fun dinners with him, but although we talked on the phone now and then, I never saw Hugh again. When he retired, he and his wife moved to England. He was a great man and a true friend.

When I returned, I brought home two dozen butter tarts from Toronto, as promised. The kids loved them and so did the neighbors.

"The tarts were a big hit," Marilyn admitted.

"I knew they would be."

"Canada has *some* good things to offer," she huffed.

"Of course it does, but making a decent living in my line of work is not one of them."

"We could get a good price for the house with the pool, the circular staircase and all the bedrooms."

"Forget it."

She jumped up, calling out, "Come on, kids, let's go and change for a swim!"

I wished she *would* change — more than just her clothes.

Meanwhile, Dwight Hemion and Gary Smith had formed a production company, Smith-Hemion, and our common agent, Lester Gottlieb, was negotiating a deal with Kraft Foods to bring back *Kraft Music Hall*. Kraft asked Smith-Hemion to develop a presentation that would convince NBC to put the show in their 1967 fall schedule, less than a year away. They called on us, the old presentation writers, and offered the same deal we had on *Hullabaloo*.

"They're paying you $12,500 *each* for this, uh, whatever it is?" Marilyn asked me, as she finished an early drink.

"It's a sales presentation."

"That seems like a lot of money for a few measly pages," she huffed.

"Do you want to phone Lester Gottlieb and tell him that?"

"You are so damn lucky!" she said, and got up to fix herself another drink.

"I know, it's a curse," I replied, only half-jokingly. I had heard this from her so many times now, it no longer made me angry. It only reminded me of my dad at his worst. Not only didn't Marilyn appreciate how hard I worked, but in all the 13 years of our marriage she had never once told me she liked — or even disliked — any of the shows I had worked on. She simply did not care.

John and I ended up sweating over the "few measly pages." We ended up with 58 of them, along with Gary's renderings of sets and various special effects. We printed up the presentation in colour, and it made an impressive-looking booklet. By the time we put the final draft of the *Kraft Music Hall* presentation to bed and handed it in, we were exhausted. When I arrived home about eight-thirty, Tommy, Marilyn and the kids were having dinner.

"Your father's home from his day on the rockpile," Marilyn said, her voice mocking.

Tommy and the kids laughed. I didn't quite see the humor.

"I'm going to pour myself a drink," I said.

Marilyn followed me into the living room. "Make me one, too," she said, slurring her words.

"Isn't it a little late for the kids' dinner?" I asked her as I poured.

"I run the house!" she shouted.

"Sorry, I thought since I'm paying the bills, I might have something to say."

"Oh sure, throw that up at me again!"

"Marilyn, I can't handle this anymore," I said quietly.

"How do you think I feel?"

"Then maybe we need some separation for a while."

"Maybe we do!"

"Fine," I said, and moved toward the stairs to go up and pack.

"Is Daddy going away again, Mommy?" I heard Robyn ask.

"He's just kidding, sweetheart," she said.

"He didn't sound like kidding," Marney said.

Melissa started to cry.

Marney was right, I wasn't kidding. I quickly filled a bag with a bunch of clothes, came downstairs, kissed the kids and told them I would see them very soon. "I'll be staying at the office, if anybody needs anything. Just call."

Marilyn was stunned as I walked past her and out the door.

Living in the office, however, was going to have its downsides.

PHIL D'ANTONI AND NORMAN BAER, who had produced big-time TV specials like *Elizabeth Taylor in London*, *Melina Mercouri in Athens* and *Sophia Loren in Rome*, wanted to work with John and me. We had many meetings at our office, and D'Antoni and Baer often brought along their secretary, Valerie Crawford. I couldn't help but notice she was very, very beautiful. She was from England, and her charming accent floated lightly through the air, even hours after she'd left the room. I hoped she might like me, too, but she was clearly not impressed that I was living in my office. Who could blame her?

On the bright side, the *Kraft Music Hall* presentation was a big hit with NBC. Kraft ordered 26 one-hour shows to be produced and directed by Gary and Dwight, with John and me as head writers. It was a huge job, so we hired two extra writers — Pat McCormick from *The Jimmy Dean Show* and Jack Burns of the comedy team Burns and Schreiber. "Two Irishmen and two Canadians," Lester Gottlieb remarked. "The only all-*goyishe* writing staff in the history of television."

Jack Burns was living in a hotel and when he heard I was living in our office, he asked if he could move in with me.

"Sure," I said. "All you need is a cot, some sheets and blankets."

"What's the rent?"

"Nothing," I said.

"Is that negotiable?"

"No chance."

"Count me in," Jack said, and I had a roommate.

It worked out really well. Like me, Jack was a big sports fan and he was as funny and easy to have around as Marilyn had been dour and difficult. He liked a drink now and then — more now than then — but what the hell, he was Irish. Life with Jack Burns was quiet and peaceful, just what I needed. Meanwhile, I kept in close touch with the kids, calling them as often as they called me. I brought them to some of the tapings of the show and every Saturday I would bring a different one of the girls into Manhattan for lunch and a movie. Marney remarked that she missed me, but she was also glad the loud arguments were over.

The *Kraft Music Hall* episode that I considered most special was the one starring Jack Benny, who had been my favorite comedian since I was 10 years old. I couldn't wait to work with him. Jack was appearing as the violin soloist with the Green Bay Symphony in Wisconsin and he wanted John and me to fly up and talk things over with him. It was the middle of winter and Green Bay was the capital of winter. Had it been any other comedian, I would have told him to forget it.

Mr. Benny met us at the door of his Wisconsin hotel suite with a joke: "The people here in Green Bay don't think it's very cold. Hell, if this isn't cold, then why is that Eskimo out there hitch-hiking with a *blue* thumb?" John and I laughed. "I didn't make that up, you know," Jack continued, "it's a joke from my radio show."

"I remember it," I said.

"You listened to me?"

"Every Sunday night at seven, Mr. Benny."

"You're a good boy. Now, what about this *Kraft Music Hall* show?"

"We thought . . ." I began.

"That's a good start," Jack said, smiling.

I told him we wanted to do a Jack Benny all-comedian string trio with him and Henny Youngman on violin and Morey Amsterdam on cello.

"That's funny already," Jack said.

"Every time there's a slight pause in the music," I continued, "one of them starts telling jokes like, 'I solved the parking problem,

I bought a parked car.' And you get furious: 'Now cut that out, Henny!' Then you all start playing again and when there's a pause, Morey stands up: 'I had dinner at my mother-in-law's and all she gave me was cold shoulder and tongue!' and you say, 'You're ruining the sonata, Morey!' Then —"

"I get it! I get it!" Jack said. "And I think it's hilarious, but let's make it a string *quartet* and we'll have a very well-known concert pianist who is very straight and professional, like . . . Rudolf Serkin would be perfect. He'll seem to be the only musician I can depend on to behave, but at the very end he comes up with a bad joke. 'Not you, too, Rudolf!' I'll shout at him."

"That'll be great!" I said.

"What an ending," John added.

"I know Rudolf very well," Jack said. "I'll call him in the morning."

Jack was pleased with the number and proceeded to show us his two very valuable Stradivarius violins. "They're beautiful," I said, "but isn't it dangerous to bring them up here? They could be stolen."

"I hope so," Mr. Benny said. "I've got them insured up the yin yang!"

The Jack Benny string quartet was the hit of the show and Rudolf Serkin played his part perfectly. Jack, of course, didn't do too badly, either. What a talent!

The show was going well, and I was having dinner with Valerie every once in a while. It was fun and very relaxing, but it all came to a halt before I could really get anything started with her. D'Antoni and Baer were leaving for Hollywood to get into the movie business and Valerie was going with them. We had a farewell dinner and that seemed to be that. After we said goodbye, I arrived back at the office to find Jack Burns having a drink with Pat McCormick.

"What's going on, guys?" I asked.

"Pat's left home and he wants to stay here with us," Jack said.

"We don't have another bed."

"I brought my sleeping bag," Pat said with a weak grin.

At that time I thought it would be nice idea — the three of us living together, writing together and drinking together. We'd develop a camaraderie, like the Three Musketeers. Instead we developed into the Three Drunken Stooges — suddenly I was on an express train to utter dissipation. And just as suddenly I was saved by my old friend Perry Lafferty, now the vice-president of CBS and head of the West Coast operation, calling from Los Angeles: "I'm having a bit of a problem with *The Jonathan Winters Show* and I'd like you to come out here and produce it."

"We're contracted for next season with *Kraft Music Hall*, Perry," I said.

"I'm sure Gary and Dwight will let you out when they hear you're stepping up in rank to producing."

He was right. Gary and Dwight wished us well and we made a great deal with CBS.

Next stop, Hollywood.

So long, roommates!

Chapter 15

◆

HURRICANE MARRIAGE AND *HEE HAW* HONEYMOON

I DROVE OUT TO THE 200-year-old coach house to tell Marilyn in person that I'd be moving to Hollywood for at least six to eight months.

"Why don't we *all* move out there?" she said cheerfully.

I was struck dumb. After 13 years of digging in her heels, pining for Toronto, envying my career and blaming it for her misery, fighting me at absolutely every turn, she had a miraculous conversion and was now suffused with the holy spirit of love, peace and understanding? I wasn't buying it.

Finally, I said, "I don't think there are any 200-year-old coach houses in Hollywood."

"No, I'm serious, Frank," she said, smiling.

"So am I. *Now* you're suddenly willing to move to Hollywood?"

"Yes, I've thought it over."

"And so have I. I've come to a different conclusion. I'm going there alone. The kids will visit me as often as they like."

"Alone?"

"Yes, alone. Without you."

"Then I'll sell the house and move back to Toronto," she snapped.

That had always been her ace in the hole. She played it whenever things weren't going just her way. For the sake of the children, I had always folded in the face of it. No more. "I wouldn't expect anything less," I said.

So ended the marriage — no bang, and not even a whimper.

When I got back to my office/home, Norman Baer called from Hollywood and offered to share his house with me. "We'll split the rent," he said. The house was in a great area just off Sunset Boulevard and the rent was reasonable.

"Why not," I said.

In Hollywood, I found Norman was living in the house with his girlfriend. Even more surprising, Valerie Crawford was living there as well. The arrangement made me uneasy, but the house was large enough for all four of us, so I could avoid any romantic complications if I wanted to. The truth was, I didn't have much choice. I had no real friends in Los Angeles. John and Nancy had rented a house in Beverly Hills and it was filled with their new babies. Furthermore, Valerie Crawford was still very, very beautiful. Besides, I had a show to write and produce, beginning the next morning. I didn't have time to go looking around for a house of my own. *Oh, what the hell,* I thought, *live a little.* In retrospect, I realize the whole scene was Valerie's setup, but right then I didn't smell it.

For the first time in our careers John and I were the bosses of a whole show — six writers, a director, costume designer, set designer, associate producer, choreographer, an orchestra, a conductor and arranger, secretaries, production assistant *and* Jonathan Winters. We had a lovely suite of offices right next to Jonathan's and we consulted with him constantly.

Perry Lafferty called us into a meeting that first week to fill us in on Jonathan's past. At one time he had been an alcoholic and pretty wild. On one drunken spree he had climbed the mast of a huge clipper in the San Francisco harbor. Eventually, he was coaxed down and taken to a hospital, and from there he went into a psychiatric clinic for a long period, where he was finally able to quit drinking. He had not taken a drink in the few years since his release from the clinic.

Perry ended the story with, "You guys may find him a little hard to handle at times, but he's so damn funny, it's worth it. And I'm here to help if needed. Okay?"

Our old friend and co-writer Shelly Keller from the Frank Sinatra special had produced Jonathan's show the previous year. He told us that unlike Como, Steve Allen and Sinatra, Jonathan Winters was uncomfortable in his own skin, which was probably why he had created all those classic, hilarious characters — Maude Frickett, High Pressure Businessman, B.B. Bindlestiff and so many others. I knew TV was such an intimate medium that the camera picked up on a performer's slightest unease, which, in turn, made the audience uncomfortable and likely to switch channels. Shelly's advice was that Jonathan should always be in character and rarely, if ever, be himself.

John and I figured we could accomplish that, but writing was only a small part of producing a big one-hour show. For each show CBS gave us $150,000 as a licence fee. That was to cover the salaries of Jonathan Winters, the guest stars, the director, the producers (John and me), the writers, the orchestra, conductor, arranger, choreographer, dancers and all the behind-the-camera workers — about 50 people in all. It also paid studio, office and equipment rental. If we spent more than the licence fee on a show, John and I were personally responsible for it. Not only did we now have to keep the show in line financially, but we had to hire everybody, approve costumes, dance routines and makeup, book guest stars — the list seemed endless. *And* we still had to come up with ideas and write them. If the show was a hit, sponsors would pay big money to buy commercial time. CBS could make many hundreds of thousands by selling ad time on a single episode of a hit show. A show's star or its producers, however, *never* share in those profits. All we earned was our salary from the licence fee. If the show was a super-hit, we might get a larger licence fee from which we could raise our salaries, but we still would never be allowed a percentage of CBS's ad-sales profits, or even know what they were.

Anne Nelson, a straitlaced woman wearing a tailored tweed suit and her hair in a bun, strode into our office after the first episode of *The Jonathan Winters Show* had aired. She was from the CBS Business Affairs Department and she carried a budget chart under her arm. She spread it out before John and me. "You're over budget on studio time, which puts your crew budget over, too," she began, pointing at a jumble of numbers.

"Maybe we could make it a half-hour show," John quipped. "That would solve it."

"That's not funny," Anne said.

As I looked at the chart, the name Red Skelton jumped out at me. He had not appeared on the show and had absolutely nothing to do with it. "Why," I asked, "is Red Skelton budgeted for $25,000 on the show?"

"That doesn't concern you," she snapped, and began folding her chart.

"Oh," I said, kind of stunned. On the one hand we were responsible for the budget, but on the other hand we weren't. Miss Nelson stood up to leave. "Uh . . . we'll try to trim as we go," I mumbled.

"I don't like the word *try*," she said, and strode out.

In our subsequent meetings with Anne Nelson, we hung on to even the slightest show of approval from her. Getting the budget under control began to take precedence over the actual content of the show. Looking back, I feel I was short-changing Jonathan. I was learning on the job, and that wasn't fair to him.

Joe Winther, the director we had inherited, always wanted things exactly his way and he annoyed Jonathan so much at times that we finally had to fire him. We brought in Bill Davis, my director buddy from Canada, and he got along just fine with our star. Better yet, he was so efficient that he cut big dollars out of the budget for us. Anne Nelson was very impressed.

Jonathan had some flights of fancy that we went along with. He wanted to do a takeoff every week of the old radio show *Jack Armstrong, the All-American Boy*. John and I loved the idea because we used to listen to the show when we were kids. Jonathan would, of course, be Jack Armstrong. We hired the very funny Charley Weaver to be Uncle Jim and we booked two talented teenagers to be Billy and Betty, Jack's pals. The satire was funny, but for some reason it didn't catch on. Perry Lafferty pointed out that anyone under 40 didn't know who the hell Jack Armstrong *was*, which meant most of our viewers had no reference point for our attempted satire. Jack got the sack.

Halfway through the season, just as the ratings were picking up, CBS fired a shot across our bow. The most expensive new show on the network that year was *Hawaii Five-O*, a big, lush weekly drama filmed on location in Hawaii. The show's ratings were low and CBS panicked, so they switched *Hawaii Five-O* to Jonathan's time period, 10 p.m. Wednesdays, and put Jonathan into the time slot where the drama had stalled, Tuesdays at nine. *Hawaii* prospered from the swap and went on to be a top 10 show that lasted over a decade and was sold into syndication for big, big bucks. *Jonathan Winters* languished in its new time slot and was canceled.

After the cancelation, Jonathan's manager blamed John and me — he said we were moonlighting on other projects while working on his show. This was absolutely not true. We gave all our time, talent, sweat and laughter to *The Jonathan Winters Show*. Still, I take some of the blame for the show's failure, because I wasn't a very good producer then. I only learned how to be one on Jonathan's back. We should have hired on an experienced assistant producer for that first year, at least. Jonathan Winters was my friend and I did not do right by him. He never spoke to John or me again. That still hurts and always will.

WHILE I WAS WORKING WITH Jonathan Winters I had regular phone conversations with my children. My accountant, Al Rettig, was sending Marilyn money to cover living expenses in the coach house. But one day when I called, their phone was dead. It was dead again the next day, and the next. I called the neighbor, Corky Voss.

"Marilyn sold the house and moved back to Canada," she said.

"When was that?"

"Oh, they've been gone a week now. The new owners moved in yesterday. Didn't you know?"

"It's the first I've heard of it, Corky. Did Marilyn give you her new address?"

"No. She left in such a rush. She said she'd write."

I was dumbfounded. The house was in both our names. How could she sell it without my knowledge, much less my signature? Not that I was sorry to be rid of the centuries-old coach house. I called my mother in Toronto. She had not heard that Marilyn and the girls were back in town. I called around, but none of my friends knew where they were, either. Finally, one of Marilyn's friends called to tell me I had to do something about Marilyn's situation.

"What situation?" I asked.

"Well, you've thrown her and the girls out with no money. What the hell's wrong with you? I used to think you were a nice guy!"

Of course, she wouldn't believe that I knew nothing about all this. I asked her for Marilyn's address, but she claimed not to have it.

The next day Robyn called. I nearly cried, I was so glad to hear her voice. She informed me in a cold, flat voice that they were penniless in Toronto. I told her they weren't penniless because her mother had sold the house and made at least $50,000 Canadian from it. Robyn didn't believe me.

"I've got to see you and your sisters, sweetie," I said. "I'll arrange for you to fly down here tomorrow. Will you do that?"

Robyn agreed. Al Rettig made the arrangements and Marilyn allowed the girls to visit for a few days. The atmosphere between us was tense, and for years they believed I had thrown their mother over without a penny. Now that I knew Marilyn's address, I had Al send her monthly support checks.

Over the past winter, John and I had taken on Bernie Brillstein as our manager. Our experience on *The Jonathan Winters Show* had taught us that agents were salesmen who brought a bushel of talent to the producer, taking out one sample after another, hoping to make a sale on somebody, anybody. A manager, on the other hand, has only a few clients and can offer more individualized attention to a career over the long term. So, it was out with the sartorially splendid Lester Gottlieb and in with the pudgy, jovial go-getter Bernie Brillstein. His first order of business was to tell us we should come up with an idea for a summer replacement for *The Smothers Brothers Comedy Hour* on CBS.

"They'll put on their own replacement," I said.

"I don't think so," Bernie said. "CBS is very upset with the Smothers Brothers. You know, too much anti–Vietnam War stuff on the show."

"I like it," I said.

"So do I," Bernie said, "but I hear that Tommy Smothers has pushed the CBS brass too far. He's refused to allow the president of CBS to view any show before it airs. The network is sure to cancel the Smothers Brothers, which means their summer replacement slot will be wide open. Dig?"

That kind of scuttlebutt was why we had hired Bernie Brillstein. We hunkered down and put our minds to the challenge at hand.

The popularity of country music was going through the roof in 1969. Albums and singles were selling like crazy and country performers were playing to sold-out audiences across the country. John and I figured that if we added comedy to the music, we could create a pretty strong variety show. Also, there had *never* before been a prime-time network country musical variety show on television. It was a vacuum begging to be filled. We came up with a 30-page presentation. Bernie's wife, Laura, suggested the perfect name for the show — *Hee Haw*.

While Bernie was trying to get a meeting with Perry Lafferty to pitch *Hee Haw*, John and I ran into Perry while we were having lunch at the Beverly Hills Hotel. We were no longer the Snowback rubes, getting drunk on banana daiquiris; we were Polo Lounge regulars, ordering "the usual, Carlos." We went over to Perry's table and told him we had an answer to his summer replacement problem. We left two *Hee Haw* presentations on his table and crossed our fingers. I don't know whether it was the presentation or the finger crossing that did it, but they bought the show.

Perry ordered 12 one-hour *Hee Haw* episodes to be taped at the CBS affiliate station WLAC in Nashville. We hired Sam Lovullo from CBS Business Affairs as associate producer. He'd be the sap who had to meet with Anne Nelson and her budget charts after every show. Bill Davis was brought in to direct, and we were lucky to get the legendary country comedian and writer Archie Campbell to join up. We also hired two more Snowbacks — Gordie Tapp, a writer/performer from CBC's *Country Hoedown*, and Don Harron, a well-known Canadian actor who did wonderful country comedy. Don was on tour in a play with Katharine Hepburn, but said he would write for us while he traveled. We brought Archie and Gordie to Hollywood to write with us at an office CBS provided.

We had only five weeks to plan and write a dozen hour-long *Hee Haw* shows. Because the time and budget were critical, our taping method would be a little radical. For instance, one weekly segment was going to be "The Cornfield" — cast members popping up from amid the cornstalks, telling a joke, then popping down again just as two more people popped up elsewhere with more jokes. The idea was to erect a huge cornfield set, a large sky backdrop and a scarecrow with a puppet crow on his shoulder. Then we could tape the cornfield segment for each of the 12 shows, one after the other. The cornfield set would be put up only once, saving a tremendous amount of time and money. Anne Nelson would have been proud of her greenhorns.

We had worked with Buck Owens and Roy Clark on *The Jonathan Winters Show* and we knew they were talented. Buck had a whole string of country hit records and Roy was a genius on guitar. He was also very funny. We decided these two performers would be the hosts and had Bernie Brillstein make a deal with them. Buck had his own band, the Buckaroos, who would be the *Hee Haw* house orchestra. Buck also had the Hager Twins under contract — they were two young singer-musicians who could really perform, and we hired them on as regulars. Jack McFadden, Buck's manager, was a slim, dark-haired, no-nonsense guy and a powerhouse on the country music scene. We brought him on to book the show's guest stars — Loretta Lynn, Tammy Wynette, George Jones and Charley Pride, to name a few. Without Jack McFadden we might never have gathered so many of the legendary stars for our show.

There would be two guest stars per show, each singing two songs. That made 24 guest singers, singing 48 songs, and all were booked to tape in Nashville over a four-day period with different sets and lighting around the WLAC studio. Those sets could be struck after four days and we would have all the guest-star numbers on tape — or "in the can," as we called it. The next day we would shoot all 24 Archie Campbell skits in the barbershop and the doctor's office with Nurse Goodbody. Gordie Tapp did a general-store sketch every show and these were handled in the same manner. Buck Owens and Roy Clark each did two numbers per show, which were all taped in two days. They also performed a two-man comedy spot in each episode called "Pickin' and Grinnin'" — all 12 taped in one day. The guest stars and cast members also did one-line jokes in close-up, which would be sprinkled through-out the show. Those we could pick up on tape as we went along, since they did not require sets.

John and I decided we needed some animated bits, so we made a deal with a small animation company in Hollywood. They did a wonderful job with the Hee Haw donkey, who appeared at the top of every show, opened his mouth and brayed, "HEE HAW!" Sexy dancing animated pigs also sashayed across the screen during certain up-tempo tunes. With banjos and guitars strumming loud and clear, we were off and running. We hired six or seven very sexy young women, dressed them up like Daisy Mae from the *Li'l Abner* comic strip and spread them throughout the show in sketches, doing jokes or just supplying very nice background.

It would take us only half a day to tape 12 skits with Roy Clark playing the hilarious desk clerk at the Empty Arms Hotel. He once told a customer he could have a room but he'd have to make his own bed.

"Heck, that's fine," the customer said, "I don't mind makin' my own bed."

"Good," Roy said, "you'll find a hammer, saw and nails and a pile of two-by-fours in your room. Next!"

Every other series of skits was taped the same way, including KORN Radio, Lulu's Truck Stop, Samuel B. Sternwheeler and the Culhanes, a family of goofballs who got everything wrong. The father said George Washington's farewell address to his troops was "So long, guys."

No one had ever produced a series of shows in this manner. Anne Nelson had turned John and me into production-efficiency monsters.

After a couple of weeks of *Hee Haw* sketch-writing in Hollywood, we realized we needed more writers. We hired our old friend Jack Burns from *Kraft Music Hall* and he suggested George Yanok, whom he had worked with on other projects. Now the six of us dug in and got as much done as we could before it was time to get on down to Nashville. Archie, Gordie and George flew down, while Jack, John and I, exhausted, took the train to get a day and a half of rest before we began our whirlwind *Hee Haw* production schedule.

Meanwhile, back at the house I was sharing with Norman Baer, his girlfriend and Valerie Crawford, things had changed. Valerie and I were now sharing a bedroom, quite happily. It had been many, many years since I could go home after work without trepidation.

Valerie and I got along so well, in fact, we soon moved to an apartment for a little more privacy. She was still working with D'Antoni/ Baer Productions and I had just completed 26 *Jonathan Winters* shows and jumped right into *Hee Haw*. I was working my brains out, which severely limited my time with Valerie. I began to sense she wasn't pleased with the way the relationship was going.

Then I left on a train for Nashville.

When the train pulled into the Nashville station, Archie Campbell was there to meet us with a wagon pulled by mules that looked like they'd been grazed on by moths. "Hop on the back," Archie said, "and we'll make a grand entrance into town."

I didn't know what he was talking about, but I leapt onto the wagon with John while Archie drove the mules, or whatever it is you do with mules. People on the street looked at us like we were crazy.

"Here's the main street," Archie announced proudly. "Wave at the folks!"

It was obvious that the people of Nashville had no idea who on earth we were, but we waved and they looked at us like we were even crazier. "They don't know *us*," John said to Archie.

"They will, they will! We're gonna give 'em a tickle they'll never forget with *Hee Haw*." Archie had more confidence than I did, but what the hell, he was a Nashville native.

A police car pulled up beside our wagon. "Whatcha got goin' on, Arch?" an officer called out the window.

"We're fine, Dave. Just gettin' the show on the road."

"If you say so, Arch, but if them critters do somethin' on the road, you clean it up."

"Will do, Dave," Archie said, and he steered the donkeys into a Holiday Inn parking lot. "Here's where y'all are stayin'. Make yourself at home."

Gordie Tapp stood in front of the motel, waiting for us. "How'd it go?" he asked.

"We were welcomed with open arms," John said.

"You could tell they loved us," I added.

"No kidding?" Gordie asked.

"*Yes*, kidding!" I said. "*Really* kidding!"

We got settled in at the motel and then met with our entire production crew in a convention suite.

"Jack McFadden, Buck's manager, is really booking some of the top country performers," Sam Lovullo said excitedly. "And get this — the top price is $1,000!"

"How come we're getting them so cheap?" I asked. On every U.S. variety show I'd ever worked, the top price was $7,500.

"Because they'll be plugging their latest records on the whole CBS network, coast to coast. That's how come."

"And that's a big deal!" Archie said.

Archie, Sam and Bill Davis had also been adding more comedy performers to the cast, including Grandpa Jones and Stringbean.

"We need a comedy lady," John said, and Bill Davis had an answer.

"Jack McFadden says there's a really funny gal who's the emcee at a strip club in Dallas. Name's Lulu Roman."

"He says she's quite a bit overweight, but funny as hell," Archie added.

"Well, let's let her be funny as hell on *Hee Haw*," I said.

"I'll tell Jack to book her," said Sam.

"What have we got to lose — it's only a summer show," John pointed out.

"This agent dropped in to see me yesterday," Archie said, a grin growing on his face. "Well, he signed this guy who was interviewed on the radio about some giant fish he caught."

"I hope it was a funny fish," John said, and the group laughed.

"Well, it damn well turned out to be just that. He played the record for me and it was *hi*-larious!"

"What else has he done?" I asked.

"Nothin'. He's not a professional, but the agent claims if you drove down to Cummings, Georgia, to meet this fella you would not be sorry."

"That sounds intriguing. Can we hear the record?" John asked.

"He wouldn't let me have it. It's his only copy."

"I have a hunch we should go down to Cummings, Georgia, tomorrow and meet this, uh, what's his name?"

"Junior Samples," Archie said.

At the time I didn't realize how important that name would be to us. Archie arranged everything with the agent, gave us the directions and John and I drove over to Cummings, Georgia, the next morning. Cummings was a little Dogpatch of a town. The sheriff was sitting in a car on the main — and only — street. We asked him the way to Junior Samples' house.

"Whatcha want him for?"

"We want to put him on a show."

"You gonna put silly old Junior in a show?" he asked, amazed.

"You never know," John said.

The sheriff pointed us in the right direction and we walked up a pebbly path to a nice little house. The front door burst open and out came a chubby man with a ruddy face as jolly as old Saint Nick's, a big warm smile, sparkling blue eyes and a bad haircut. "You the fellas from the new *Hee Haw* show? I'm Junior Samples and this is my wife."

When he said the word *wife*, a woman's head popped out from behind him. She looked older than Junior, but I think everybody did. He just seemed so full of fun and energy.

"We're having lunch outside in the garden." He motioned us into his house. The interior was cramped, with odd bits of furniture, but the place was clean and neat as a pin. The garden Junior mentioned was out back. It was a real garden with rows of what looked like vegetables, just starting to sprout. "You sit there, Mr. Frank, and you there, Mr. John." The chairs were painted nail kegs with cushions on top. They looked strange, but they were comfortable. Mrs. Samples began placing bowls of food on the wooden table. When the table was fully loaded, she stood behind Junior, holding a tree branch covered in leaves.

"This here is homemade turtle salad," Junior announced, pointing to a dish.

I heard John's sharp intake of breath when the word *turtle* was mentioned. I'd heard of turtle soup, but I had never heard of homemade turtle salad. I'm sure store-bought turtle salad was out of the question.

Junior continued with his menu: "And this is fried okra with fried bass fillets. I caught the bass this mornin'. And this here is a pitcher of turtle gravy that goes over the bass and it's homemade, too. So dig in."

John and I both dug in as ordered and found that all the strange food was wonderful — even the turtle salad. As we ate, Mrs. Samples started waving the leafy branch over the food. I looked at Junior with a question on my face.

"Keeps the flies away," he said.

That seemed like a reasonable explanation, so I simply nodded and went on eating.

"I could use a glass of water," John said.

"There's a dipper and a pail there, right beside you," Junior pointed out. "The water's real cold, right from the well." The ice-cold well water was great — no chlorine, nothing but pure spring water.

During lunch Junior told us fishing stories that had us both *really* laughing. "If this guy can handle a camera," I whispered to John, "we've got a real find."

John nodded and smiled. "Would you like to be on the new *Hee Haw* show, Junior?"

"I would be real tickled," he said, beaming.

"Well, you're hired," I said. "We'll phone you about when to come to Nashville." I took some money out of my pocket. "Here's $400 on account." As I handed him the money, Mrs. Samples stopped shagging flies, snatched the money from Junior's hand, shoved it into her apron pocket and scooted into the house, never to be seen again. We left Junior, knowing our *Hee Haw* cast was now complete.

BACK IN NASHVILLE, EVERYONE WAS in town, including Buck, Roy and their managers. The cue cards had been written for all 12 shows. The cornfield set was up and we were ready to begin the next morning.

Our manager, Bernie Brillstein, showed up before we started taping and asked to look over the budget. "There's nothing in here for music arranging and copying," he said.

I explained that the musicians and backup singers in Nashville had their own musical system. They listened to a song and then wrote down their parts with a series of numbers. I don't know how it worked, but it sounded great and eliminated arranging and copying.

"That'll save a bundle of bucks," Bernie said with a large smile.

"The harmonies and everything come out perfectly," I assured him.

"You'd never get away with all that in L.A. or New York," Bernie pointed out.

"We're not getting away with *anything*, Bernie," John said. "These people are smart. They invented their own system."

"By the way," Bernie said, "Nick Vanoff called me."

"You going to represent him?" I asked.

"No, he and Bill Harbach want to be your partners."

"We've already been through that with the Five Incorporated thing," John reminded him.

"Nick isn't mad at us anymore?" I asked.

"Apparently not," Bernie answered. "Nick and Bill would like to buy half of your company and give each of you $50,000."

"Nancy won't let John go in with Nick, Bernie."

"Well, that's the deal. It's up to you."

"I think I could convince Nancy," John said.

"How?" I asked.

"I've got 50,000 reasons!" he exclaimed.

"Okay, I'll have the papers drawn up. What's the name of your company again?"

"Yonge Street Productions," I said.

"What's that stand for?"

"Yonge Street, Y-O-N-G-E, it's Toronto's main street."

"That figures," Bernie said with a chuckle.

Now we had new partners and new money. Nick and Bill called to congratulate us and told us they were getting a Yonge Street Productions office in Beverly Hills. They wondered if we would be interested in producing their *Hollywood Palace* show in the fall. We said yes and agreed to have dinner as soon as we returned.

"Are you keeping track of everything?" I asked John.

"It ain't *easy*," he laughed, shaking his head in disbelief.

When Junior Samples arrived in town, we tested him on camera. We gave him a joke to tell and he managed to screw it up in a very funny way. The camera *loved* him.

"You got a winner there!" Bill Davis said. "He jumps out at you."

Things were going smoothly and everything was on schedule. The TV crew at the Nashville station were terrific. They knew their stuff and did everything they could to make the show work. It was the same team feeling we all had on the Andy Williams summer show, 10 years earlier in 1959.

The night before we were to start taping, excitement streamed through the Holiday Inn. John and I were just having an after-dinner drink in my suite with Jack Burns and George Yanok when the phone rang. It was Roy Clark's manager — he wanted to see John and me in his room right away.

Roy's manager was sitting in an easy chair, holding a drink and wearing a silk bathrobe. He had straight dark hair, piercing hazel eyes, a smooth young face and he tried very hard to let you know that a manager from Tulsa knew his way around.

"Pour you a drink?" he asked.

"No, we're fine, Jim," I said.

"You wanted to see us?" John asked.

"I've got a problem," he said with a grimace.

"And it is . . . ?" John asked.

"I'm not happy with Roy's billing."

"You mean 'Starring Buck Owens and Roy Clark' is a problem?" I said.

"'Starring Roy Clark and Buck Owens' would be better."

"For you it would, you mean," John said. "By contract Buck Owens is in the first position."

"We'd accept changing that every other week."

"Or what?" I said.

"You start taping tomorrow and I wouldn't want to interfere with that schedule."

"We'll talk to Jack McFadden," I said. "I'm sure he'll understand."

"Is he fucking crazy?" Jack McFadden fumed in a room down the hall. "Buck is the star, the million-record seller!" Jack had been Buck's manager forever and he protected his star like he was Fort Knox.

"Then you're saying no to Jim's suggestion?" John asked.

"Hell," Jack said, "do you even have to ask me that?"

"No," I said meekly as I watched Jack impatiently tighten the belt of his woolen bathrobe around his slim figure. He turned his back on us and poured himself a drink. End of conversation.

We trudged back to Roy's manager down the hall.

"He says you're crazy, Jim," I said.

"I know. I heard him."

"Then that's that," John stated, and turned to leave.

"Not so fast," Jim said firmly. "That's not definitely that. We'll compromise and give Buck the first six shows and give Roy the last six. Seems only fair."

"To you, maybe," I said. "We'll see."

"*Fair!*" Jack McFadden yelled when we told him the latest proposal. "The man *is* fucking crazy! Just tell him no. We have a contract."

Back at Jim's room, I began, "Look, Jim —"

"I know! I've got ears. McFadden's being unreasonable."

"He's got a contract," I reminded him.

"And I've got Roy Clark."

Jim wasn't stupid; he knew we depended on Roy for a lot of comedy as well as his musical magic on four or five instruments. *We* knew that CBS wanted Buck because he was one of the top country performers in America. We had to stop the bathrobe-to-bathrobe trek we were on, right now.

"Look, Jim," I said, slapping my hand on his coffee table, "we are going to start taping *Hee Haw* tomorrow morning *with* or *without* Roy Clark!"

"It's up to you, Jim, and the billing stays the same!" John added sternly, and we left the room.

As we walked down the hall, Jack McFadden leaned out of his door and gave us a thumbs-up. We could also hear people clapping from inside all the rooms on the floor. The Holiday Inn had very thin walls.

"What if Roy doesn't show up?" I said to Bernie Brillstein.

"We'll sue his ass!" he said, and put his arms around our shoulders.

Chapter 16

✦

HEE HAWING ALL THE WAY TO THE BANK

THE NEXT MORNING ROY CLARK showed up at the studio, on time and ready for work. His manager, however, was nowhere to be seen.

Things were really coming together. The cornfield set filled the whole studio and it looked wonderful. The cast caught on to the rhythm of the quick joke scenes right away. After lunch Junior Samples and Roy popped up in the cornstalks together and both of them cracked up. Junior couldn't even talk, he was laughing so hard. His laughter jiggled him right off his feet. Bill Davis had the camera follow Junior as he hopped between rows of corn, doubled over. Eventually, everybody, including Buck, was howling hysterically, even the technicians and Bill up in the booth.

I ran upstairs to the booth and said, "Save that shot, Bill! We'll cut it up into little segments of Junior's hysterics and get close-ups of three or four of the cast saying, 'Let's see if Junior enjoyed that.' Then we'll cut to one of the clips of Junior, laughing his ass off in the corn."

That was how so many things on *Hee Haw* happened — on the spur of the moment. Another time, Junior was sitting on a chair, waiting to go on, when he fell sound asleep. Bill had the camera pan to him and we created another series of clips of Junior *not* enjoying something. We were all having so much fun, and we knew it would be reflected in the show. That had to be good. At the end of that first day, Bill announced over the PA system, "Thanks for all your hard work today. Keep up that energy for tomorrow. You can all go home now."

The next morning the cast showed up — everyone, that is, but Junior. I phoned the motel where he was staying and they told me that Junior had taken Bill at his word, hopped in his car and gone home to Cummings, Georgia.

I phoned Junior in Cummings. "What's going on, Junior?"

"Mr. Bill told me to go home and here I am."

"He meant for you to go back to the hotel, Junior."

"The hotel is not my home."

"I know but —"

"Cummings, Georgia, is my home, not the Holiday Inn."

"You should have asked somebody."

"Why, Mr. Frank? I *know* where my home is."

"Well, you're not supposed to be there."

"Does it mean I'm fired?"

"Not at all, you see —"

"Do I have to give back the $400?"

"Of course not, just get on back here, okay?"

"Sure, but don't nobody tell me to go home again."

I warned Bill to *never ever* mention the word *home* at the end of the day.

DURING THE MIDDLE OF THE second week, Marcia Minor, our brilliant executive production assistant, told John and me, "Senator Albert Gore Sr. would like to see you two at his home tomorrow at 10 a.m."

"Tell him we're very busy right now," John said.

"John," Marcia said, "Senator Gore is the power in this state, especially in Nashville. I suggest you comply."

We were still getting to know Marcia, but we already had great respect for her. Under her sleek blond exterior was a woman of great intelligence, experience and common sense. She wound up staying with *Hee Haw* for 21 years. The series couldn't have run one year without her.

Senator Albert Arnold Gore Sr. had been in Washington, D.C., for 31 years — 13 in Congress and 18 in the Senate. His son, Al Junior, was just out of college and working at a local TV station. We arrived at the senator's modest mansion at 10 to 10, naturally.

"The senator will see you in the library," an aide said. "Follow me."

Senator Gore was sitting at a large, impressive desk, surrounded by a zillion books. When the aide had said "library," he wasn't joking. The senator was very senatorial-looking, grayish hair and not too tall. He sized John and me up with friendly, discerning blue eyes and gave us an election-campaign handshake that was more than firm.

"So, you two gentlemen are the producers of this new *Hee Haw* show?"

"That is correct, Senator," John replied.

The senator continued, not acknowledging John. "Through certain channels I have heard what is going on at the station WLAX."

I said, "We're taping the show there —"

The senator spoke right over me: "You're not making fun of our state, our city or our people, are you?"

"Not at all, Senator!" I said. "Just celebrating country music and having plain old country fun."

"You're welcome to come down anytime and see for yourself," John added.

The senator continued, completely ignoring anything we had said. "Because if I find out you're looking down your Hollywood noses at us or in any way making us the butt of your *Hee Haw* jokes, I'll stop you as fast as a brick wall stops a bull. Understand?"

"Perfectly," we both said.

"Well, then." He stood up. "It's been real neighborly having this nice little chat with you boys." He smiled and put out his hand for a second bruising handshake.

Without another word, the aide quickly ushered us out the door.

"How'd it go?" Marcia Minor asked when we got back to the studio.

"We told him to fuck off!" John snapped.

Marcia laughed. "No, seriously, he could cause us big trouble."

"We figured that, Marcia, and we were polite and agreed with everything the senator suggested," I said.

"You're good boys," Marcia said, patting us on the back. "It's the smart thing to do. When in Rome, right?"

"Oh, so right," John agreed, and we took our Hollywood noses back into our corny cornfield.

When I got back to the motel that night, there was a brief letter from Valerie. Since she was no longer working for D'Antoni/Baer, she was bored all alone in our apartment. So she was going home to England.

For a week, a month, forever? Valerie didn't say, though she did leave a phone number. It was a little disconcerting, to say the least.

Bernie Brillstein showed up for a visit that same evening with more bad news, but some good news as well. He told us that ABC had canceled *Hollywood Palace*. In September we'd be unemployed, but at least we had two new partners in unemployment, Nick Vanoff and Bill Harbach. The good news: Doris Day's manager had called and wanted to know if we'd be interested in taking over *The Doris Day Show* next year. Here was another major movie star in TV trouble. Doris Day's lackluster sitcom had run with moderate ratings for its first season.

"Of course we'd be interested, Bern," I said, a little annoyed, "but why is it we get called in to a show when the old staff is let go and we have to try and save things?"

"It's a compliment," Bernie said, trying to look at the bright side.

"The hell it is," John exclaimed. "They put us in a very tough position."

"They know you can do it."

"That's bullshit, Bernie. Do what? We didn't save Perry Como, we didn't save Judy Garland, or Jonathan Winters," I almost shouted.

"Well, are you interested?'

"Of course we are," I said.

"Then what was all that crap you just gave me?"

"This *Hee Haw* show is the first time since our early days in Canada that we've been able to start a show from scratch. It's so much more fun this way, without any inherited problems."

"Look, Bernie, we're just getting it off our chests, okay?" John said.

"Then I take it that's a yes and I'll tell Doris's manager you'll call him."

We finished taping *Hee Haw* in two months and we left Nashville for Los Angeles with 32 miles of videotape to edit down to a dozen hour-long shows. When the first show was edited, we screened it for Perry Lafferty and his staff at CBS.

"It sure is different," Perry commented, noncommittally.

Bob Tamplin, Perry's young assistant, said, "I don't think you should keep that old lady who sang on that front porch set."

"Old lady?" I said. "Bob, that old lady, as you call her, is Loretta Lynn, the Judy Garland of country music. She's the queen! Besides, she's only 34 years old."

"Oh," Bob said, "I had no idea. I'm not exactly a country music fan."

"Let's put it out there," Perry said, "and see what happens. Thank you, gentlemen. Your work was stellar."

This was hardly an enthusiastic response. John and I reminded one another that *Hee Haw* was just a summer replacement series and summer shows tend to come and go without much notice. In 1969 country music was considered a second- or even third-rate art form in the entertainment capitals of New York and Los Angeles. Hillbilly music, they called it. ASCAP, the American Society of Composers,

Authors and Publishers that had licenced and collected royalties for most musical artists since 1914, had not allowed country composers to be members until the mid-'60s. (ASCAP also shunned black and Latino artists.) Country music in 1969 was also thought to be politically incorrect, or "not cool," as Barbara Mandrell sang. Many country musicians tended to be culturally conservative, while the prevailing mood on both coasts was defined by psychedelic hippie peaceniks. John and I knew we were pushing a boulder up a hill with *Hee Haw*.

I CALLED VALERIE IN ENGLAND. She was staying with her parents, Alec and Della, who lived in a small town outside London. She suggested I fly over so we could talk everything through. I didn't quite know what she meant by "everything," but when all the *Hee Haw* shows were edited and ready for airing, I bought a round-trip ticket for London. Valerie met me at the airport. She had booked us a room at the Grosvenor Hotel on Park Lane.

"My parents are anxious to meet you," she said as we settled down in our room.

"I believe that can be arranged," I said, and gave her a kiss.

"I've missed you," she said.

"Me, too."

"I hope we can be together for a while."

"All the *Hee Haw* shows are done. We have a meeting with Doris Day in two weeks and that's about it for now."

"I know what 'for now' means in your business."

"Can't be helped. I do what I do."

"I know, but if we could get a house it would make such a big difference."

The word *house* scared the hell out of me, but I did think about her proposal. We went out to dinner and when we came back to the hotel I had a message to call John in L.A.

"You won't believe it!" he shouted over the long-distance line.

"What? What?" I asked.

"*Hee Haw* is No. 1 in the ratings. The first two episodes, No. 1! Perry Lafferty and everyone at CBS are thrilled."

"I can't believe it! Wow! All that work and the turtle salad paid off."

I hopped the next plane for L.A. I asked Valerie to come along, but she said no.

The show remained No. 1 for all 12 weeks of its run, Sunday nights at nine. Some critics hated it and others loved it as a piece of mined gold Americana. Whatever it was, somebody out there liked us. It was a good feeling.

That good feeling got even better at the end of that summer when we were invited to the Country Music Awards. Charley Pride and Glen Campbell announced that Frank Peppiatt and John Aylesworth were the country music men of the year. They called us up to the stage and presented us each with an engraved silver statuette of a Stetson. *Hee Haw*, they said, had given a huge boost to country music all over America. A simple little country show sure was making waves.

When Valerie returned to Los Angeles, I bought a nice, normal house on Doheny Drive, just off Sunset Boulevard. Valerie seemed much happier once we had moved in. I guess I was, too. I felt a little more like I belonged somewhere.

BEFORE OUR FIRST MEETING WITH Doris Day, her manager warned us not to mention booze or cigarettes or anything off-color in front of her. So it was with great trepidation that we rang her doorbell in Beverly Hills.

A maid answered and led us into a beautiful living room where the beautiful Doris Day was waiting for us.

"Sit down, guys," she said. "My name is Doris Day."

"We know," I replied, sensing the humor in her voice, "but I never would have guessed. Right, John?"

"Never," John said. "You're much prettier live than in the movies."

She laughed and picked up a glass from the coffee table. "I'm having a gin and tonic. What'll you have?"

"That suits us just fine."

"Linda," she called, "two more gee and tees!"

We couldn't believe it — two gin and tonics from Doris Day. She was so damn nice, down-to-earth, and she did have a great sense of humor. We talked about her show, explaining some changes we had in mind, and she seemed to like our proposals. Finally, she said her manager would talk with our manager, but as far as she was concerned, she wanted us to work with her.

We called our manager with the good news. Bernie's response was "She wants you guys only because you're not Jewish."

That hurt. I wondered whose side my manager was on. As for Doris Day, we saw absolutely no evidence of any bias. Bernie had taken a cheap shot at Doris, John and me.

Meanwhile, over at CBS they were beginning to air the new *Leslie Uggams Show* on Sundays at nine. The ratings were nowhere near those *Hee Haw* earned in that time slot during the summer. Perry Lafferty called us in for a meeting. "Could you get your *Hee Haw* show ready to go on in early December?" he asked.

"I don't see why not," John said. "The sets and costumes are all stored in Nashville."

"Look, you guys, please keep this under your hat, but I think we're going to have to cancel *Leslie Uggams* soon. Can you really be ready?"

"We have to give the talent some warning," I said.

They did indeed cancel *The Leslie Uggams Show* and gave *Hee Haw* the green light. We explained to Doris Day that *Hee Haw* had to take precedence over her, since it was our very own show. Doris understood and wished us luck.

We called Nick Vanoff and Bill Harbach, our new partners, to share the news.

"Can you do it in time?" Nick asked.

"It will be easy if we can hire the same staff," I said. "They already know the ins and outs of *Hee Haw*."

"Does Yonge Street Productions have offices in Beverly Hills yet?" John asked.

"Be ready in a week," Bill Harbach said.

"That'll be our *Hee Haw* headquarters," Nick explained.

"Can you get part of your staff from *The Hollywood Palace* to work there?" I asked.

"No problem," Nick said.

Sam Lovullo started arranging the studio crew in Nashville, Bernie Brillstein began re-booking the summer cast and Jack McFadden got busy booking guest stars. We'd be doing around 20 shows with a much bigger budget. We had a lot of writing ahead of us.

Nick and Bill had chosen a wonderful location for the Yonge Street Productions offices on North Canon Drive in downtown Beverly Hills, and the place was a hive of activity. We decided to plan and write the first 10 shows in Hollywood and then move on to Nashville and continue writing based on the rewrites of the first few shows.

CBS moved our show to Tuesday nights at nine, and put *The Glen Campbell Goodtime Hour* in our old slot, Sundays at nine. Suddenly, country was cool at the network. We weren't No. 1, but we did damn well — some weeks in the Top 10, other weeks in the Top 20. CBS was very pleased.

My relationship with Valerie was also much better. I was home a lot more and it was *our* home. We went out to dinner often and she had met some nice girlfriends. Valerie seemed to understand that I had to leave her in October and stay in Nashville through November. A lot of money was involved.

THE SHOW WAS SCHEDULED TO air the first week in December, and we made it with a half day to spare. The editing machine was still hot when the donkey brayed "HEE HAW!" that first Tuesday night.

During that year, I met one of the funniest men I would ever know, Gailard Sartain. Gailard drove to Nashville from Tulsa to audition for us in 1971. I was blown away by his talent and hired him on the spot as a regular for the 1972 season. After the audition Gailard and I spent a couple of days making our way through every bar in town, keeping each other in stitches and hangovers. It was the beginning of an unshakable friendship. Everything Gailard did was funny and he added a lot to *Hee Haw*, where he turned out to be a regular for two decades.

I invited my children to come down to Nashville for spring break. I had not seen them for more than a year, not since their brief visit to Los Angeles shortly after their mother had spirited them off to Canada. In the meantime, Marilyn had a lawyer send me a separation agreement with generous provisions for alimony and child support. I signed it, no questions asked, and honored the document to the letter, month after month, year after year. Though I had heard Marilyn was still telling anyone who would listen that I had abandoned her and the girls without a penny, she had quietly bought a big house in a tony section of Toronto and was driving a brand-new Cadillac. I never confronted her about the sale of our New York house or what she did with the money. I was just relieved to be rid of both Marilyn and that damned 200-year-old coach house.

My darling girls, on the other hand, I missed terribly. I had broken a sacred bond with them. Could I ever repair it? Could I ever forgive myself? Would *they* ever forgive *me*?

The day their flight was to arrive, I was at the Nashville airport, anxiously waiting to see them. Three full-blown teenagers ran up and hugged me. What had happened to my little girls? How could they have changed so much in less than a year? Robyn was 14 now, Marney was 12 and Melissa 11. What joy, kissing and holding them again!

"I've got loads of Dog Sam stories for you," I said.

"Oh, Dad!" Melissa snorted, rolling her eyes. "Dog Sam is for babies."

During their stay in Nashville, I took them with me to the studio every day and they had great fun with the cast and crew. After work we went out for long, quiet dinners. We took up where we had left off the year before, and yet I sensed a new space between us — dark, deep and very sad. In a flash the week was over and I tearfully saw them off at the airport.

I had been so busy I had not realized how much I had missed them. I promised them they could come back in the summer if the show was renewed. They liked that idea a lot and so did I. They wound up coming to Nashville many, many times over the next decade. When Robyn was old enough, she even worked on the show during summers.

WE FINISHED OUT THE SEASON, and I returned to Valerie and L.A. Then, in May, CBS renewed *Hee Haw* for another 26 shows, so off I went again to Nashville for six weeks, taped 13 shows and brought them back to L.A. to edit. In late summer we returned for six more weeks and taped another 13 shows, completing another successful season. At least, we *thought* it was a successful season, until the new president of CBS, Robert Wood, announced that he was going to urbanize the network. In 1971, he canceled all the country shows, including *The Andy Griffith Show*, *Green Acres*, *The Beverly Hillbillies* and, of course, *Hee Haw*.

We sat around our Yonge Street offices, absolutely stunned. "The show is too damned successful to drop out, damn it!" Nick said.

"What's the answer?" I asked.

"Syndication," Sam Lovullo said.

In those pre-cable days, each of the networks — ABC, CBS and NBC — had contracts with affiliated stations across the nation to play the shows they produced in New York and Hollywood. By canceling us, CBS had thrown us off all their affiliates. Networks never picked up shows that had been canceled by other networks. However, there were hundreds of independent, non-affiliated, locally owned stations across America. They tended to play local programs and reruns that had been sold to each of them individually by a "syndicator." No syndicator would touch an original show because it was too risky — many producers had lost their shirts trying to circumvent the networks by going straight to syndication.

"Sam's right!" Nick said. "We'll send a telegram to every TV station in America, saying that next year we will make 26 new *Hee Haw* programs available to them, for free."

The reaction to Nick's plan was amazing. In less than two weeks we had heard from over 200 stations that wanted to carry our show. Ironically, many of those stations were CBS affiliates who had been sorry to see us go and had spare hour slots to fill, especially in the early evenings. It was a good deal for the stations: there were a dozen 30-second commercial positions in each show, and we would give the stations six half-minutes to sell locally and keep the fees for themselves. Yonge Street Productions would keep six half-minutes of commercial time plus a station break that we would sell to national sponsors, thus eliminating the network middleman.

We had to raise a million dollars cash to produce the first 13 shows. Nick and I put up our new houses as collateral for a million-dollar bank loan. John couldn't participate because he didn't own a house at that time. Nonetheless, I gave him half of my share, for nothing. Bernie Brillstein told us we were crazy, that we should just swallow the CBS cancelation and move on. He refused to help the enterprise in any way. But we had the money and we let our cast and crew know that we were back in business. The local stations, for their part, were having no trouble selling their six half-minute commercial slots at very good prices.

Now it was up to us to sell our minutes. Nick and I went to New York's Madison Avenue ad agencies very confident, because the previous year's ratings had been excellent. Confidence didn't turn the trick, though, because the sophisticated New York advertising people turned their big-city noses up at *Hee Haw*. But even if it had not been a country show, CBS had canceled us, making us damaged goods. From ad agency to ad agency, day after day, up and down Madison Avenue, I can still hear the doors slamming in our faces. It was beginning to look as though Nick and I would be bankrupt and finished in show business. As we walked to yet another agency appointment one day, Nick clutched his chest and staggered against a store window on Madison and 57th Street. He thought he was having a heart attack. Frantic, I shoved him into a doorway and massaged his chest vigorously for several minutes. Finally, he straightened himself up and said, "Thanks, that feels better."

"How much better?" I asked anxiously.

"Enough to keep going and *sell* this fucker!" he screamed. Sweat poured down his face. Passersby did double takes. Even in blasé Manhattan we had created quite a scene.

We did not sell the fucker, though.

During that nightmare trip we ran into Loretta Lynn and related our problem to her.

"Why, heck," she said. "I've been the national spokeswoman for Crisco since forever! I'll just call the big boss and tell him to buy half a little ole minute on the *Hee Haw*."

We went on the air with only one commercial — Crisco. Good as that was, it wasn't nearly enough to cover the costs of producing 26 hour-long programs. But there was no turning back. We were contractually obligated to provide all our stations with 26 new shows. We were losing money fast. One small commercial along with public service spots by the likes of Smokey the Bear did not nearly break us even, much less add up to a profit. The public service spots were free, after all — we gave the damn things away.

Near the end of the first 13 weeks, the national syndication show ratings were published. All 13 *Hee Haw* episodes emerged as No. 1 in

America! When he read the ratings results, Nick Vanoff said, "We're gonna make those Madison Avenue fuckers pay through the nose, Frankie!" A headline in *Variety* read, "'Hee Haw' picks and grins its way all the way to the bank."

The slammed doors on Madison Avenue suddenly opened and in one day we sold all of our half-minute spots, plus the full-minute station break, for very big prices. We were No. 1! For many years we did not raise the rate for good old, loyal Crisco. They had made a sweet deal, indeed. Now we were off and running. Big money was coming in, our houses were saved and we were putting hundreds of good, talented people to work for years to come.

Suddenly, we also found ourselves at the pinnacle of the Hollywood social scene. Nick had hired a publicist for Yonge Street Productions who told us we needed to have a big lavish party to publicize our phenomenal success. Not much of a party monster, I wasn't interested, but Nick pointed out that it was all tax deductible and wouldn't cost us much in the long run. The next day the publicist submitted a guest list for the party. It included names like Gregory Peck, Bette Davis, Charlton Heston, Maureen O'Hara, plus the heads of all the major film and TV studios and talent agencies. I thought the publicist had to be delusional.

"I've never met any of these people," I said, handing the list back to him.

"That doesn't matter, Frank!" the publicist said. "I've been doing this for many years. Believe me, they'll come."

And he was right. Most of them did come to hover like moths around the bright light of new money.

Chapter 17

✦

DROWNING IN MONEY

AFTER WE HAD FINISHED OUR first 13 *Hee Haw* shows for the '72–'73 season, we had a few months off to rest. I really needed it. I was looking forward to spending some time with Valerie in the nice, normal house I had bought on Doheny Drive. But no such luck. Gary Smith and Dwight Hemion called from England and asked John, Jack Burns and me to write eight one-hour specials called *The Kopykats*. The show would star five or six of the best impressionists in the business, including Frank Gorshin, George Kirby, Marilyn Michaels and Rich Little, the Snowback who, since his Judy Garland debut, had become a big star in the world of impressions.

Valerie was excited by the idea because she wanted to go home and visit her family and friends. So Bernie Brillstein made a very sweet deal and we were off to London. I asked John if Nancy would be going and he informed me that they were getting a divorce. He had not said one word to me about any problems with his five-year-old second marriage, which had resulted in four babies. As usual, John kept his troubles private.

In London, we were each supplied with a lovely apartment on Hill Street behind the Grosvenor Hotel. A car and driver picked us up every morning and drove us to the vast, fabled Pinewood Studios,

Frank Peppiatt

outside the city, where we had plush offices and where the show would be taped. As the impressionists arrived, they were asked to autograph a large sign and list the various voices they did. Frank Gorshin had the most impressive list — around 20 — until Rich Little came and listed 62, all of them spot on, as the Brits put it. He was amazing. The shows were fun to write, especially since Gary and Dwight booked such interesting hosts, including Orson Welles, Robert Young, Raymond Burr, Steve Lawrence and, believe it or not, Ed "Tonight we've got a really *big shoe*" Sullivan.

The U.S. presidential election was imminent and almost all the impressionists were very interested, though not politically. They wanted to be sure they could imitate whoever was elected. Only Marilyn Michaels wasn't paying any attention to the campaign. Even if she could imitate the future first lady, who would care? The performers were always stopping John and me in the hall or the parking lot, assailing us: "I do a great Bogie now, sweetheart"; "My Gary Cooper is dead on"; "I can sing like Cary Grant"; "If you need John Wayne, I'm here, mister"; "What kind of fool am I? Anthony Newley. Right?" One day Rich Little walked into our office with voice No. 63. "Ladies and gentlemen," he announced, "the Broadway star, Miss Carol Channing!" He sang half a chorus of "Hello Dolly" and it was perfect. If you closed your eyes, you'd swear Carol Channing was in your office.

The week Ed Sullivan hosted the show, there was more comedy off camera than on. We were rehearsing a sketch where Ed was dressed as an American Indian. He had a large feather headdress, leather pants, beaded doeskin shirt and jacket, and his face was covered in war paint. Halfway through the rehearsal Ed said he had to go to the washroom.

The stage manager directed him. "Turn right, out the door, then go to the first hallway, turn left, and it's the second door on the right. You can't miss it, Mr. Sullivan."

From the director's booth Dwight announced, "Take 10, everybody." Ten, 15, 20 minutes went by, but Ed didn't return. Apparently, he had taken a wrong turn and was lost in the halls of the monster-movie studio, wearing a full Indian costume, complete with war paint.

Gary Smith was checking his watch with a very worried look. "Billy," he called, "you better go and find him."

"Right," the prop man said, and went out the door. After a minute or two a uniformed security guard came in. "We're holding a geezer at the main gate who's in an Indian getup and sez he's Ed Sullivan, whoever that is."

"Would you please bring him in here?" Gary said.

"You're welcome to the bloke," the guard said, and left.

At last Ed came back, led by another security guard. "'Ere's your red Indian — says 'e's some mucky-muck named Ed Sullivan."

"I *am* Ed Sullivan," Ed said, wrenching his arm out of the guard's grasp, "and my *big shoe* is on Sunday night, everywhere!"

"It ain't on 'ere, Eddie me boyo, believe my fish and chips."

"Do you own a television?" Ed demanded of the guard.

"Yes, I surely do."

"Then you must know my *really big shoe!*"

"Not from Adam, me lad."

"Your show is not on in London, Ed," Gary said.

"Well! I'll fix that when I get back home!"

"I'm sure you will, Ed. Now let's get on with rehearsal. You just come in as Sitting Bull and you —"

"I've got to go to the washroom."

"I thought you went," Gary reminded him.

"I couldn't find it."

"Okay, go ahead, and you go with him, Billy," Gary ordered. "And *bring him back!*"

Ed was excellent, and his Indian was a really big hit on the *shoe.*

Valerie brought her mother, father and younger sister up to

London to watch some of the taping and they didn't know who Ed Sullivan was, either, but I didn't mention it to Ed. She also invited her cousin Arthur and his wife, Anne, to a taping. Afterward all of us, including John, went out to dinner in London. Throughout the dinner John was giving Anne the eye; I didn't think anything of it at the time.

The eight *Kopykats* shows aired all over Great Britain and on ABC in the United States. It was hard work, but the shows came out well and received good critical reviews. I was also more tired than ever. All I wanted was some time off in my Doheny Drive house, where I had slept but a few nights in the year since I had bought it. But there was no reprieve. We had to get back to Nashville to write and produce the last 13 *Hee Haw* shows for that season.

And there was more. Nick Vanoff called us in Nashville and told us he was going to produce the new *Julie Andrews Hour* on ABC. Julie told him she loved *The Kopykats* and would like to use the show's writers. Nick told her that since John and I were his partners, he could give Julie a Yonge Street package and toss in Jack Burns to write and Bill Davis to direct. She and ABC agreed.

In the 1960s Julie Andrews was one of the biggest movie stars on the planet. She had little, if any, interest in television and probably felt disdain for the medium. However, in the late '60s and early '70s, she made two very expensive and monumentally unsuccessful films — *Star* and *Darling Lili*. All at once she was box-office poison and rumored to be in a tight cash squeeze. ABC offered her a huge sum to star in *The Julie Andrews Hour*. Reluctantly, she accepted.

We all assumed, incorrectly as it turned out, that the many big stars who had worked with Julie on the big screen would clamor to be guests on her television show. But Julie's movie co-stars had as little interest in TV as she did. Nor could Yonge Street Productions pay guest stars anything near as large a fee as Julie's. They all said, "No thanks."

Nick, Bill Davis, John and I, plus our writing staff — Jack Burns, Jay Burton (my old *Como Show* pal), George Bloom and Lila Garrett — sat around our new ABC offices, pondering what to suggest. There was a long, nerve-racking silence. The opening show *had* to be spectacular. No B-list stars would do.

An idea flashed into my head. "We can book two big stars!" I began. "One has an Academy Award and the other has a Tony Award."

"And they'll do the show?" Nick asked anxiously.

"I guarantee it!" I said.

"Okay, who? Frank, who?" Bill Davis asked.

"Eliza Doolittle and Mary Poppins."

Everyone looked at me as though I were slightly deranged.

"Jesus!" Nick finally said, and turned to our director. "Could we do it, Billy?"

"Yes," Bill answered. "It'll take a little extra time, but yes, and it could be sensational!"

Julie loved the idea, and we started writing with Doolittle and Poppins in mind. We screened both *Mary Poppins* and *My Fair Lady* to get us in the mood, and everything started to click.

My daughter Robyn was 18 now and she had just graduated from my old high school, Lawrence Park Collegiate. I flew her down to Hollywood for the summer. She lived with Valerie and me on Doheny Drive and worked as a production assistant on the show, assisting Julie and running errands until she went back to Toronto in the fall to start college. She thrived at the job and became friendly with Julie and, thankfully, with Valerie, as well. I drove her to work every day and home every night. I was really getting to know my talented daughter and maybe she was starting to understand her father a little better, too.

We completed the script for the first show and, believe me, the newspapers gobbled up the idea that our guest stars were Eliza Doolittle and Mary Poppins. We had also hired, as regulars, our favorite impressionist, Rich Little, and a wonderful comedic actress, Alice Ghostley. The music was arranged and conducted by Nelson Riddle, with whom we had fallen in love on the Frank Sinatra special. He was the best.

When the first *Julie Andrews Hour* went on the air, it caused a sensation. The reviews were raves and the show won 11 Emmys, including best comedy variety show. Julie won an Emmy, our director Bill Davis won one, and Nick collected the best show Emmy and thanked John and me from the stage, as had Davis. We were nominated for a writing Emmy, but we were beaten out by the *Laugh-In* writers. All in all, things turned out pretty damn well.

During the year we could see that Julie was exhausted. "It's like doing a fucking movie every week," she said. The word *fucking* sounded refined the way she said it with her English accent. It was Judy Garland all over again — one or two movies a year was fine, but not 26 in a row. Julie started wanting the show simplified — more songs, less comedy and maybe some drama. She had seen the English actor, Keith Michell, doing Shakespeare on the BBC, which aired here on public television, and wanted to bring him on board.

"But nobody knows him here," Nick explained to her.

"He was just on PBS."

"Nobody watches that, Julie."

"Well, they should, he was wonderful. I want him as a guest. We could do something meaningful."

"Okay, it's your show," Nick said. He shrugged and left to make a phone call.

Keith Michell showed up in all his Shakespeareiousness, and he and Julie decided to do a scene from the Bard. They also wanted to do another scene from a modern play, something dealing with a more up-to-date theme. It had to be about five minutes long, she told us. Julie's request was a bit of an insult to John and me and our writing staff. We were professional writers and she was asking us to do research.

We didn't have much time for play reading and we didn't have much luck finding anything suitable.

"Screw it!" Jack Burns said. "Let's write one."

"They'll know," John said.

"I'll bet they don't," Jack stated firmly.

We wrote a five- or six-minute scene where Keith played a sprite dressed in leaves and flowers who was saving the world from parking lots, highways and landing fields that obliterated nature. He met Julie in the forest and proceeded to convince her that his view of the world was the only right one. We had a lot of laughs writing it.

When we read the piece to Julie and Keith, Julie held back — she was not as well versed in the classics as Keith.

"Hmm . . ." Keith began, stroking his Shakespearean beard. "Interesting . . . even humorous . . . in spots. Who wrote it?"

"Joyce Aspern," Jack said, poker-faced.

"I don't believe I know her and —"

I interrupted Keith, "Joyce is a man."

"Oh, of course!" Keith said, "Now I remember Joyce Aspern. He's good!"

"Then let's do it," Julie said, smiling brightly.

They performed the scene on the show and it turned out very well. I have never told this story before — I hope Julie doesn't get angry. We were only trying to help. If there *is* a Joyce Aspern who is a writer, we're sorry.

The ratings for the show began high, but slid continuously afterward. By the 24th show the ratings were so low that ABC canceled *The Julie Andrews Hour*. Apparently, America wasn't ready for Keith Michell as a wood nymph. Julie took her enormous fee and returned to London.

A WEEK BEFORE THE 1973 Emmy show, where we expected to win a dozen awards, Valerie moved out and took her own apartment.

Although I had set her up in her own antiques store (which she aptly named A King's Ransom), paid for all the antiques in it, as well as the shipping from England and the import tariffs, she felt out of place in the Doheny house. Valerie wasn't one to verbalize her discontents — she *acted* them out. Her attempted manipulation just made me angry. I was hurt, too. I closed up my house and went to Nashville to work on the first 13 *Hee Haw* shows of the '74–'75 season, and I watched the Emmy Awards alone in my Nashville hotel room.

Back in L.A., I sold the Doheny house and rented on Malibu Beach in the Colony. It was peaceful and beautiful there. Finally, I had a whole summer to rest. Marney and Melissa were ecstatic when I invited them to come down and stay with me for the summer. They swam in the ocean every day and got to know some of the movie stars' kids on the beach.

Halfway through the summer, things were going just fine and dandy. Two of my kids and me, the beach, the ocean and peace and quiet. Then, one day, Bernie Brillstein showed up. It was a pretty good drive from Bernie's office to Malibu, so he wasn't just dropping in. He was there for a reason and I didn't like the feeling I had — trepidation.

"Good news," he began. "Jackie Gleason's people want you and John to be head writers on a *Honeymooners* Thanksgiving special."

"I don't think so, Bern. My kids are here and I want to relax before we start another 13 *Hee Haw*s.

"John needs the money."

"Then let *him* do it!" Deep down I knew John couldn't get a job without me. Bernie knew it, too, which was why he had driven all the way out here. Neither one of us said it out loud. "Besides, he's making plenty on *Hee Haw*, not to mention all we made on Julie Andrews." Even though, throughout our careers, John and I made the same money, he was always on the verge of financial ruin.

"Well," Bernie sighed, "he married Anne."

"He *what*? Valerie's cousin's wife?" I was speechless. John had never said anything to me about Anne.

"Yes, and he pays his first wife and two kids alimony and child support *and* he pays Nancy and *four* kids."

"And he and Jack Burns take those goddamned cruises at a hundred grand a pop. Jack can afford them, since he doesn't have a family, but John can't. Besides, I pay hefty alimony and child support to Marilyn, too, you know."

"I know, Frank. Give John a break." Bernie flashed me his salesman's smile.

"When do they want us?"

"Next Monday."

"Shit, Bernie, I'll have to send my kids home!"

"Please, Frank. John's really on the edge of disaster here."

"Why didn't he come out here and ask me himself?"

"He's embarrassed. You've always got your shit together."

"I wish!"

"Sure you do, Frank. That's why you can do this."

"Oh, hell! Okay!"

Marney and Melissa were not at all pleased about going home a month early. I tried to convince them I owed it to John. The hell I did! I couldn't even convince *myself*. And I sure as hell have never forgiven myself for disappointing Marney and Melissa so badly. To this day I don't really understand why I did that.

I FLEW TO FLORIDA WITH two other writers from Hollywood, Alan Katz and Don Rio. We were given a condominium at Gleason's golf course and spa. John showed up with his new wife, Anne, her 10-year-old-son *and* a nanny. How sweet it was, as Gleason might say.

We met with Jackie and presented some ideas the four of us had come up with. Mr. Gleason didn't remember John and me from that sleepy, sappy Saturday on the golf course nearly 10 years before. We didn't remind him. We pitched an idea for an hour-long Thanksgiving episode of *The Honeymooners* that would be a musical comedy, but Mr. Gleason would have none of it. He knew exactly what he wanted. The first half-hour would feature a *Honeymooners* Thanksgiving in the Kramden's dreary apartment with his wife, Alice, and neighbor, Ed Norton. The second half-hour would star Reggie Van Gleason and his liver, with no mention of Thanksgiving.

Why he had decided on this format, I had no idea. He almost dictated the whole show to us. My God, why had he flown us in from Los Angeles, put us up in style, paid us top dollars, only to tell us what to write? I couldn't figure it out then, and probably never will.

After Jackie had practically written the show by himself, he wanted us to concentrate on opening jokes or maybe even a mono-logue, and to shove the material we'd written under his front door at the end of every day. We started working on the jokes, and he never said whether he liked the stuff or hated it. We weren't sure he even read it. He just told us to keep on writing.

When the taping of the show was about to start, Mr. Gleason came into the writers' room. At last, we'd get some feedback on our writing — or so we thought.

"I'll take it from here," he announced. "You guys can go home."

Jackie Gleason was a monumental comedy talent — he made America laugh for many years. He made me laugh, too, but I would not answer a help wanted ad from Mr. Gleason.

BACK IN L.A. I RENTED a different house on Doheny Drive, this time just south of Sunset. It was tiny, but very comfortable for me. I also bought a two-bedroom condominium in Palm Springs. I went over to the King's Ransom to see how business was going. I had told Valerie when she moved out of the house that I would no longer back her store, and now she told me she had sold a few pieces at a profit. I reminded her that she hadn't figured in the cost of shipping and duties, which came to nearly as much as the value of the antiques.

"Oh," she said. Math wasn't her strong suit. All her smarts went into manipulation.

I then told her I had sold the big Doheny house.

"Gee," she said. "You didn't have to go that far!"

I also mentioned my little bungalow and the Palm Springs condo.

"Could I go down there and see it?" Valerie asked.

"It's not really furnished yet, but sure, let's go down this weekend."

"This is nice," Valerie said, walking around the almost empty condo a few days later. "I'd love a chance to furnish it."

"Be my guest," I said. "Surprise me."

Before driving back to Hollywood, we stopped for lunch in Palm Springs.

"You know, if we were married, I'd feel a lot more secure about everything," she said.

"I know what you mean, but I *am* married."

"But you've been separated for seven years. Are you going back?"

"No, I'm not." I was quiet, lost in thought. At last, I spoke again. "So why aren't I divorced?"

"I'm not asking you to get a divorce, Frank," she protested softly.

"I know. It's *my* idea, and it's a good idea after all this time."

"It's up to you."

"And *we* can get married."

"Yes," she said, flashing a big smile. "I would love to have our wedding in England."

And that's exactly what we did. Valerie flew to London to get things moving, wedding-wise. I went to Nashville to finish off the second 13 *Hee Haw*s of the year.

Marilyn, however, was very upset about the prospect of a divorce. But when her lawyer made an even better alimony and child support deal with me than she'd had during the separation, she finally agreed.

When all the pieces were in place, I arrived in London for the wedding and a big reception at the Grosvenor Hotel on Park Lane. All of Valerie's relatives attended. I was more than a little surprised when *I* got the bill.

"Isn't this bill for your father?" I asked Valerie.

"His money is all tied up in investments right now. He'll square it with you later," she said.

I had heard that song before. Marilyn's dad had had some financial problems, too. It had rankled then and it rankled now. Not an auspicious beginning. I remembered my dad's warning: "They could move in with you. Mark my words, sonny boy!"

Before I left L.A. for the wedding, I had moved out of the Doheny bungalow and rented a much larger furnished place with a pool in Beverly Hills. When we arrived back in L.A., we moved right in.

"This is okay," Valerie said, "but we have to look for a house with a tennis court. A house to *buy*."

"Why the tennis court?" I asked.

"A definite social advantage right now."

"I haven't played tennis in 30 years, Valerie."

"Were you any good?"

"No."

"We'll practise. You'll get good. You're an athlete."

"But why?"

"Believe me; it's very important — socially." She said this with a strength of conviction I had never seen in her before.

Who is this woman? I wondered. She had known me for six years now. She had to have noticed that I was not a partygoing kind of guy. I worked very long, hard hours at a job I loved. When I got home, I wanted peace and quiet. I didn't give a damn about "socially important" things, especially in Hollywood. I thought she understood that. It's the way it had been with us for years. Where had all this social stuff come from? I didn't quite get it.

Valerie went out with real estate agents every day, looking for some kind of social advantage. Hopefully, there were no old coach houses available. I checked with my accountant, Al Rettig, and he said it was a very good time to buy because the housing market in Beverly Hills was moving up every day.

Valerie was coming home exhausted from her house hunting, and her need for the tennis court made it all the more difficult.

"How'd the hunting go today?" I asked as I got home one evening.

"It's hopeless," she sighed, "but I think I found the answer."

"Skip the tennis court, right?"

"No, Frank, no! The agent showed me a fabulous acre of land, just off Coldwater Canyon and the owner *has* to sell. It's a steal."

I showed the land in question to my accountant and he agreed it *was* a steal. We purchased the property, but I prefer to think we stole it. The land had plenty of room for a tennis court and a pool. Valerie hired an architect, then a builder, and workers began erecting a house. It was going to cost a lot of money, but Valerie and the architect convinced me it was worth it.

Hee Haw had another very successful year and Yonge Street Productions continued making really big money. "You can afford the house," Nick said. "It's better than investing in the stock market." He set my financial mind at ease and I went about getting next year's *Hee Haw* ready to tape.

While the house was being built, we were talked into three extra bedrooms and a guest house. *What the hell*, I figured, *in for five hundred thou, in for a million.* I remembered my father saying that from time to time, only his version involved dimes and dollars. Valerie spent almost every day at the site, telling the builder what he was doing wrong. The builder phoned me at the office one day. "Mr. Peppiatt," he pleaded, "does she have to be there every fucking day?" At least she wasn't wearing overalls and workboots.

I went back to Nashville for two months and when I returned, the house and all the trimmings were only half-finished, but over budget — by a lot. "If she doesn't stop changing things," the builder complained, "it's gonna cost you even more!" Easy for him to say. The train had left the station. The money was disappearing quickly and I needed another source.

With impeccable timing, Nick came to the rescue. "Cher's new solo show is not working," he said. "CBS has talked her into letting Sonny come back and they want to bring us in to produce and write it. Whaddaya think?"

"I think yes. The house is killing me and I can really use the extra money."

"John can, too," Nick said. "Those cruises he takes with Anne and Jack Burns are really adding up. Tell Bernie to call me and we'll set it up."

I was feeling a hell of a lot better. Nick made a deal for Cher to hire Yonge Street Productions as a corporate team, which saved a lot of taxes. We, in turn, hired a female writing team as well as a male team. Cher loved the idea of lady writers, as she called them, being involved in the creative process. Cher invited the entire creative staff to dinner at the Beverly Hills Hotel. Sonny, her ex-husband now, was also there and Cher managed to nurture a great feeling of camaraderie among us. She was a smart cookie.

We developed some new running concepts for the show, and she and Sonny were very cooperative. Sonny certainly should have been cooperative; Cher was paying him $1 million to return. I had a fine time doing *The Sonny & Cher Comedy Hour* — the ratings were good and the publicity around Sonny and Cher reuniting didn't hurt. All in all, everyone was happy, CBS included. John and I and all the writers were nominated for a writing Emmy and this time we were beaten by Carol Burnett's writers. Cher told us how sorry she was, and that was nice. At least we got a plaque that said we'd been nominated. It was suitable for framing.

VALERIE'S AUNT AND TWO GROWN daughters wrote and told us they were planning to come visit us in Hollywood — we had invited them at the wedding reception. Valerie wrote back and told them to wait until the house was finished, and six months later, on the very day we were finally moving into our new home, her relatives arrived — the aunt, her two daughters, their husbands, a pair of small children, a babe in arms and a dog. We had plenty of room because we had added the three bedrooms, but it turned out they weren't here for just a visit. They had picked up stakes in England and were planning a permanent move to the United States — a move right into our house. My father's prophecy had come true.

I liked Valerie's relatives, but it was hard to keep liking them, week after week, month after month after month, ad infinitum. When I'd get home from the office, they'd be frolicking in the pool, whacking tennis balls around on the court, playing pool on my brand-new table or sitting around waiting for din-din. Valerie had hired a cook to handle the 25 or so meals a day we were eating. She also hired a butler to look after the housecleaning, sheet changing and general upkeep. The butter, eggs and milk delivery every day was immense. At least the milkman was smiling. When the relatives were finally dislodged from our house six months later, the milkman had tears in his eyes.

"Where did they move to?" he wanted to know. "Maybe they're on my route."

JOHN DIDN'T WANT TO DO the second year of the *The Sonny & Cher Comedy Hour* because, he said, he was tired of taking orders from women like Judy Garland, Julie Andrews and Cher. He had never mentioned this before. Given that John was always in need of money, it must *really* have pissed him off to have a lady boss. He couldn't afford to turn down work. With John now gone, Nick became executive producer and I was now the producer, which brought me into a much closer relationship with Cher. I don't remember her *ever* issuing any "orders." If she didn't like something, she simply said so, and we changed it.

As the season wore on, I could tell Cher was getting tired of the weekly grind. I was tired, too. Not only was I writing and producing Cher's show, but there was still *Hee Haw*. From the late '60s through the '70s we produced and wrote dozens of other shows not previously mentioned here. There was *Shields and Yarnell* (22 shows), *Hee Haw Honeys* (24 shows), *International Showcase* (in Munich — 10 shows), four Dinah Shore specials, three Mohawk Carpet specials, two Herb Alpert specials, one *Princess Grace in Monaco* special, a *Heck's Angels* pilot, the movie *Wake Me When the War Is Over* and various other unproduced screenplays. There were also six months of a nightly talk show in Toronto called *Almost Anything Goes*. This I agreed to do so I could spend time with my daughters, of whom I didn't see nearly enough.

Just as the fatigue was beginning to drive me insane, Cher approached me one day and said, "This is my last year on the show. It's too damn tiring."

"What if the network wants you to keep going?" I asked.

"They can go fly a kite. I'm going to be in the movies and maybe even become a star, Mr. Peppiatt," she stated firmly.

I understood, but I was sorry the show had to end. I had grown very fond of Cher. She had it all — talent, smarts and character. The last episode aired in 1977 and Cher did go into the movies and she did become a movie star. Eleven years later she won an Academy Award for best actress in a movie called *Moonstruck*, directed by that Lorne Greene academy graduate and my old Canadian friend, Norman Jewison. Cher showed 'em, and how!

The summer of '77, John and I returned to Nashville to write and produce another 13 *Hee Haws*. Marcia Minor pointed out that the next year would be *Hee Haw*'s 10th anniversary.

"We should do a *Hee Haw* anniversary special," Bill Davis suggested, and we took the idea to Perry Lafferty at CBS.

"Look, gentlemen," he said, "we canceled *Hee Haw*. Why would we celebrate that it's still going strong?"

Perry had a damn good point, so we took the idea to NBC and they bought it.

"You guys are going to be damn busy in Nashville this year," Nick pointed out. "Twenty-six *Hee Haw* shows and a 90-minute *Hee Haw* anniversary special."

"We can handle it, Nick," John said.

"I worry about your health, guys. We're not kids anymore."

Nick was right. I had just turned 52 and I was feeling it. I was edgy and forgetful and I was drinking to wind down from the constant pressure. My daily schedule was so complex, not even my excellent full-time secretary could keep it straight. I'd come home late every night and I'd be so tired that I just wanted to fall into bed. Then I'd lie there, unable to sleep, my mind racing with everything I had to do the next day. I'd get up and drink until I passed out and got a few hours of sleep. The next morning, hungover, I'd drag myself to my car and get myself to the office or the studio or the airport to fly to Toronto, Monaco or Nashville.

"You're becoming an alcoholic, Frank," Valerie said late one night after finding me nearly passed out on the kitchen table.

"Hardly an alcoholic," I said.

"You remind me of my father and I don't like it. It's very upsetting."

"I'm working hard, Val, and a drink or two relaxes me."

"If it was just a drink or two I wouldn't mind."

"Okay, I'll cut down."

"It's not *just* the drinking," she went on. "We have this beautiful house and we hardly ever have a party."

"We've been through this a hundred times, Valerie. You know I don't like Hollywood parties. They're fake."

"We should be entertaining every weekend with tennis parties and have the guests back for dinner. We have a fine cook and butler who would love it."

"Then invite them for tennis and dinner."

"Oh, you are the absolute limit, Frank Peppiatt!" she said, and stomped out of the room.

The butler woke me the next morning. Valerie wasn't there beside me in bed. "Mrs. Peppiatt is on the phone and she'd like to talk to you," he said.

"I can't take it anymore, Frank," Valerie said when I lifted the receiver. It was like she was accusing me of beating her or something. "I just can't live with you any longer."

"You want a divorce?"

"Maybe."

"Look," I said, "in two days I'm going to Nashville for the 10th anniversary special. While I'm gone you come and live here and in two weeks when I get back, we'll talk. Okay?"

"Okay, but I've made up my mind."

"Fine, but we have to talk first."

If things were rocky at home, they were hectic as hell in Nashville. The anniversary show was being produced at the brand-new Grand Ole Opry in Opryland, U.S.A. After the taping we hosted a huge cocktail party and dinner for the cast, crew, all our guest stars plus the governor of the state and everybody else who was anybody. Over the course of the evening, Nick, John and I made speeches, thanking everyone for their help and their belief in the show. The party was a big success.

I flew back to Los Angeles late the next day and arrived home about 10 p.m. The cook and the butler were there, but Valerie was staying with a girlfriend, they told me. I was dead beat and went right to bed. In the morning the cook made me a nice breakfast, and then

I headed to the garage and got in my car.

I sat behind the wheel with the keys in my hand. I felt dizzy. Suddenly, I was overcome with panic. I had no idea what the keys were for or, for that matter, what *anything* was for. The steering wheel looked foreign to me, the pedals on the floor seemed strange, and all the buttons and gadgets on the dashboard were just a maze of nothing. *What am I doing here?* I wondered. *What am I supposed to do?*

I had no answers. I just sat there in a daze.

"Mr. Peppiatt?" A voice broke into my blur of thoughts. "It's nearly noon. You have been sitting here for hours. Are you all right?"

"No, I'm not all right," I confessed as the butler helped me out of the car.

I knew a psychiatrist in Beverly Hills whom I'd played poker with. I called him, told him what had just happened and he agreed to see me immediately. The butler drove me to the doctor's office.

"This is serious, Frank," the psychiatrist said after a long interview. "You still feel you can't drive?"

"I can't seem to remember how."

"You're suffering from overwork and a massive depression that is muddling up your senses."

"I should start coming to you regularly, I guess."

"That's not enough. You need treatment, every day, in a controlled situation."

"But I have work to do."

"That's your problem. Do you want to get better?"

"Of course."

"Then I want you to fly to Boston tomorrow."

"Now, wait a minute!"

"No, Frank, you wait a minute. This is serious. I'm going to register you at the McLean Hospital and they will take complete care of you. Now, go home and pack. I'll book you on a plane leaving tomorrow morning and the doctors at the institute will be expecting you tomorrow afternoon."

The next morning I was on a flight to Boston — and then God knows where and what and who and whatever.

I was scared to death.

Chapter 18

✦

DEPRESSION WITH SHRINK

THE GROUNDS OF THE McLEAN Hospital were beautiful — rolling hills, lots of trees and stately houses dotting the landscape. I was taken to one of the houses and led to a nice, sunlit room. This was where I'd be staying.

"Take your time, Frank," the young staffer said. "Unpack, put your things away. You can relax in the common sitting room right outside your door and read or watch TV."

"Thank you," I said. This wasn't nearly as bad as I had feared.

"Tomorrow morning you'll be starting your treatment. Get a good night's sleep, and good luck." He shook my hand and left me alone.

The sitting room was large and tastefully furnished. There was a TV, magazines and a few books. Quite a few doors like mine led off the sitting room — I figured other patients were behind them. On the wall hung a map of the grounds that showed where the dining hall was located.

"Welcome to McLean," a pleasant lady's voice said. I turned and saw a woman who looked to be in her 20s, dressed very well, with curly black hair, friendly brown eyes and a welcoming smile.

"My name is Julia and I'm here to help you and make sure you help yourself."

"Good to meet you, Julia. My name is Frank and —"

"I *know* your name, Frank. I'm a psychiatric assistant and the patients in this house are my responsibility. If you don't feel like eating in the dining hall, there's a fully equipped kitchen right here. You can buy your own food and prepare it here, if you wish."

"Thank you, Julia."

"You're welcome," she said, and left me alone in the sitting room with my thoughts.

I wondered what my treatment tomorrow morning was going to be like. I pictured myself lying on a leather couch with a Viennese Dr. Von Psycho analyzing me, his face hidden behind a shaft of light shining directly into my face. That's the way I would have written it in a sketch on one of my shows.

Dr. Von Psycho turned out to be Dr. Fairfield, a tall blond man, 40ish, with kind blue eyes. There was no leather couch, just a nice comfortable chair, a well-lit room and a smiling doctor sitting opposite me.

"How are you feeling?" he asked.

"A little nervous, Doctor."

"Only natural. It's your first time."

"Yes, it is."

"Well, just relax and we'll talk a little."

He knew all about the loss of my ability to drive and he didn't seem surprised by it. He wanted me to go back to my early childhood and slowly bring him up to the present.

I had sessions with Dr. Fairfield every other day. I also participated in group sessions with the other patients in the house, conducted by another psychiatrist. I was given a complete physical examination and a complicated series of written tests, ink-blot tests and memory exams.

There were 18 other patients in the house and they had varying problems — eating disorders, alcoholism, depression, personality disorders, fear of not being clean, fear of being touched. We discussed everyone's problems in our group sessions. In show business I had met more than my share of unstable people; in fact, sometimes my profession seemed like a veritable nut magnet. I thought I had seen it all, but I was amazed at the number of disorders that existed among my fellow patients.

In my first week at McLean one of the female patients woke up screaming and ran out the front door, stark naked. She yelled that she wanted to die. Six male and female nurses appeared, it seemed from nowhere, and took her away to God knows where. The next morning someone came to pack up her things. That was the last we ever saw of her. Our group psychiatrist had us all talk about how the event had affected everyone. It had scared the crap out of me. I realized how fragile my situation was.

But after two weeks with Dr. Fairfield, I felt things were going along just fine. And then he began a session by saying, "It's been a nice little fairy tale you've been telling me, Frank. Can we stop the bullshit and get down to some serious business?"

"I don't know what you mean, Doctor."

"I have the results of all the tests you've been given, and whether you want to admit it or not, you are terribly depressed and it's going to show itself in many more serious ways than just forgetting how to drive."

I was stunned. "I don't know what to do," I said quietly.

"Don't worry, we'll do it together," the doctor replied. "We have to get one thing straight in your mind. You entertain millions of people every week, big stars want you, producers want you, networks want you, but the three people closest to you don't really care."

"Hold on there, Doctor, I feel —"

"That's the problem you haven't allowed yourself to confront. Your father thought what you were doing was trivial. He wanted you in a court of law, not in a silly Superman outfit on TV. Your first wife thought you were just lucky, that you had everything handed to you. Your present wife, it seems, just wants the money to keep coming in, whatever you do. Your father and your first wife were jealous, Frank. So they had to believe your success was a fluke. Your present wife just doesn't care. Down deep, you know this, Frank. On top of that, you work yourself ragged, taking job after job to prove something, and we'll find out what that is."

A 52-year-old man started crying in Dr. Fairfield's office, and it was me. I had not cried in almost two decades, not since that terrible year when my father and my best friend had died. All my buried sadness started coming out in a garbled, blubbering rush. This went on, session after session, with increasing clarity and less and less garbling and blubbering.

The weeks rolled into months and I knew now that I was getting better. I could feel it. My head was clear. I hadn't had a drink since I'd entered the institute, but that wasn't the reason it was clear. Dr. Fairfield was the reason.

Three months into my stay at McLean, Valerie paid me a visit. She seemed pleased that I was looking so good. She wanted to meet Dr. Fairfield. The doctor showed Valerie into his office while I sat just outside in the waiting room. I had no trouble hearing their conversation.

"He's looking so much better, Doctor," she said.

"He's responding very well," he said.

"Do you think you can cure him of his alcoholism?" she asked.

"He has no problem with alcoholism, Mrs. Peppiatt."

"He's an alcoholic."

"No evidence of that. He's had no withdrawal symptoms."

"That's wrong. I *know* he's an alcoholic!" she yelled.

"No, Mrs. Peppiatt," he said calmly. "Your husband was suffering from a deep depression, which I am happy to report is getting better by the week."

"You're no goddamned psychiatrist if you don't know an alcoholic when you see one!" She was screaming now.

"Please keep your voice down. There are other patients here," he said. His voice was even.

"Well, good luck to them with *you* around!" she shouted.

"Nice meeting you, Mrs. Peppiatt. Now, I have other things to attend to," he said flatly.

The office door opened and Dr. Fairfield looked at me with a smile. "Mrs. Peppiatt will see you now, Frank, and I'll see you tomorrow, right?"

"Damn right!" I said.

Valerie was in a total fury. She wanted me to leave the institute immediately. I refused. That enraged her even more. She took a plane back to Los Angeles the next day.

I stayed at McLean until the end of August, six and a half months in all. Dr. Fairfield gave me the name and number of a psychiatrist in Beverly Hills and told me to call him if I had any problems.

"Thank you, Doctor. You've given me new life."

"That's my job, Frank. It's been a pleasure working with you."

Back in L.A., Valerie was living with the butler and cook in the big house off Coldwater Canyon. I looked for a house at the beach, but there was nothing available in Malibu. I had to go farther north to Broad Beach.

I called Nick and told him I was back.

"How are you feeling, Frankie?"

"Like new, Nick, like new. It was amazing."

"That's great!" he said.

"How's *Hee Haw* going?"

"Sold out again. Hey, you remember that presentation we wrote for a show we called *The Nashville Palace*?"

"Sure. We did it just before I went away. It was good."

"Well, John and Bernie are pushing it really hard at NBC."

"John and Bernie? Aren't you involved, Nick?"

"We *both* should be, but let's see what comes up."

"Okay, I'll see you at the office tomorrow."

I drove in to Yonge Street Productions the next day. When I walked into the office, all the staff looked at me strangely. They were very polite, of course, but they seemed frightened, as though I were an escapee from an insane asylum.

"Frank!" a familiar voice called. It was Sam Lovullo. "You're back."

"It seems so, Sam," I said.

"We're going to Nashville in October. Can we count on you?" he asked.

"Definitely."

"Great. I'll give you the dates," he said, and went into his office.

I entered the office I shared with John. John was sitting at his desk. Beside him on a sofa was a young writer, Barry Adelman. Bernie was sitting at my desk. He'd never done that before. He did not get up to give me my chair. They all froze, as though they were looking at a ghost.

"Frank," Bernie said, "what are you doing here?"

"Coming into *my* office. I've been on the road for six months."

"Good to see you back," John said, without a shred of sincerity.

"We can finish this meeting after lunch, guys," Bernie said, getting up from my chair.

"We should hear from NBC tomorrow," Barry Adelman said.

"Oh, *The Nashville Palace*," I said. "Nick told me about that." I turned to John. "I remember when we wrote the presentation."

"That's all changed," John said, not meeting my eyes.

"Isn't it still modeled after *The Hollywood Palace*?" I asked.

John didn't answer.

"Sort of," Barry said, "but it's much different now."

"I'd like to read it," I said.

"We'll get you a copy after lunch," Bernie quickly assured me, and tried to flash his best salesman's smile. It didn't quite come off.

"No hurry," I said.

All three of them threw odd glances at one another. I couldn't believe what I was seeing.

"If you need any help on the Nashville project, I'm available," I offered.

"We might add another writer down the line," John said.

That was a punch in the gut. My partner of almost 30 years telling me he *might* have a little writing job for me somewhere down the line! I don't know what the three of them saw on my face, but they beat a hasty retreat out of my office, without another word.

I walked into Sam's office. "Sam," I said, "are you working on this *Nashville Palace* deal?"

"Not yet," he answered, "but they'll probably need me on the budget."

"What's with John and Bernie? They acted scared when they saw me just now."

"Look, Frank," Sam said, "Bernie just got married again and his new wife is very shy and retiring. John's wife, Anne, took her under her wing and they became best of friends."

"And Bernie's grateful," I said.

"So he's helping John succeed at something on his own," Sam explained.

"What do you mean?" I asked. I was beginning to feel queasy.

"You and Nick have always been the strong ones in the partnership and John has always been itching to fly solo and show the world what he's made of. You know?"

"No," I said, "I didn't know that." Here was John springing another huge surprise on me, and it was a doozy — a double doozy.

"Anyway," Sam continued, "Bernie is helping John with all that."

Now I got it. My own manager and my lifelong partner were screwing me. I get sick for six months and a couple of worms turn. I'm lucky I wasn't sick any longer or I probably would have been screwed out of *Hee Haw*, too. This is another fine mess you got me into, Stanley!

I was ready to run out and hire a lawyer and sue their asses. I don't know much about law, but this was an open and shut case, if I ever saw one. I phoned Nick and told him what Sam and I had discussed.

"Relax, Frankie," Nick said, "everything's going to be fine. Just let them run with it."

Nick calmed me down somewhat. I took a very confused drive back to my new beach house. The phone was already ringing when I walked in the door. It was Bill Harbach. He wanted to know if I was okay now. "I'm not crazy anymore, Bill, if that's what you mean."

"Great!" Bill exclaimed. "I want you to come over to Steve Allen's house right now."

"Fine," I said.

"Great! Great!" Bill shouted happily. "I'll see you here in half an hour."

"Hold it! Hold it, Bill! I have to know how to get there!"

Bill hadn't changed. It was the old "corner of Walk and Don't Walk" again.

I drove to Steve Allen's place in Thousand Oaks. Steve was there with his manager, Irvin Arthur, and Bill Harbach, along with an executive from NBC. I shook hands all around and Steve's manager started things off. "You've been away for a while, Frank."

"That is correct."

"Are you okay now?"

"I'm fine. I'm even allowed to leave my keeper in the car." Everybody chuckled, warily.

"We've got a problem," Irvin continued. "Steve has a deal with NBC for five comedy specials. They will be pilots for a late-night series, following Carson's *The Tonight Show.*"

"The production isn't going well," the NBC exec went on. "We want Steve to get a new staff and start from scratch."

"Does Steve agree?" I asked.

Steve nodded and smiled. "I'd like you and Bill to produce for me, get some funny writers and go for it."

"That sounds good to me. What's the schedule?" I asked.

"Tape the first show in mid-October," Mr. NBC said.

"We'll do it," Bill Harbach yelled, filling the room with his irrepressible optimism, "and we'll do it *funny!*"

So I was back in business — on my own, not as one of John's maybe-somewhere-down-the-line writers. I was damned if I was going to let Bernie set this deal for me. He'd probably get John the job. I made my own deal with Steve's manager. And I did very, very well for myself.

"Steve wants to handle getting a conductor and arranger," Bill said, and Steve nodded in agreement.

"Fine," I said. "I'd like to hire Shelly Keller as head writer. We worked really well together on *Frank Sinatra: A Man and His Music.*"

"Shelly's great!" Bill yelled, keeping things up-tempo.

"Bill," I said, "you hire the office staff and an associate producer. You know the deal."

"Been doing it all my life. We're in the old Merv Griffin offices on Vine Street."

"See you there tomorrow morning," I said.

I drove back to the beach, and the first thing I did was phone Shelly. He was thrilled.

"John not involved with this?" Shelly asked when we met the next morning.

"He and Brillstein are doing something together."

"Oh, I see." Shelly got the picture, but said nothing about it. "So . . . let's choose four or five writers and get this show on the road!"

Our budget allowed us to hire some very good writers. As soon as they were settled in, we started putting together a show. Steve had a promising running concept called "Eye Witless News." He was the crazy anchor, showing zany film clips and interviews, really dumb weather forecasts and sports. We had a ball writing it and it was very funny. When Steve had done the first *Tonight Show*, back in the early '50s, he did a very funny segment called "The Man on the Street," which we revived, using guests like Steve Martin, Rich Little, Jonathan Winters, Joan Rivers and Kay Ballard as ordinary people on the street being interviewed by Steve.

It was kind of a crazy show and it reminded me of my early days at the CBC in Toronto. It was a lot of fun and my new head was doing just fine. After work I'd often go and hang out at Shelly's house in the Hollywood Hills. Then I'd have to face at least an hour drive back to Broad Beach and, in the morning, an even longer drive back through rush-hour traffic. It was lonely out there with nothing but the surf and the silence.

"Hey, Frankie," Shelly said one morning, "that beach living doesn't seem to agree with you."

"I'm not really an ocean person, Shel."

"Then why don't you get out of there and move in with me until you get your life straightened out?"

"Seriously?" I asked.

"No, I'm just joking," Shelly said. "Of course I'm serious. I've got two extra bedrooms."

I moved in with Shelly on the weekend. He was great company and we also got some extra work done. Shel was going out with a very attractive woman and he suggested that we double date.

"I'm not dating anybody, Shelly."

"I can fix that, Frankie," he said confidently. "I know a beautiful lady who would be perfect for you. Her name is Caroline. What do you say?"

"What do I say about what?"

"I'll phone her and we'll see. Okay?"

"Well, okay."

Shelly phoned Caroline, spoke to her briefly and handed me the phone.

"Hello," I said.

"Look, Frank, I don't like blind dates, but since it's Shelly, I'll go for a drink. No dinner, just a drink. You can pick me up at six. Shelly will tell you how to get here. No dinner."

"Just a drink," I said, and she hung up.

"How'd it go?" Shelly asked.

"She didn't exactly sound thrilled."

Caroline lived in the hills above Laurel Canyon in a tiny bungalow. I parked, got out of the car, and a large brown dog jumped up and licked my hand.

"Frank?" a very sweet voice called.

"Yes," I answered.

"Iggy likes you," she said.

"And I like Iggy."

A woman came out the front door. "I'm Caroline," she said.

Wow, I thought, *is she something, or what!* Blond, blue eyes, a beautiful figure and a smile that could light up anything it wished to.

"I figured that, and it's a pleasure," I said. "Where would you like to go for our *one drink*?"

"There's a nice little bar on Sunset Boulevard," she said.

It *was* a nice little bar and we found a table for two in the corner. We ordered our drinks and the conversation was effortless. We had a lot in common temperamentally, philosophically and politically. We found we knew many of the same people and we were amazed that we'd never met before. I felt really comfortable with her and she must have felt okay, too, because she allowed a second drink. I drove her home about eight o'clock and she invited me in for a glass of wine. Wow, a third drink.

We talked and laughed for a couple of hours. I told her I had recently been released from the McLean Hospital after six months of treatment for a new head. She told me that many years ago she'd had a similar long stay at a psychiatric hospital on Long Island in New

York. We were both psychiatric graduates. No diplomas, but feeling okay.

As I was leaving, I asked if I could call her. "Sure," she said.

"Maybe we could have dinner?" I asked.

"That would be nice."

"Just *one* dinner," I said, and she laughed.

I drove back to Shelly's in one of the happiest moods I'd experienced in a long time.

MEANWHILE, STEVE ALLEN'S SHOW, WHICH had been going along in fine style, skidded to a stop. The rumor was that Johnny Carson wanted his own company to produce the new late-night show that would follow his *Tonight Show*. He also wanted to choose the star. In conjunction with NBC, Carson chose a young comedian named David Letterman. That seemed to be that.

NBC announced that they had purchased a limited run of *The Nashville Palace*. Nick Vanoff called a meeting of all the Yonge Street principals to discuss it.

"I want everybody here to know," Nick began, "that I registered *The Nashville Palace* presentation with the Writers Guild, right after John, Frank and I wrote it up."

The Writers Guild has a registration system into which any writer can deposit a copy of what they have just written — script, book, play, essay, presentation or outline. The work is officially stamped and dated by the Writers Guild Registrar. If anyone comes along later and claims the work as their own, the original writer can prove otherwise by means of the Registrar's stamp, which is accepted as irrefutable evidence in any court.

Nick continued, "I'm also quite aware that John and Bernie have sold the show to NBC with John as producer. Since Frank and I are co-owners of the concept, we will retain our usual profit participation, when profits develop."

Bernie and Barry Adelman were dumbstruck by Nick's statement.

John, however, forged ahead. "I understand that, Nick, and I accept it. But I must have complete creative control and a producing fee of $50,000 per show."

Now Nick and I were the ones taken aback. Nick recovered much faster than I did. He turned to Bernie. "That fee is a little over the top, Bernie."

"Not these days, Nick," Bernie said with a smirk.

"Okay," Nick said, "John gets creative control and the $50,000 is his only fee, even for all other runs of the show."

Smugly, Bernie nodded at John. He thought he'd won.

"That's fine," John said.

"Fine with me, too," I added. I saw the ruse Nick had played.

That night I took Caroline downtown for dinner at the Windsor Hotel. It was one of the few nice places in town where we wouldn't run into any showbiz types. We had a great meal and a wonderful evening.

I was happy as a lark until my Aunt Charlotte called me in the morning and told me my mother was dying. Wasting no time, I grabbed a flight to Toronto. But when I arrived, I was told my mom had died while I was in the air. The wonderful, understanding woman who had always backed me up was gone. All her sisters and brothers, their spouses and many friends attended the funeral. Marilyn and the three kids were also there. My mother was buried beside my father. It was a sad day.

IT WAS GETTING CLOSE TO Christmas, and the kids — they were actually young ladies now — persuaded me to stay over for the holidays. I also had things to clear up with my mother's estate. I was staying at a hotel downtown, but the girls and Marilyn insisted I stay in her big house on Strathallan in the Lawrence Park neighborhood. I had a lovely room, and everything worked out quite well. Marilyn and the girls cooked Christmas dinner and I handed out gifts I had purchased for everyone. My girls were doing great: Robyn had finished college and was about to move to Nashville to help on *Hee Haw* and do some other television work there. Marney and Melissa didn't attend college; they both had decent-paying jobs in Toronto. In spite of the sad events that had brought me there, it was wonderful spending the holidays with my daughters.

However, I found myself thinking about Caroline all the time. I couldn't get her out of my mind. I flew back to Los Angeles the day after New Year's and was welcomed by Shelly. I didn't waste any time in phoning Caroline to wish her a happy New Year.

"What happened to you?" she said.

I told her about my mother's death, spending the holidays with my kids and seeing to my mother's estate. "Are you available for dinner tomorrow night?" I asked.

"I sure am."

"I've missed you," I said.

"We had only two dates and already you missed me?"

"Yes, I did and I'm sorry it happened so quickly."

She laughed. "Pick me up at seven," she said.

Caroline and I started seeing a lot of each other. I wasn't working and that gave us a chance to spend a whole bunch of time together. As the kids used to say in high school, we were going steady.

In the midst of this romantic bliss, Bernie Brillstein called me and said Valerie wanted us to get back together.

"Not interested, Bern."

Al Rettig called with the same request and he received the same answer.

When Caroline and I finally made love in her little house, it was sensational! It was more than sex. I realized I was in love for the very first time in over 50 years. It was great to be alive and feeling this way.

"I have a place in Palm Springs," I said.

"I know. You told me," Caroline replied.

"Let's take Iggy, go down there for the weekend and see if we can get some Palm Springs tongues wagging."

"Let's!"

When we walked into the condo a few days later, Caroline said, "Who decorated this place — the King of Morocco's gay nephew?"

I laughed. "I had nothing to do with it. Valerie did the deed."

In spite of the decor, we managed to have fun and games, and lots of love and laughs. And the dog loved it, too. She and Caroline ran up the mountain every morning and the rabbits stayed in their holes when Iggy was on the loose. We spent some great weekends in Palm Springs, but it was getting close to summer — summers in Palm Springs are so hot it's almost uninhabitable.

"Let's rent a house and move in together," I suggested.

"You mean *live* together?" she said with a smile.

"That's precisely what I mean."

"I vote yes," she said.

"Then it's unanimous."

Caroline found a really nice house and pool for us on Outpost Drive in the Hollywood Hills. I said a fond goodbye to Shelly. He wished us luck, and Caroline and I moved in. The place was beautifully furnished and comfortable. It was summer. We had the pool and each other and we were happy as all hell.

When it came time for me to go to Nashville to do *Hee Haw*, Caroline and I decided to drive there and see some of the country. Our first big road trip was a blast.

Working with John again, however, was quite awkward. He seemed oblivious to what had gone on between us. Same old John, completely out of touch with himself. I quickly got all the comedy finished so that Caroline and I could head home to Outpost Drive.

It wasn't long before we decided to get married. I got a lawyer, Valerie got a lawyer, and after a couple of meetings we worked out a deal. Valerie and I sold our house and tennis court for twice what I had paid for it. When the divorce was at last final, Caroline and I went down to Los Angeles City Hall. It was very busy at the marriage office, so the clerk took us in 10 couples at a time. In the confusion, I nearly married a Rosalita and Caroline almost became Mrs. Garcia. Afterward, the two of us had a wonderful lunch at the Biltmore with a great bottle of champagne. And for our honeymoon, we did something special — we went home.

I GOT A CALL FROM NBC. They wanted to meet with me about *Barbara Mandrell and the Mandrell Sisters*, which was currently on the network. I walked into the meeting at NBC and who should I see but Saul Ilson, my writing buddy from Canada. He was now a big program executive with the network.

"Good to see you, Frank," Saul said.

"Same here, Saul."

"You know Barbara, right?"

"Sure, she's been on *Hee Haw* a lot."

"Well," Saul went on, "Barbara doesn't feel her current producer knows much about country and she's probably right. I suggested you to produce the show this year and Barbara agreed. What do you think?"

"I'd love to work with Barbara and her sisters, if we can work things out."

"I'm sure that won't be a problem. I'll tell Barbara you accept."

"Thank you, Saul."

"You've helped me a lot, Frank. Now it's my turn."

I flew to Nashville for a day and met with Barbara and her husband on their boat. I shared with her a couple of thoughts I had, and she liked them.

As I was leaving, she said, "Frank, I don't think it's a good idea to book *Hee Haw* people."

"You're country enough," I said.

"Exactly!"

I was back in L.A. the next day, hugging my wife.

In the meantime, Nick had made a deal to sell *Hee Haw*, Yonge Street Productions and all the costumes and sets to Gaylord Entertainment of Oklahoma City. They paid us $15 million for the whole kit and caboodle. My share was fantastic. So was John's, even though he hadn't put up a nickel of his own money back when Nick and I had risked everything we had.

WORKING WITH BARBARA MANDRELL WAS great fun. She is very talented and extremely smart. She knew what was best for her and was usually right. She had damn good ideas for every guest we had on the show and I did everything I could to make them work. But I could see Barbara and her husband were unhappy being away from Nashville. They really didn't like Hollywood, and I think she thought Hollywood didn't like her. She would much rather have done her show in Nashville, but NBC would have none of it. So, at the end of the year she decided to quit, even though the ratings were good.

"See if you can make her change her mind," Saul Ilson asked me.

"It's no use, Saul, the show has hurt her record sales and she hates it out here on the coast."

"Yeah," Saul said, heaving a sigh. "All the big music acts have found lately that many of their fans won't bother to buy their records or concert tickets, if they can be seen for free on network TV every week. Times are changing, Frank."

After the last episode of *Barbara Mandrell and the Mandrell Sisters*, she kissed me goodbye. She was smiling ear to ear, knowing that she, her husband and their kids were going home.

But even with the end of that series, opportunities kept coming my way. I had an offer to produce a new game show by Mark Goodson and Bill Todman, which I turned down. The show never got on the air. I was also offered a new Nashville talk show, which I also turned down. It didn't make it to air, either.

The Nashville Palace, which I'd been squeezed out of, was canceled before Christmas after only five episodes. John had his wish. The whole world got to see what John Aylesworth could do on his own. NBC had nothing to put on in place of *The Nashville Palace*, so they reran all the shows in the new year. John did not participate in the rerun revenues. He had already collected his entire producing fee. Nick and I kept the rerun production fees all to ourselves and made out very well without having done a lick of work. John was fucking furious.

Caroline and I felt that something new was happening in the kingdom of television. Variety was being deposed. It was 1981, and MTV had just been born, playing nothing but music videos, all day, every day. Once, the networks had aired 15 or 16 variety series every season; now there were only a couple left, with no new ones in the pipeline. The variety show had faded like the mustache cup, vaudeville, the big bands and panty girdles.

Chapter 19

✦

CANADIAN SUNSET

I DIDN'T WANT TO BE an old fart, sitting around Nate 'n' Al's Deli, remembering about the good old days. In Hollywood, if you weren't working on a show or movie, you were nobody. I was nearly 60, which was prehistoric in that town. There were thousands of 20- and 30-year-olds clawing at the showbiz gates. Most of them wouldn't make it in, but they wanted their chance and they wanted it *now*. Hell, they had a right to their chance, just as I had 2,500 shows ago.

"Let's ride off into the sunset," I said to Caroline.

"Fine, pard," she said. "Time to sell the ranch and saddle up."

"Where to?" I asked.

"I'd like to try Canada," she said. "Besides, I think you have some unfinished business with your daughters there."

We bought a big house on a hill overlooking a lake just north of Toronto. By the summer of 1985 we were moved in. Our relatives visited regularly and Marney and Melissa spent many weekends with us, while Robyn came up from Nashville as often as she could. Reconnecting with my daughters made me very happy. Old Toronto friends from way back in the Superman-suit era dropped in, sometimes staying too long, but what the hell, it was summer and we had a ball — swimming, boating, water skiing, cooking on the terrace, playing poker till all hours. In winter we were snowed in by December, but we skied across the frozen lake every day. We had our first white Christmas in many, many years, then our first white New Year, followed by a white Valentine's Day, a white St. Patrick's Day and a white April Fool's day. Nick Vanoff called from Los Angeles and asked me to come down to work with him on Dolly Parton's variety show, *Dolly*. It was the first time I ever turned Nick down. I had never been so happy in all my life.

In early May, as the ice on the lake was finally breaking, I got a call from a Toronto television production company offering me the executive producer job on *Check It Out!*, a situation comedy being shot in Toronto and starring Don Adams. I had known Don from the old Perry Como days, when he had been a semi-regular on the show. *Check It Out!* had been on the air for two seasons and the syndicators were not going to renew it for another year unless major improvements were made. The show needed work, lots and lots of work. They offered me $200,000, and though I didn't need the money, it was a sum worthy of my attention. *Besides,* I thought, *I don't have to leave home to do the job.* But commuting from the lake every day was too much, so Caroline found us a little Yorkville townhouse where we could stay during the week. The show was so bad I had wondered why Don was staying with it. He had made a fortune on *Get Smart*, which was still running in syndication some 20 years after its original airing. Then I remembered that back in the Como days Don had been an inveterate gambler — horses, cards, casinos, whatever.

In my first meeting with Don he said to me, "Frank, why are you fucking doing this? You don't need the money, do you?"

"No."

"Then why?"

"I thought it might be fun."

"You're close to my age, Frank, and believe me, this will not be fun."

"Why do you say that?"

"Because you're walking into a thornbush of trouble. Trust me!"

Some fun! Don was right — I quit after three shows. There were so many intrigues raging throughout the staff that it was impossible to get anything done. No one but Don and the syndicator wanted to change anything. I realized I had been brought on only to mollify the syndicator and make them sign on for another year. Now that the ink was dry on that contract, I was only getting in the way of all the intrigues.

Back at the lake house, Don Adams called me and uttered three words: "Smart move, Frankie." In truth, I don't think I could have done the show, even if all the conditions were perfect. I finally had to admit to myself that I was out of gas.

THE YEARS WENT ON HAPPILY, and we spent most of our time at the lake and a day or two a week at our little Yorkville townhouse. I loved that place. It had the same look and size of my Grandpa Grant's house on Glebeholme Boulevard. It was just big enough for Caroline and me. But sometimes, late at night, I sensed the whole Glebeholme crowd was there with me — my mother and father, Aunt Millie, Uncle Dunc and my dear, dear Grandpa Grant.

Now and then I got job offers from Los Angeles, but I turned them down. I worked on a few local projects — *Durante the Musical*, some Canadian plays and television specials — but it wasn't much more than dabbling.

I was getting to know my daughters' friends and boyfriends. One winter weekend Robyn brought home a handsome, sandy-haired man named Doug and announced that they were engaged. They wanted a big wedding and I was happy to oblige. Naturally, I wanted to step in and take over the production, but I managed to remain in the background, writing the checks. It was a beautiful September wedding. As I was about to walk down the aisle with my daughter-bride, she whispered, "Thanks for being here to give me away, Daddy."

"I am just walking you down the aisle, sweetheart," I said. "I will never give you away. I just got you back."

A few months later Melissa and her boyfriend eloped to Las Vegas. Marney's boyfriend moved into her house. Before I knew it, I was a grandfather four times — two boys and two girls. Who said variety was dead? It's been fabulous watching these new Peppiatt peanuts grow up.

IN 1996, THE CBC SURPRISED us by devoting an hour of prime-time to John and me, with a special called *A Tribute to Peppiatt & Aylesworth: Canada's First Television Comedy Team.*

The day before the show aired, a young CBC newscaster who was doing the promo editorialized on the air, "Peppiatt and Aylesworth? I've never heard of these two guys!" She hadn't even been born when "these two guys" were prancing around, live and in black and white. Regardless, I loved doing the show. John and I, Norman Jewison, Jill Foster and her playwriting husband, Bernard Slade, sat around for an hour, playing old tapes and remembering the days of struggle and fun. Rich Little showed up and played a tape of his first appearance on *The Judy Garland Show.* It was an entertaining hour, even for the young newscaster who had never heard of "these two guys."

The next year the girls told me their mother was dying. Except for at Robyn's wedding, I had not seen Marilyn in a couple of decades. My daughters told me it was their mother's last wish that I attend her funeral. I was reluctant, and Caroline said, "Do what you like, Franko, just leave me out of it." My daughters continued to pressure me about the funeral until I relented and agreed to attend. "Oh thanks, Dad!" the girls said, hugging me.

It was a well-attended service and I knew almost everyone there. All of Marilyn's best and oldest friends had turned out, as well as her two brothers, who glowered at me as though I had murdered their sister in cold blood. I sat alone near the back of the church. I was puzzled when the main eulogist came to the pulpit. I had never seen or heard of him before. With all of Marilyn's daughters, brothers and best friends there, why was this stranger delivering the eulogy? Apparently, he had just flown in all the way from Vancouver. The stranger gave a long, emotional recitation of Marilyn's life, the gist of which was that despite being abandoned by her husband and left penniless, she had managed somehow to raise three fatherless daughters all by herself.

Was this an elaborate practical joke? I looked around at the crowd. Nobody was laughing. They were all taking in the gospel of bullshit emanating from the pulpit. So this is why Marilyn had wanted me at the funeral. One last kick at the can. I wanted to get up and storm out of the church, but a warped sense of Canadian decorum stopped me. I was glad Caroline wasn't there. She would have raised one hell of an un-Canadian fuss.

Once the service was over, I tried to sneak out the door, but got caught up in the reception line by my daughters and the two glowering brothers-in-law. My anger was just about to boil over, which didn't bode well for the brothers-in-law. Blood would surely be spilled.

But just then my four grandchildren emerged from the crowd. "Grandpa! Grandpa! Grandpa!" they squealed excitedly. They jumped into my arms, kissing and hugging me.

My heart melted instantly and I was filled with love. Ah, the power of grandchildren!

I glanced at the glowering brothers-in-law. They looked on at me and the children, their mouths agape, confused by this display of love and affection. I was on top of the world. If there is a heaven and if Marilyn made it in, maybe she was looking on at me and her grandchildren. Maybe she would finally forgive me for my ambition and the love I gave to my work. Maybe my dad was looking on, too. Maybe he would finally forgive me for not being Perry Mason. I pictured the two of them together in overalls and tool belts, renovating the Pearly Gates.

From the *Globe and Mail*, August 17, 2010

I REMEMBER JOHN AYLESWORTH
by Frank Peppiatt

I REMEMBER I WAS FRESH out of the University of Toronto, working at an ad agency, writing a Javex radio commercial, when a man walked into my office, introduced himself as John Aylesworth, the new copywriter, and pulled up a chair to my desk. For the next 60 years, he was my friend and partner — he even got his own desk.

John and I were the company cut-ups, so when television came to Canada in 1952, we were given a comedy show called *After Hours*, which we wrote and starred in. Some stars! My mother made the costumes.

For a Superman sketch, John — as Perry White, in his own suit, tie and pipe — had to keep a straight face as I leapt in wearing long underwear, dyed blue with a Superman logo sloppily painted on the chest, trailing a beach towel for a cape. It was a live broadcast and there was no time for me to change costumes. So I just slapped on a fedora and glasses to become the mild-mannered Clark Kent. John fell down laughing. Luckily, all of Canada laughed with him.

Soon we were off to New York to write for Perry Como. Next stop, Hollywood and *The Judy Garland Show*. She invited us to her house for dinner at seven. Being Canadians, we were there sharp. The butler answered, buttoning up his uniform, his shoelaces still untied. The only person in the living room was Glenn Ford, the big movie star, lying on the sofa, reading a script. John said, "Hi, Mr. Ford! We're Canadians, too!" Ford glanced up, very briefly, turned his back to us and continued reading. A couple of hours later, when Judy emerged, she gave us a warmer welcome.

There followed decades of shows with Frank Sinatra, Jonathan Winters, Sonny and Cher, Julie Andrews, etc., etc. Back in Canada, it was said that we were lucky. But they weren't there all those many, many nights John and I burned the midnight oil, writing, rewriting and rewriting a script that was going into rehearsal the next morning and on the air the day after.

In the spring of 1969, we created a little temporary summer replacement show. When taping was finished, I went off to vacation in England, certain I'd seen the last of that project. It was called *Hee Haw*. A few weeks later, John called me from Los Angeles and said, "Get back here. *Hee Haw* is the number one show of the summer and the network has ordered 16 new shows to run the whole winter." The show ran for 25 years.

My worst memory was of July 29. My daughter Francesca called with the news of John's death the night before. He was half of me for many, many years and will always be in my memories. I remember John Aylesworth. How can I forget?

INDEX

INDEX

INDEX